"This excellent and practical book builds on Mike Smith's personal engagement with and study of leadership. In it, he distils the product of many meetings with leading individuals and workshops and conferences he has led addressing the subject."

Sir Mark Moody-Stuart, Chairman, UN Global
Compact Foundation and Former
Chairman of Shell Group

"Mike Smith has been pursuing an urgent conversation on the new leadership for longer than most companies have realized they needed it. If you want to understand where leadership in the business world is going, you could ask for no better global guide."

Margaret Heffernan, Texan entrepreneur, Huffington
Post blogger and best-selling business author of
Wilful Blindness *and* A Bigger Prize

"Mike Smith shares profound insights into the DNA of good business. His easy, narrative style makes these insights both accessible and persuasive. A thoroughly recommended read for all those who care about a better business ethos."

Professor Roger Steare FRSA, Corporate Philosopher,
Cass Business School, City of London

"Some people write about the failings of capitalism and some people write about the achievements of individuals. What Mike Smith does uniquely well is to tell inspiring stories of individual achievement in a manner that points the way towards a better capitalism."

Mark Goyder, Founder, Tomorrow's Company

"Mike Smith's work on ethical business is both extremely well researched and enormously timely. We are in an age when business as usual is no longer an option, either for the planet or its populations. *Leading with Integrity* tells the stories of some of the businesses that are making most difference and leading an ethical revolution. It deserves a very wide readership."

Tony Bradley, Lecturer in Social Economy & Enterprise
and Lead Researcher in Sustainable Business,
Liverpool Hope Business School

"Taking 'time out' to contemplate what is right action going forward is a transformative leadership habit. Mike Smith shows us, through many powerful stories, how leaders tapped into their own values compasses to create ethical and sustainable businesses."

Anita Hoffmann, founding CEO of Executiva, and
author of Purpose & Impact: How Executives
Are Creating Meaningful Second Careers

Leading with Integrity

Thanks to global news and social media, we are the most informed and socially conscious generation in history. But what are the sources of inner inspiration that guide our daily conduct and motivations in the workplace?

Far from the old Machiavellian dictum that "the ends justify the means", the reverse is often the case: the means determine the ends. This book presents the stories of business leaders who have aimed to build trust in the economy, and have delivered value through integrity, cooperation, stewardship, purpose and sustainability. It proposes the eight Cs of trust which can define the culture of organizations: contracts, covenants, competences, character, conscience, conviction, courage and change.

The book makes the clear link between personal decision-making and global outcomes and demonstrates how positive decision-making can lead to change inside organizations and beyond.

Michael Smith is a freelance journalist on the topic of values in business and the economy. His articles have appeared in the *Financial Times*, the *Guardian* and *Guardian Weekly, The Times*, the *Independent*, the *Scotsman*, the *Herald* (Glasgow) and the *Pioneer* (New Delhi). He serves on the Swiss steering committee of Ethical Leadership in Business forums and was Head of Business Programmes at Initiatives of Change, UK, from 2010 to 2017.

Leading with Integrity
Creating Positive Change in Organizations

Michael Smith

Routledge
Taylor & Francis Group

LONDON AND NEW YORK

First published 2019
by Routledge
2 Park Square, Milton Park, Abingdon, Oxon OX14 4RN

and by Routledge
711 Third Avenue, New York, NY 10017

Routledge is an imprint of the Taylor & Francis Group, an informa business

British Library Cataloguing-in-Publication Data
A catalogue record for this book is available from the British Library

Library of Congress Cataloging-in-Publication Data
Names: Smith, Michael, 1947 July 14- author.
Title: Leading with integrity : creating positive change in organizations / Michael Smith.
Description: First Edition. | New York : Routledge, 2019.
Identifiers: LCCN 2019003328| ISBN 9780367200695 (hardback) | ISBN 9780367200701 (pbk.) | ISBN 9780429259456 (ebook)
Subjects: LCSH: Leadership. | Organizational change. | Social change.
Classification: LCC HD57.7 .S6487 2019 | DDC 658.4/092--dc23
LC record available at https://lccn.loc.gov/2019003328

ISBN: 978-0-367-20069-5 (hbk)
ISBN: 978-0-367-20070-1 (pbk)
ISBN: 978-0-429-25945-6 (ebk)

Typeset in Times New Roman
by Taylor & Francis Books

MIX
Paper from
responsible sources
FSC
www.fsc.org   FSC™ C013985
Printed in the United Kingdom
by Henry Ling Limited

Contents

About the author

Michael Smith is a freelance journalist and author of books on values in business and the economy. His articles have appeared in the *Financial Times, The Guardian* and *Guardian Weekly, The Times, The Independent, The Scotsman, The Herald* (Glasgow) and *The Pioneer* (New Delhi).

He was Head of Business Programmes at Initiatives of Change (IofC), UK, from 2010 to 2017. He was on the steering committee of a series of international conferences on Trust and Integrity in the Global Economy (TIGE), held each year in Caux, Switzerland, for ten years, from 2006 to 2016. Since 2017 he has been on the Swiss steering committee of Ethical Leadership in Business forums, held each summer in Caux.

In the early 1970s he was production manager at *Himmat* newsweekly in Mumbai for three years and has revisited India many times since then. Returning to Britain, he cut his teeth in journalism as a volunteer on the editorial staff of *The Industrial Pioneer*, a monthly shop-floor newspaper published in the West Midlands. In 1986, following a year in the USA, he became a founding co-editor, then managing editor, of *For A Change* magazine, where he remained till 2006. He was Head of Communications for IofC UK before his role as Head of Business Programmes.

More recently he has given a series of lectures, on Pillars of Trust in the Economy, to MBA students in business schools and other audiences in the UK and around the world, including Denmark, Latvia, Sweden, Beirut, Pune and Chandigarh in India, as well as to 200 business lecturers at a Businet conference in Vilamoura, Portugal, where he was the opening keynote speaker.

His previous books include *Beyond the Bottom Line* (2001), *Trust and Integrity in the Global Economy* (2007) and *Great Company* (2015). As well as writing on business issues, he has written over 60 obituaries for *The Independent, The Guardian, The Times, The Daily Telegraph, The Scotsman* and other newspapers.

He and his wife, Jan, lived in Wimbledon for 36 years, following their marriage in 1981, and now live near Dorking in Surrey. They have two adult children.

Preface

The stories and perspectives in this book draw on a wide range of sources. They include case studies presented by business leaders and other economic players at a series of international forums on Trust and Integrity in the Global Economy (TIGE)—of which I was one of the organizing hosts—held each summer from 2006 to 2016 in the Swiss Alpine village of Caux. Since then the business forums there have continued under the title Ethical Leadership in Business.

Some of the stories also draw on the Asian work of Caux Initiatives for Business (CIB renamed Initiatives of Change in Business (ICB) since 2019) and its international conferences held biennially at Asia Plateau, the Indian centre of Initiatives of Change, in Panchgani, Maharashtra, since 2006.

These two programmes have been drawn together, since 2018, under the umbrella title of Initiatives of Change in Business and the Economy (ICBE).

My own involvement in both was as Head of Business Programmes for Initiatives of Change UK, a position I held from 2010 to 2017. In declaring this interest, I hope I have approached these stories with objectivity, though I unashamedly admit to an advocacy of the values and virtues that Caux and Asia Plateau stand for.

By no means can all these stories be attributed to the influence of the two centres, though they do all reflect the same ethos. Caux and Asia Plateau tend to act as a magnet for like-minded individuals and organizations in the business and corporate world, and part of the role of the two centres is to "connect the dots"—to bring people together in coalition as catalysts for wider change in society and the global economy. The two centres act in a way similar to the term used by Dr Katrin Muff, former Dean of Business School Lausanne: a "collaboratory"—a powerful space for educating, enabling and engaging at the individual, organizational and societal levels. (See Chapter 13.) They are transformative and can leave a permanent mark on those who visit them.

The book concludes with a series of recommendations for transformational practices in organizations and at the personal level: not so much as didactic "do's" and "don'ts" but more as sources of inspiration for constructive action.

This is my fourth book on ethical values in business and the second since the crash of 2007–2008. Since then, the evidence of the extraordinary power of human and, indeed, spiritual motivation to change things for the better has been surprising, as I have drawn these stories together. Any errors in reporting them are entirely mine and not due to the subjects of the stories themselves. They themselves are the inspiration for this book which is written in tribute to them.

I should also make it clear that any hint of my political leanings, whether to the Left or the Right, that readers may surmise from this text should be regarded as being mine alone and not those of the organizations with which I have been associated. These charity organizations remain party-political neutral.

My thanks go especially to my colleague Simone Mueller for her helpful insights and incisive comments on the original manuscript. My thanks also go to my colleague Talia Smith, Project Manager for the business programmes of Initiatives of Change UK, 2012–2016, for her research and thoughtful inputs into the chapter on "Time for self-reflection".

I hope readers will find the stories in this book encouraging, inspirational and instructional.

Michael Smith, April 2019

References

Muff, Katrin (editor) et al., *The Collaboratory: a co-creative stakeholder engagement process for solving complex problems*, Greenleaf Publishing, 2014

1   Why this book?

The purpose of this book is to highlight the human motivations that lead to positive change in organizations in the context of the great global challenges—human, environmental, social, cultural and political—and how such motivations can be incubated, encouraged and nurtured at the individual and organizational levels. The book addresses the role played by a leadership of integrity in business and, by extension, the global economy.

Integrity builds trust, which was seriously damaged by the banking crash of 2007–2008, and which, according to the authoritative Edelman Trust Barometer is only now, a decade later, beginning to be restored.[1]

The book contains some 60 case stories of ethical best practice, stories of inspiring people and organizations, which I hope the reader will find engaging and from which lessons can be drawn.

A golden thread running through all these stories is a leadership of integrity, based on individuals' character, displayed by all those in positions of influence. Indeed, we all influence those around us by our practices and behaviours, whatever our positions.

The book looks at the effect of people's inner motivations which affect outcomes. Far from the old Machiavellian and Leninist dictum that "the ends justify the means", the reverse is often the case: the means determine the ends. This was dramatically shown, to devastating effect, in the human drives combined with deregulation in the financial services industry which led to the crash of 2007–2008. Equally, organizations that are shown to be led by a leadership and character of integrity have positive outcomes, as we shall see throughout this book.

The *way* we do things is as important as what we do. Our aims—those of business leaders and all of us—are all important. They can be driven solely by a spirit of acquisition, often interpreted as a materialistic motivation of greed. Or they can be driven by contribution, in service to society and the wider good.

Critical to this choice are, firstly, the moral, ethical and spiritual dynamics that lie deep in the heart of a person, which affect behaviours. The people

---

1   The 2018 Edelman Trust Barometer reported a "recovering belief in CEOs"—up from 37 per cent to 44 per cent year on year—as they are rewarded for speaking out on global issues.

quoted in this book draw on an inner inspiration which encourages correction, direction and best practice for themselves and their organizations, especially through times of self-reflection and silence. They often make this a regular or daily habit. Secondly, this encourages a sense of purpose for themselves and their organizations towards the wider good. Thirdly, none of them claim to be paragons of virtue, though they have an intention, a willingness, towards best practice. We shall see at the end of the book how such best practice can be encouraged at the organizational and personal levels.

Business leaders and all those engaged in shaping the global economy have particular skills sets. But in other respects they are just like the rest of us with all the combination of human emotions: fear, greed, hate, lust, revenge, power and self-interest; or love, selflessness, a desire to serve, integrity and a mutual interest in the welfare of others, in providing the goods, services and jobs the world needs. The choice runs through every human heart and the book touches on this aspect.

Why is the issue of a leadership of integrity in business and the economy important to me? I don't have a business degree or an MBA. I am essentially a journalist rather than a businessman, as reflected in the stories in this book, though I was on the board of a small, independent publishing house, Grosvenor Books, in London for several years in the 1990s. As I listened to the stories captured in this book, I was more and more intrigued and inspired by them. I wanted to gather them together and write about them in the press.

My late father, Neville Smith, and his brother Basil were the fourth generation running a family wool textile mill in Bradford, Yorkshire. It was founded in 1840 by their great-grandfather, John Smith, a dalesman who started washing and combing sheep's wool for cloth manufacture where there was a plentiful supply of water on the banks of the river Aire. His son, Isaac, became the Mayor of Bradford, twice elected by his fellow aldermen, in the 1890s. (I presented to a recent Lord Mayor of Bradford a large silver platter, inscribed to Isaac Smith by his fellow aldermen, for the City Hall's splendid silver collection, after I inherited it from my father.)

Isaac, my great-grandfather, was one of four Bradford business leaders who, in 1893, bought and took over the running of the world renowned Salts Mill in the village of Saltaire. Its founder, Sir Titus Salt, had died in 1876 but his sons had not been able to stem the company's debts. Isaac chaired the new consortium owning the company.[2] Sir Titus Salt had famously introduced alpaca wool into the British textile industry. In the village next to the huge mill, Salt had provided housing, a library and a chapel for his workforce in the paternalistic culture of Victorian businessmen. Salts Mill and Saltaire village are now World Heritage sites and the mill has been turned into a splendid arts and crafts centre famed for exhibiting paintings by the Bradford-born artist David Hockney.

Isaac Smith's Fieldhead mills in Bradford were said to produce the finest manufactured wool tops (long fibres) anywhere in the world. My grandfather,

---

2 *Salts Mill*, Maggie Smith and Colin Coates, Amberley Publishing, 2016; *Salt and Saltaire*, Dr Gary Firth, The History Press, 2009.

Harold, expanded John Smith and Sons (Fieldhead Mills) in the 1930s till it employed 1,100 people. At the outbreak of World War II, my father and uncle were deemed to be in a "reserve occupation", producing the wool needed to make uniforms for the armed forces and, it was said, the wool for King George VI's shirts and pyjamas. So Neville and Basil were never called up into active war service.

Shortly after I was born, after World War II, the family, including my two elder brothers, moved to Bank Top House, one half of an old stone farm building at the top of a bluebell wood overlooking Salts Mill. We lived there till I was 14, loving the ample garden—lawn, apple orchard, paddock and kitchen garden. After we moved from there the garden was sold and turned into a modern housing estate.

Sad to say, there were management misjudgments in running the family owned business. Harold, in the anti-Semitic culture of his times, refused to do business with the men's clothing retailer Montague Burton, simply because he was Jewish. I have no idea if Harold was overtly anti-Semitic or if he simply feared the good opinion of his peers. But it was a costly decision. Burton bought his wool elsewhere and expanded his retail outlets into a national chain, eventually taken over by the Arcadia group. A contract with him might have secured our family's textile mill.

Harold also borrowed money from the company in order to buy a splendid family home, Ranby Hall, in the village of Ranby, Nottinghamshire, on the edge of Sherwood Forest. It had 50 acres of estate and 11 paid staff: cook, butler, housemaids and gardeners. This was where my father grew up as a teenager. This was all very well but the good trading, which Harold expected would cover the cost of this grandeur, never came, not least due to competition from the rise of artificial fibres and rival textile businesses in southern Europe. The family business failed to invest in new technology to keep up with the competition. My grandfather had to sell Randy Hall and rent Moor Park, a country house outside Harrogate, which was, nonetheless, on a grand scale with an enormous, sweeping staircase from the entrance hall. This was where my parents got engaged. (The building has long since been converted into flats.)

The company floated on the stock market to raise capital. But it was all too late and in a sale of shares, not anticipated by my father and uncle, the company was taken over in the 1950s by a competitor group. From one day to the next, my father and uncle were told that they were out of a job. The mill was soon closed down by the new owners and the only evidence of its existence now is the name of Smith Street in the centre of Bradford, on one side of the site where the mill once stood.

Having lost everything, my parents moved to a small bungalow in the seaside village of Selsey in West Sussex, where I spent my teenage years. My tiny bedroom had to be built into the loft. For my father, it was a far cry from the splendour of Ranby Hall. Yet he remained remarkably free of any sense of bitterness over his loss.

My mother, Joan, the daughter of a tartan cloth and gabardine manu-facturer from Ilkley, called it "the rise and fall of the Smith empire". Her ancestor in Lancashire, great-uncle Samuel Turner, had been the inventor of the use of asbestos as a heat insulator. Children would play in piles of asbestos dust outside the factory as if it was snow. No one in those days had the slightest knowledge of the appalling health hazards to lungs and life that asbestos dust posed. Having this in my family history makes me all the more aware of the environmental damage that industrial processes can cause.

My elder brother, Nigel, spent most of his working life in the Bradford textile company which had taken over our family's business, becoming its training and personnel manager, before he too retired with his wife to live in Selsey.

For myself, I had to carve out a different identity, called to serve the international network of Initiatives of Change through writing and journalism. But I could never wholly divorce myself from our family history and have retained a certain fascination with the world of business and industry, its core motivations and its impact on the world.

My baptism into the world of trade unionism came when my colleagues and I at the publishing house where we worked joined one of the print trade unions and became active London branch members for several years. We had to be union members or the artwork we generated would have been boycotted by the printing press operators in an era that militantly defended the closed shop which barred non-union labour. I was the father-of-the-chapel, the printers' term for a shop steward, and at one time we put forward a motion to the London district council of the erstwhile National Graphical Association print trade union, in support of the international development issues raised by the Brandt Commission Report, published in 1980.[3] The motion was carried almost unanimously and was opposed, surprisingly, by only one person in the packed hall: a left-wing member of the Trotskyite Militant Tendency.

I hope the stories in this book, highlighting core motivations, are a source of inspiration and enlightenment to young and seasoned entrepreneurs alike. The challenge is to raise and encourage a generation of young entrepreneurs, the world's next business leaders, who are prepared to put into practice the highest moral and ethical standards they know.

Michael Smith, April 2019

References

Smith, Maggie and Colin Coates, *Salts Mill*, Amberley Publishing, 2016
Firth, Dr Garry, *Salt and Saltaire*, The History Press, 2009

3   https://www.sharing.org/information-centre/reports/brandt-report-summary

Part 1
The global context

2 Skin in the game

The global economy is all pervasive. It affects the daily lives of everyone on the planet—from the largest urban conurbations to the remotest villages.[1]

- The global economy provides all the goods and services for our daily lives. It includes the jobs, incomes, education, skills, housing, health care, economic wellbeing—or otherwise—and a degree of human and social security for the billions of people around the world.
- It includes all those employed in, and supplying, the big corporations, small and medium sized enterprises, and public sector organizations which service the global economy.
- The global economy includes the purchasing choices we make about our food and clothing and their origins; the road, rail and air transport we use; our carbon footprint and our energy use.
- The global economy affects the quality of the air we breathe, the water we drink, the diseases we suffer—and the plastic we throw away, polluting rivers and oceans and killing wildlife. It dramatically impacts on climate change.
- It includes the information technology and social media we use, provided by some of the world's biggest corporations.
- And it includes the taxes we pay—or fail to pay—to provide for our public services.
- The global economy encourages the conditions for peace, such as the Schuman Plan which integrated coal and steel production in France and Germany after World War II, laying the foundation for the European Economic Community.
- Or it exacerbates the conditions for war and conflict over natural resources, from oil in the Middle East to blood diamonds in Africa.

Anyone who says they don't have an interest in the global economy needs to understand that the global economy has a great deal of interest in them.

---

1   The economic prospects of families in the remotest villages of African countries, for instance, can be transformed by a simple piece of intermediate technology: a bicycle. See Hans Rosling's talk "Don't panic" at: https://youtu.be/FACK2knC08E

We all have a financial stake, whether we are owners, employees, investors or simply purchasers. We all have skin in the game.

Capital and social market economies have lifted millions out of poverty in the last three decades, not least in the BRIC countries (Brazil, Russia, India and China). Yet the capitalist economy has also led to enormous economic disparities between the world's richest and poorest, as well as within organizations—the gap between boardroom pay and average wages. Such injustices all too easily fuel the humiliations and anger that lead to extremism and violence.

It is arguable that a consequence of the financial crash of 2007–2008 was the backlash against remote political and economic elites, alongside fears of immigration, which led to Brexit and the election of Donald Trump. The voice and feelings of the disenfranchised is too easily overlooked by political and economic elites, leading to unexpected political outcomes. As Ed Conway, Economics Editor of Sky News, wrote: "Look for a common theme among voters around the world and you'll find anger at an unelected elite, whether in Brussels or Washington. The message is simple: we never voted for the version of globalization you've given us and we want more control."[2]

Trump's election gave rise to the notion of "fake news" perpetrated by Trump and others, for or against him, particularly on social media platforms. It was noticeable from the moment he claimed that the crowds attending his inauguration ceremony were far greater than the news footage actually showed. Trump repeatedly accused the media, including *The New York Times*, of being "the enemy of the people". The mendacity at the heart of government led to what American author Michiko Katutani of *The New York Times* calls The Death of Truth.[3]

There is, of course, nothing new about "fake news". During the Cold War it was known as disinformation. Pope Francis wryly commented that the first fake news was the serpent's reassurance to Eve that eating the forbidden fruit in the Garden of Eden was okay!

By January 2018, trust in the giant social media companies (about which more later in this chapter) had fallen to an all-time low in the UK, accused in part by spreading fake news, according to the 2018 annual Edelman Trust Barometer. Less than a quarter of people trusted Facebook and Twitter. Most Britons thought that the social media companies were doing too little to tackle extremism, cyber bullying and child safety on their platforms.[4]

Since the growth of the Internet from the 1990s, the World Wide Web, emails and file sharing have transformed the world and led to the all-pervasive social media.

Such rapid technological changes in the last 30 years are likely to be matched in the next decades. A child born today is likely to live, if they are in the

2   *The Times*, 3 November 2017
3   *The Death of Truth*, Michiko Kakutani, reviewed in *The Times*, 28 July 2018
4   The 2018 Edelman Trust Barometer: https://www.edelman.co.uk/wp-content/uploads/Website-Edelman-Trust-Barometer-Press-Release-2018.pdf

wealthy, more secure economies, through the whole of the 21st century. What revolutionary developments—in science, health-care, space exploration, environmental protection, relationships between individuals and between nations—will they experience by the time they reach old age?

On many fronts, the world is getting dramatically better. The late Swedish statistician and friend of Bill Gates, Hans Rosling, spells this out in his book *Factfulness* (2018).[5] In 1800, 85 per cent of the world's population lived in extreme poverty—living on $2 a day at today's prices—and life expectancy was only 30 years. Twenty years ago, 29 per cent lived in extreme poverty. Now it is nine per cent and still falling. "This is absolutely revolutionary", he writes. "I consider it to be the most important change that has happened in the world in my lifetime." Moreover, the global average for life expectancy is now 72 years. Cereal yields have almost trebled since the 1960s; and about 88 per cent of us enjoy clean water supplies compared with 58 per cent in 1980. Rosling calls this "the secret silent miracle of human progress". But there is no excuse for complacency: a billion people still have to survive on about $1 a day.

Rosling sees five global risks that we should all be worried about: the possibility of a global pandemic (such as the Spanish flu which killed 50 million people after World War I); another financial collapse, crashing the global economy; World War III ("It's a huge diplomatic challenge to prevent the proud and nostalgic nations with a violent track record from attacking others", he writes.); Climate Change which requires "a strong, well-functioning international community", such as the UN, to address it; and extreme poverty, a daily reality affecting some 800 million people around the world, and often fuelling the desperation and extremism that leads to terrorism.

It is clear that we still need a far more just global economy.

At least we are globally aware. We are the most informed generation in human history, thanks to the impact of global communications, electronic news gathering and the World Wide Web. These have encouraged in today's generations a strong sense of social conscience.

The Third and Fourth Industrial Revolutions, in the four decades since the 1980s, have had a huge impact on the world—the digital revolution of computing power, the Internet, and information and communications technology (ICT), transforming the daily lives and practices of much of the world's citizens; and now the Fourth Industrial Revolution (Industry 4.0) with technological breakthroughs in robotics, artificial intelligence (AI), biotechnology, nanotechnology, quantum computing, cryptocurrencies, 3D printing and "autonomous" or driverless vehicles. AI alone will have the potential to both destroy and create jobs, and save lives through the early detection of diseases ranging from cancer to Alzheimer's.

Industry 4.0, claims Joe Kaeser, President and CEO of Siemens AG, with some hyperbole

---

5   See also review of *Factfulness: ten reasons we're wrong about the world—and why things are betting than you think, The Times*, 28 April 2018.

is the greatest transformation human civilization has ever known... transforming practically every human activity: the way we make things; the way we use the resources of our planet; the way we communicate and interact with each other as humans; the way we learn; the way we work; the way we govern; and the way we do business. Its scope, speed and reach are unprecedented... That's why the Fourth Industrial Revolution is not just about technology or business; it is about society.[6]

The challenges are enormous, says Kaeser:

If we get the revolution right, digitization will benefit the nearly 10 billion humans inhabiting our planet in the year 2050. If we get it wrong, societies will be divided into winners and losers, social unrest and anarchy will arise, the glue that holds societies and communities together will disintegrate, and citizens will no longer believe that governments are able to fulfill their purpose of enforcing the rule of law and providing security.

The Fourth Industrial Revolution, writes Klaus Schwab, the founder of the World Economic Forum in his book of that title, requires that we nurture four types of intelligence: "contextual (the mind), emotional (the heart), inspired (the soul) and physical (the body)". "In other words", comments Matthew Taylor, CEO of the Royal Society of Arts in London, reviewing Schwab's book, "technological development must be matched by a great leap forward in wisdom and empathy".[7]

In this new paradigm, "the Fourth Industrial Revolution will eliminate millions of jobs and create millions of new jobs", adds Kaeser.

I believe that the next step on the path to inclusiveness is to significantly raise standards for business as far as social responsibility and sustainability are concerned. Contrary to Milton Friedman's maxim, the business of business should not just be business. Shareholder value alone should not be the yardstick. Instead, we should make stakeholder value, or better yet, social value, the benchmark for a company's performance.[8]

According to a 2018 McKinsey report, "AI has the potential to deliver additional global economic activity of around $13 trillion by 2030, or about 16 percent higher cumulative GDP compared with today. This amounts to 1.2 percent additional GDP growth per year."[9]

For the pioneering IT entrepreneur Bela Hatvany, who funded the creation of the online donations platform Just Giving, "The Internet and social media

---

6   Kaeser was addressing the World Economic Forum, Davos, 25 January 2018.
7   *The Fourth Industrial Revolution*, Klaus Schwab, Portfolio Penguin, 2016
8   Kaeser, ibid.
9   https://www.mckinsey.com/featured-insights/artificial-intelligence

are the new fire—a great servant but a terrible master." He says: "We need to move from the growth economy to the care economy. We must stop destroying the earth for profit." He adds: "The care economy depends on the right balance between male and female leadership."[10]

The new millennium has seen the astonishing rise of social media: the use of the Internet by tech and social media companies to link up and transform the world. The growth of the social media tech firms in the first decades of the new millennium has indeed been phenomenal. By the end of December 2017, the world's largest companies by market capitalization were Apple, Google, Microsoft, Amazon and Facebook.[11] Then, in August 2018, Apple became the world's first trillion dollar company.

Even so, there is still a huge digital divide in the world. 2018 was the first year in which over half the world's population had access to the Internet, three decades after Tim Berners-Lee invented the World Wide Web. Billions are still excluded. Berners-Lee, marking the 29th anniversary of his invention in March 2018, warned against the concentration of power in the huge tech firms that "control which ideas and opinions are seen and shared". Google, for instance, accounted for some 87 per cent of online searches worldwide. His concern was that the giant tech companies, including Facebook, Google and Twitter, were built to "maximize profit more than to maximize social good". Berners-Lee continued: "A legal or regulatory framework that accounts for social objectives may help ease those tensions." Business, governments, civil society, academia and the arts all needed to be involved in the debate.[12]

Facebook, which also owns WhatsApp, Messenger and Instagram, has become one of the world's most influential media outlets. Its impact is measured not in millions, like traditional broadcast and print media, but billions. It claims to have 2.38 billion users every month, and growing, while some 1.56 billion people check their Facebook pages every day. Its arch competitor, Alphabet, which owns Google and YouTube, has 1.5 billion monthly users. There has been nothing like it before. Yet Facebook is hardly a news organization in its own right so much as a publisher. It simply acts as a platform for users' content. They are the authors. Individuals worldwide create their own networks among friends and families: small interlocking communities which combine, like fractals, to contribute to Facebook's global reach.

Despite this, there is a "malignity" at the heart of Facebook, according to the award-winning writer John Lanchester, not least because of its use as a platform to disseminate fake news. "In September [2017], details of what the Russians had done started coming out", Lanchester writes. "Kremlin-connected propaganda outfits bought $100,000 of Facebook advertising to use it to target 10 million Americans." The aim had been to damage Hilary

10 Hatvany was addressing the opening ceremony of the 2018 Caux Forum, "Developing potential for human change", Switzerland, 28 June.
11 *Financial World* magazine, London, February/March 2018
12 Olivia Solon, *The Guardian*, 12 March 2018

Clinton and support Donald Trump in the presidential election campaign. Facebook's founder, Mark Zuckerberg, had to backtrack on his remark, after the election, that "I thought the idea of misinformation on Facebook changed the outcome of the election was crazy." Now, he said, "Calling that crazy was dismissive and I regret it. This is too an important an issue to be dismissive."[13]

Another "malignity" of Facebook, writes Lanchester, is the way it gathers information about its users in order to target them with advertising. "Facebook", he writes, "is in the surveillance business. Facebook, in fact, is the biggest surveillance-based enterprise in the history of mankind. It knows far more about you than the most intrusive government has ever known about its citizens." Knowing our interests and preferences, Facebook's advertising revenue boosted its profits in 2017 by 73 per cent to an enormous $17.6 billion, fuelled by a 46 per cent jump in turnover to $40 billion.[14] Yet the controversies surrounding Facebook caught up with the company when, on 26 July 2018, more than $100 billion was wiped off its stock market valuation—a 19 per cent drop and the biggest one-day fall in Wall Street's history. Facebook's users were spooked by privacy concerns and regulations, prompting a drop of three million European users.[15]

The case for regulation of the social media industry had become overwhelming when, earlier in March, reports emerged that the data of 60 million Facebook users, mostly Americans as well as a million in the UK, were "harvested", without their knowledge, and passed on to the data company Cambridge Analytica. The London-based company boasted that they used the data to target American voters with messages encouraging them to vote for Donald Trump in the US Presidential elections and to "vote leave" in the UK's EU referendum. Facebook's founding CEO, Mark Zuckerberg, acknowledged the need for regulation.[16] Advertisers took fright and Facebook's share price and market capitalization plummeted. Meanwhile, Cambridge Analytica lost so many customers, frightened by the controversy, that it had to close down that April.

As well as economic and political influence, at the heart of all these developments is the influence on, and impact of, millions of "ordinary" citizens, their dreams and decisions. Stuff happens because millions of individuals—including those in leadership and those with enormous talent—make it happen. Zuckerberg had created Facebook from his Harvard dormitory room as a relationships and dating platform for students at Harvard and other US universities. No one could have anticipated its phenomenal growth, making Zuckerberg the world's youngest billionaire.[17]

13 John Lanchester, *The Sunday Times Magazine*, London, 29 October 2017
14 Danny Forston, *The Sunday Times*, 28 January 2018
15 *The Washington Post*, 26 July 2018
16 *The Times*, 23 March 2018
17 See especially the Hollywood film *The Social Network* (2010).

Human motivations, person by person, group by group, society by society, as much as "impersonal forces", play a critical role in the march of history. Stuff happens, for good or ill, because of all the gamut of mixed emotions and motivations—hate, fear, greed, lust and corruption; love, courage, integrity and forgiveness—played out in the hearts and minds of individuals and in the affairs of the world.

When John Major succeeded Margaret Thatcher as the leader of the Conservative Party and Prime Minister in 1990 he famously called for "a nation at ease with itself". I reflected at the time that, while this was a fine ideal, it could only truly come about if the nation's citizens, individually and collectively, were at peace with their consciences. Today we are far from the notion of a nation at ease with itself. The British have been deeply divided over the choice for or against Brexit and appallingly uninformed about the economic implications surrounding that choice. The United Kingdom has become a nation deeply at dis-ease with itself.

We need not only a "conscious capitalism"—conscious of the needs of society—that liberates "the heroic spirit in business", in the words of John Mackey and Raj Sisodia,[18] but also a conscience-based economy and society that is inspired and informed by the indwelling of the human spirit in individuals.

In a VUCA world (Volatile, Uncertain, Complex and Ambiguous), business and political leaders—and all of us—often under the great pressure of events and information overload, all the more need an anchor, a daily source of stability and inner inspiration in our lives. What, therefore, are the spiritual resources that inform and strengthen today's generation of business, economic and political leaders as well as students—the world's future leaders? How do such resources apply in practice? Thanks to the global and social media, we are the most informed, and socially conscious, generation in history. But what are the spiritual norms, the sources of inner inspiration, which guide our daily conduct, motivations and perspectives?

This book aims to look at these issues. It gives case studies of those who aim to build pillars of trust in the economy, including integrity, cooperation, stewardship, purpose and sustainability. In so doing, they also reflect eight Cs of trust which define the Culture of organizations: Contracts, Competences, Covenants, Character, Conscience, Conviction, Courage and Change.

Above all, the book addresses human motivations—the personal factor—and the spark that governs them, particularly in the business and economy context. This, again, is the golden thread running through the case stories. The book provides tools for decision-making, including the eight Cs of trust, "self-reflection" and "inner motivation", and how these might be encouraged inside organizations.

In an age that is seeing the growth of automation and artificial intelligence, threatening traditional jobs and creating new ones, the need is space for

---

18 *Conscious Capitalism: liberating the heroic spirit of business*, John Mackey and Raj Sisodia (2014)

reflection—for intuitive intelligence, for emotional and spiritual intelligence, for conscience-based intelligence and decision-making in business, economic, political and personal life.

References

Kakutani, Michiko, *The Death of Truth*, William Collins, 2018

Mackey, John, and Sisodia, Raj, *Conscious Capitalism: liberating the heroic spirit of business*, Harvard Business Review Press, 2014

Rosling, Hans, with Rosling, Ola, and Ronnlund, Anna Rosling, *Factfulness: ten reasons we're wrong about the world—and why things are better than you think*, Sceptre, Hodder & Stoughton, 2018

Schwab, Klaus, *The Fourth Industrial Revolution*, Portfolio Penguin, 2016

3 Narrowing the world's rich-poor gaps

While the booster rocket of economic growth in recent decades has helped to give unprecedented levels of wealth to over a billion and a half people, what about the rest? Oxfam's 2018 briefing paper, "Reward work, not wealth", was published that January, just as the world's business leaders met for their annual gathering at the World Economic Forum in Davos, Switzerland. Oxfam said that over 80 per cent of the world's wealth created in 2017 flowed into the coffers of the world's wealthiest one per cent. At the same time, the poorest half of the world's population—3.7 billion people—saw their wealth flatline. An emphasis on leading with integrity needs to be in the context of this reality, if we are to create a fairer, more just global economy.

"Something is very wrong with a global economy that allows the one per cent to enjoy the lion's share of increases in wealth while the poorest half of humanity misses out", said Mark Goldring, Oxfam's UK chief executive. Oxfam quoted data from Credit Suisse, published in November 2017, which showed that the world's 42 richest people owned the same wealth as the poorest half of humanity.[1]

Such disparities, as well as the enormous wealth gap between boardroom pay and average wages, seem to call into question the whole capitalist edifice. Yet, as we have seen from Hans Rosling's book *Factfulness*, the world is greatly better than it used to be: global poverty has declined sharply from the 1800s to today. But the benefits are by no means evenly distributed. In Mexico, Rosling points out, the peak number of the population live on less than $8 per day, while in the USA the peak numbers of people live on closer to $100 a day. Many of the wealthiest in Mexico have much the same income as the poor in the USA.

In India rapid economic growth has benefitted millions but left millions of others still in grinding poverty. The nation's growth has mostly benefitted its four wealthiest states, say Jean Dreze and Amartya Sen in their seminal book *An Uncertain Glory: India and its contradictions* (2013). There is still a huge need for investment in both physical and social infrastructure: from transport

---

1 https://www.oxfam.org.uk/get-involved/campaign-with-us/inequality-and-poverty;
   https://www.oxfam.org/en/research/reward-work-not-wealth

and energy supplies to health care and education. Above all there is a far greater need for what Dreze and Sen call "participatory growth" whereby the benefits of economic growth are more evenly distributed. Yet growth in India, the world's most populous democracy, was critical to the target set by the UN's Millennium Development Goals of halving global poverty by 2015.

It was an issue addressed by Anup Mukerjee, former Chief Secretary of Bihar (2009–2011), one of India's poorest states, during the biennial Caux Initiatives for Business conference in Panchgani, in November 2013. Bihar was becoming a safer state to live in and its infrastructure was improving, claimed the senior Indian Administrative Service officer. He is a man of renowned personal integrity, who has been compared by his fellow IAS officers to Gautama Buddha, thanks to his frugal lifestyle. So his word could be taken at face value. In Bihar, "access to education for the poor, particularly the girl-child, and empowerment of women, have all contributed towards creating a trend of participatory growth", Mukerjee claimed.

Oxfam urged governments to adopt a range of measures to close the wealth gap. These included clamping down on tax dodging by corporations and individuals; sharing the tax burden fairly, shifting taxes more towards capital and wealth and away from consumption; introducing minimum wages and a "living wage" for all workers; and equal pay for men and women. An important question is what the world's wealthiest people are doing with their enormous fortunes. Bill and Melinda Gates, for instance, have invested over $30 billion in two decades to help eradicate diseases, particularly polio and malaria, through their foundation.[2]

Pneumonia is also a child killer in developing countries. An investment of $0.40 per person in inoculations could save 5.3 million lives by 2030, according to Save the Children. It reports that 450 million children globally will face chronic malnutrition over the next 15 years. And 150 million children are engaged in child labour, depriving them of a normal education.[3]

Another disturbing trend is the widening gap between top boardroom pay and mean wages inside organizations, a gap which seems to have grown exponentially, and which fuels disaffection in society as a whole. The issue has led to concern on both sides of the Atlantic. In the UK, it affects the morale of employees, according to a survey by the Chartered Institute of Personnel and Development, the body which represents human resource managers. CIPD surveyed over 1,000 workers in 2015 and warned that there was now a "crisis" over inordinate pay increases for top executives. Three out of five workers felt "demotivated" by high pay awards in the boardroom. "The growing disparity between pay at the high and lower ends of the pay scale for

2   https://www.gatesfoundation.org/; https://www.theguardian.com/world/bill-and-m elinda-gates-foundation

3   Email to the author from Christine Wu, General Counsel, Asset Control, and area representative of Save the Children, 18 December 2017; www.savethechildren.org. uk

today's workforce is leading to a real sense of unfairness", said Charles Cotton of the CIPD. That was impacting on employees' motivation at work.[4] The trend so concerned Prime Minister Theresa May that her government drew up a Green Paper that would force companies to publish their pay gaps.[5]

In the USA, according to the Washington DC think-tank the Economic Policy Institute, income inequality had risen in every state since the 1970s. "For the United States overall, the top 1 per cent captured 85.1 per cent of total income growth between 2009 and 2013. In 2013 the top 1 per cent of families nationally made 25.3 times as much as the bottom 99 per cent", stated the report.[6]

The Northern Irish businessman Peter Brew, who ran the Asia-Pacific regional arm of the International Business Leaders Forum from Hong Kong (2008–2011) highlights

> the quite obscene levels of remuneration within the business sector. If you invent something and you put all of your resources behind it, then you deserve to gain the benefit of that. But the vast majority of business leaders are short-term trustees of the companies in which they are operating. They usually don't stay for more than five or six years and yet they receive benefits that are far beyond any rational level of payment. Back in the 1970s, the ratio between the CEO and the average pay was something like seven to one. It's now in the order of 500 to one.[7]

Such gross disparities fuel anger in society, at a time when, according to the authors of *The Spirit Level*, Kate Pickett and Richard Wilkinson (2010), the more that societies are equal the better and more satisfying they are for everyone. The alarming alternative, in grossly unequal societies, is the cry of the anarchists at the time of the Russian Revolution to "loot the looters", as they seized the property of aristocrats. This, in effect, is what happened to banks and retailers during street riots in London and other British cities in the summer of 2012.

Remuneration committees, too often in a cosy relationship with the board rooms they serve, have to bear responsibility for taming the gross, and often unfair, rewards that they award to top executives. It is an issue which builds—or undermines—trust in society. It also cuts to the very heart of status—how do I compare with my peers?—and human satisfaction in life. When John D Rockefeller was asked, "How much is enough?" he is said to have replied, "Just a little more". The demand for more becomes insatiable. The American chairman of one of the world's leading medical technology companies told me

---

4　*Daily Telegraph*, 18 December 2015
5　*The Independent*, 29 November 2016
6　Economic Policy Institute, 16 June 2016; https://www.epi.org/publication/incom e-inequality-in-the-us/
7　Peter Brew said this during his public Caux Lecture, Switzerland, in July 2013.

in Caux, Switzerland, that he had done very well out of the US stock market and that he was now concerned about how to use his wealth for social purposes, including which charities to support. "After all, I can only sail one yacht at a time!" he remarked.

There are, of course, renowned organizations such as the John Lewis Partnership, the UK-based retail chain, that have deliberately limited the ratio between boardroom pay and mean wages.

Perhaps the most unusual story of leadership by example comes from the former boss of JAL (Japan Airlines), Haruka Nishimatsu, President of the JAL Group from 2006 to 2010. CBS News carried a TV profile of him walking to work, having an open-door policy to his staff after knocking down the walls to his office, having lunch in the company cafeteria, and minimizing his salary, which one year was as low as $90,000. "Nishimatsu says a CEO doesn't motivate by how many millions he makes, but by convincing employees you're all together in the same boat", wrote CBS journalist Barry Petersen.[8]

So what else do business leaders need to do to build a fairer, more just society? Milton Friedman's notion that the sole purpose of business is to maximize the profits for shareholders, articulated in the context of the Cold War, is now largely obsolete. New models of ownership are emerging, from social enterprises and cooperatives to employee owned companies and "benefit" corporations (B corps). In India, individual companies in the Tata group, one of the world's most reputable companies, are publicly quoted, whilst the parent company is 60 per cent owned by its charitable trusts. The company can never be subject to a takeover bid.

New boardroom motivations are emerging in the "stakeholder economy", which serve the interests of all stakeholders, from owners, customers and employees to wider society and the legacy for future generations yet unborn. Another Japanese example came from the late Ryuzaburo Kaku, Chairman and CEO of Canon Inc. of Japan, who would speak about the need for *kyosei*. The Japanese word can be understood as symbiosis—a relationship of mutual benefit—but which he interpreted as "living and working together for the common good". By this he also meant the legacy left for future generations, and particularly the environmental impact of business activity on society. This was why he opened a factory in China, employing 300 people, solely for the purpose of recycling Canon's products such as printer ink cartridges.

Kaku's emphasis on environmental concerns was born out of his traumatic experience in Nagasaki, where he was a 19-year-old conscripted shipyard worker when the atom bomb fell. Having studied nuclear physics at university, he knew immediately what had happened, and urged his colleagues to remain underground for three days to avoid the effects of radiation, so saving their lives.[9]

New company laws are also being enacted to strengthen boardroom's responsibilities towards all their stakeholders—their "fiduciary duties". Perhaps

8   https://www.cbsnews.com/news/japan-airline-boss-sets-exec-example/
9   Obituary of Ryuzaburo Kaku by Michael Smith, *The Independent*, 10 July 2001

these would have addressed the grossly inadequate due diligence investigation carried out by Royal Bank of Scotland into the state of affairs at the Dutch bank ABN Amro, during RBS's ambitious and disastrous takeover of the Dutch bank in 2007, a situation which should never happen again.

At the global level we should not be pessimistic. In the choice between capitalism and centrally planned command economies, especially since the fall of the Berlin Wall in 1989, the former seems to have won the battle and be delivering the goods. Despite capitalism's disparities and corruptions, Douglas A. Irwin, Professor of Economics at Dartmouth College, goes so far as to assert that the spread of capitalism is the "ultimate antipoverty program".[10]

Irwin quotes a World Bank report of 9 October 2014, indicating that

> the share of the world population living in extreme poverty had fallen to 15 per cent in 2011 from 36 per cent in 1990. Earlier this year, the International Labor Office reported that the number of workers in the world earning less than $1.25 a day has fallen to 375 million in 2013 from 811 million in 1991.

"Such stunning news," Irwin continues, "seems to have escaped public notice, but it means something extraordinary: the past 25 years have witnessed the greatest reduction in global poverty in the history of the world."

To what could this be attributed? Irwin asks.

> Let's be blunt: the credit goes to the spread of capitalism. Over the past few decades, developing countries have embraced economic-policy reforms that have cleared the way for private enterprise.
>
> China and India are leading examples. In 1978 China began allowing private agricultural plots, permitted private businesses, and ended the state monopoly on foreign trade. The result has been phenomenal economic growth, higher wages for workers—and a big decline in poverty. For the most part all the government had to do was get out of the way. State-owned enterprises are still a large part of China's economy, but the much more dynamic and productive private sector has been the driving force for change.
>
> In 1991 India started dismantling the "license raj"—the need for government approval to start a business, expand capacity or even purchase foreign goods like computers and spare parts. Such policies strangled the Indian economy for decades and kept millions in poverty. When the government stopped suffocating business, the Indian economy began to flourish, with faster growth, higher wages and reduced poverty.
>
> The economic progress of China and India, which are home to more than 35 per cent of the world's population, explains much of the global

10 http://www.dartmouth.edu/~dirwin/

poverty decline. But many other countries, from Colombia to Vietnam, have enacted their own reforms.

Irwin acknowledges similar progress in African countries.

According to the IMF, Ghana, Nigeria, Ethiopia and Kenya have all had growth rates above five per cent. And according to the World Bank, six sub-Saharan African countries were predicted to have the world's fastest growth rates in 2018: Ghana (8.3 per cent); Ethiopia (8.2 per cent); Côte d'Ivoire (7.2 per cent); Djibouti (7 per cent); Senegal (6.9 per cent); and Tanzania (6.8 per cent).[11]

This is hugely significant, as it indicates where new markets are likely to be growing, alongside population growth.

Stephen B. Young, the global executive director of the Caux Round Table group of business executives, writes that Irwin's commentary "reminds us why it is important to work towards a moral capitalism, one that serves humanity's material needs and its desire for more equality of opportunity and possession of wealth, while also serving a more transcendent desire for justice".

Far too many people still live in degrading poverty and the threat of killer diseases such as ebola. For capitalism, the market economy, and the companies and organizations that work within them, five pillars of trust—integrity, sustainability, purpose, stewardship and cooperation—are more than ever needed.

In summary, the world is getting far better—including poverty reduction over recent decades—than public perception realizes. Yet the benefits are patchy at best and need to go much further. There are still enormous economic disparities, in which private and public sector business organizations can play a crucial role.

References

Dreze, John and Sen, Amartya, *An Uncertain Glory: India and its contradictions*, Penguin, 2014

Pickett, Kate and Wilkinson, Richard, *The Spirit Level: why equality is better for everyone*, Penguin, 2010

Rosling, Hans, *Factfulness: ten reasons we're wrong about the world—and why things are better than you think*, Sceptre Hodder & Stoughton, 2018.

---

11 *The African Exponent*, 10 July 2018; https://www.africanexponent.com/post/the-6-fastest-growing-economies-in-africa-36

4 Banking on the brink

It quickly became apparent that the financial crash of 2007–2008 impoverished the world. According to the World Bank, the crash led to a drop of 20 per cent in world trade and threw 100 million people into poverty.[1] It was every bit as damaging to the world order as the 9/11 terrorist attacks of 2001.

"I honestly believe that September and October of 2008 was the worst financial crisis in global history, including the Great Depression", commented Ben Bernanke, Chairman of the Federal Reserve Bank at the time.[2]

In this chapter we shall look at the causes of the crash and its aftermath. In the midst of the crisis key individuals took courageous action, motivated, I believe, by a leadership of integrity—the urgent need to do the right thing.

In the US the government's Troubled Asset Recovery Program (TARP) authorized a bail out of the troubled banks to the tune of an incredible $700 billion, signed into law by President George W. Bush in October 2008. The nation of private ownership and free enterprise pumped in billions of taxpayers' money to save the system from total collapse. The sum was subsequently reduced to $475 billion and by the end of 2012 the US Treasury had received repayments of 97 per cent of the $418 billion actually disbursed.

In the UK, Alistair Darling, the Chancellor of the Exchequer in Gordon Brown's Labour government, took decisive action to save RBS (Royal Bank of Scotland) from imminent collapse, as we shall see later in this chapter.

Other individuals stand out.

"Paul Moore here. Who are you?" This abrupt phone call in the spring of 2010 was my introduction to the man who had become internationally known as the HBOS whistleblower. He was calling after I had left a message for him at *The Tablet*, a leading UK Catholic newspaper. I hadn't anticipated that he would call back so quickly.

Moore is a devout Roman Catholic. He and his wife Maureen live in the North Yorkshire village of Helmsley near Ampleforth Abbey, a Benedictine monastery. He had been educated at Ampleforth College. I had read an article about him in *The Tablet*, in which he said he was looking to set up a

1   Figures quoted by Gordon Brown in his book *Beyond the Crash* (2010)
2   *The Times*, London, 28 August 2014

business think-tank with a Christian ethos. I had surmised that the Initiatives of Change (IoC) UK business programme, of which I had recently become the head, perhaps might fit the bill, even if we embraced people of other faith traditions and none. So, over the phone I explained myself to him. Would he come to address a group of us in London? He readily agreed. Thus began our friendship.

Moore, a barrister by background, had been a partner at KPMG in London from 1995 to 2002, where he had been an advisor on financial regulatory issues to a number of FTSE 100 clients. In 2002, he joined HBOS (Halifax Bank of Scotland) to become head of group regulatory risk, based in Halifax, Yorkshire. As such, he had policy setting and oversight responsibility for the executive board's compliance with the UK's Financial Services Authority (FSA) regulations.

In 2004, he warned the management board that the bank's aggressive sales culture had become markedly out of balance with its "systems and controls" and, in particular, with risk management. They were expanding too fast, not just in lending but also in relation to the sale of all other financial products, such as Payment Protection Insurance. He also reported this to the FSA. The issue had been particularly focused for Moore when an employee in a Scunthorpe branch had told him, "Paul, we'll never reach our sales targets and sell ethically."

A few weeks after his warning to the board, its Chief Executive, James Crosby, called Moore into his office. Moore assumed that Crosby wanted to talk about how to address the risk culture in the bank. Instead, much to Moore's shock, Crosby said that he was making Moore redundant. "You can't make my job redundant", Moore responded. "The regulating system requires my job to exist." Moreover, there was no justification; he had not done anything wrong. "Oh, yes, I can", Crosby replied. He replaced Moore with a sales manager who had no previous experience of risk management.

Devastated, Moore left the building and in tears on the street outside called his wife. "He's given me the sack", he told her. Her immediate reply was: "Don't worry, Paul. This is all part of God's plan." It was not the kind of response you would expect even from the saintliest of spouses. But Maureen is the rock in his life. They had first met on Christmas Day 1988, when he was hang-gliding in the Chilean Andes, she coming from Anglo-Colombian parentage. They are used to personal risk assessment themselves.

Moore duly sued the bank for wrongful dismissal and in 2005 settled for a payment of more than £500,000. Part of the settlement was a gagging order which forbade Moore from talking about his dismissal publicly. However, in February 2009 he heard that a Treasury Select Committee in parliament was investigating risks taken by UK banks prior to the credit crunch of 2008. Moore felt a compelling urge to submit his evidence. He had already decided to go public but now found that he would be protected by parliamentary privilege. Whether or not this was the divine will—Moore was inclined to see it as such—he felt his time had come. He sent the committee dozens of pages.

One member got back in touch with him to say that his evidence was "explosive". They had not received anything like it from anyone else within the industry. His evidence became sensational news, with double-page spreads about him in the Sunday newspapers. The media dubbed him the HBOS whistleblower.

Sir James Crosby resigned as Deputy Chairman of the FSA on 11 February 2009, ostensibly to protect the FSA's reputation. It had employed KPMG to investigate Moore's concerns but KPMG, HBOS's auditor, had failed to uphold them. Yet Gordon Brown, the Labour Prime Minister of the day, had to rescue HBOS from collapse by injecting £21 billion of taxpayers' money, and supporting the take-over of HBOS by Lloyds Banking Group. Crosby later surrendered his knighthood.

Moore was further vindicated when in 2012 the Parliamentary Commission on Banking Standards castigated HBOS's former leadership, prompting an apology from Crosby to the commission for the bank's near-collapse, saying "I am very sorry." He was one of the few bankers ever to offer an apology.[3]

Eight years after his dismissal, Moore told the *Financial Times*: "It's like the parting of the Red Sea. I feel a massive shift has taken place. I think most people knew I was right and had a lot of admiration for me but could not associate with me because of risk to themselves. Now they see I spoke up from conscience and competence, not hatred."[4]

Nonetheless, like other whistleblowers, Moore has paid a high price. Headhunters ignored him and it was only in December 2012 that he became, for a while, non-executive chairman of Assetz Capital, a peer-to-peer lender. The trauma of his experience led to bouts of depression and he has never worked in banking since then.

Moore called for a far-reaching reform agenda of the global financial system backed by an "Arab Spring" of public opinion. Most ordinary people, he believed, saw the banking crisis as a symptom of much deeper problems in the world. "The majority of ordinary people on this planet know very well in their hearts and souls that a profound change is needed in the way we live" to avoid the potential for a global disaster brought about by excessive consumption and the climate change that it causes. "Almost everyone I meet seems to know that the pervasive culture in the developed world of 'me, more, now', in which GDP and continuous economic growth seem to be the only mantras around, is not the true road to well-being for all of us, let alone social justice. We have totally lost our way in a sea of greed and vanity." The need was "to rebuild our public policy around the financial sector in a way that not only serves the real economy but also the common good of the whole of humanity."[5]

Earlier, speaking on "Capitalism towards the common good: regulation or culture and character?", in the London centre of Initiatives of Change,[6]

3   *Financial Times*, 4 December 2012
4   Dina Medland, *Financial Times*, 5 June 2013
5   Moore was addressing the 2011 business conference in Caux, Switzerland.
6   23 November 2010

Moore called for a review of corporate governance, including a separation of powers between executive boards and "those accountable for overseeing their actions and reining them in". Risk professionals, such as himself, needed to report to non-executive directors rather than the main board, in order to have influence and to protect their positions. The non-executive directors in turn needed "competence, independence, integrity and diversity", to avoid a "cosy relationship" with executive boards.

"You can have the best governance processes in the world but if they are carried out in a culture of greed, unethical behaviour and an indisposition to challenge, they will fail", Moore said.

The date of 09/15/2008 was never likely to be embedded in the public's consciousness as much as 09/11/2001. No buildings physically collapsed, no television cameras caught the same scale of utter devastation. There were no horrific, visceral images. But the date of 15 September 2008 should be equally remembered nonetheless. It had as great an impact on the global economy. The collapse of Lehman Brothers on that date represented a nadir in the financial crash of 2007–2008, leading to the international credit crunch. Banks lost trust in each other's creditworthiness and interbank lending seized up.

It was the largest bankruptcy in US history. Lehman held toxic debts of around $60 billion. The bank was seriously over-leveraged in its borrowing to finance its expansion in the housing market, and heavily over-exposed in the sub-prime mortgage market. In the second fiscal quarter of that year, Lehman reported losses of $2.8 billion and decided to raise $6 billion in additional capital. By 10 September, Lehman announced a loss of $3.9 billion. Investor confidence collapsed after the Korea Development Bank pulled out of negotiations to take over the US bank, plunging its stock value by 45 per cent.

The sub-prime mortgage market was always a chimera; investing in it was a monstrous gamble that would never pay off, built as it was on a dishonest assessment of individuals' creditworthiness. Sub-prime mortgages were essentially those taken out by people who had no collateral and were bound to have difficulty in keeping up their repayments, especially if they suffered unemployment, ill health or divorce. Yet the percentage of lower-quality sub-prime mortgages, originated in the US market during a given year, rose from an historical eight per cent to approximately 20 per cent from 2004 to 2006, with much higher ratios in some parts of the US. No amount of "slicing and dicing" of the "mortgage backed securities" and collateralized debt obligations (CDOs), the instruments sold between banks to finance the debt, would protect against the underlying risk. Mortgage backed securities turned out to be anything but secure. As Alex Brummer wrote in his book *Bad Banks: greed, incompetence and the next global crisis* (2015, p 105): "People gambling with money that is not their own are more likely to be relaxed—cavalier even—about betting it when they know that losses will be borne by the investor and gains will swell their own earnings."

A collapse in US house prices from a peak in 2006 and subsequent mortgage "delinquencies" (non-repayments) and foreclosures triggered the crisis. It was also brought on by the doubling of fuel prices in the USA between 2005 and 2008, which hit consumers, particularly commuters, hard.

As adjustable rate mortgages soared, so too did delinquencies. The crisis had severe, long-lasting consequences for the US and European economies. The US went into a deep recession, with nearly nine million jobs lost during 2008 and 2009, roughly six per cent of the workforce. An estimate of lost output from the crisis came to at least 40 per cent of the 2007 US gross domestic product. Housing prices fell nearly 30 per cent on average and the US stock market fell approximately 50 per cent by early 2009. By early 2013, the stock market had recovered to its pre-crisis peak, and continued to soar, but housing prices remained near their low point.

In the light of the crash, the Dodd-Frank Wall Street Reform Act set the size of banks' assets for regulatory oversight at $50 billion. However, in May 2018, Congress passed a roll-back on this figure to $250 billion, thus applying to only the top 10 US banks. This was seen as a victory for President Trump who had promised to "do a big number on Dodd-Frank."[7]

The knock-on effect of the great crash was huge elsewhere. Lehman's collapse "exposed the vulnerability of the entire international banking sector", wrote Alistair Darling, the UK's Chancellor of the Exchequer from 2007 to 2010 (*Back from the Brink*, 2012). The Icelandic banks nearly collapsed. In the UK there was a run on Northern Rock in September 2007, with customers queuing outside branches to withdraw their deposits. The bank collapsed and had to be nationalized. Then disaster struck Royal Bank of Scotland, the world's largest bank according to its balance sheet, which was also heavily exposed in the sub-prime mortgage market. When RBS joined a consortium to take over the Dutch bank ABN Amro, its board of directors failed in their fiduciary duty to their stakeholders; there was no adequate due diligence investigation into the state of ABN Amro's sub-prime exposure. It was the world's largest ever bank take-over and turned out to be disastrous. RBS came within hours of collapse and had to be bailed out by the British government which nationalized the bank. At the time, RBS's liabilities were thought to be around £1.9 trillion, Darling wrote, compared with the UK's entire GDP of around £1.5 trillion. The takeover cost UK taxpayers £15 billion, making them owners of more than 70 per cent of the shares.

Ten years later, in 2018, RBS came to a provisional settlement with the US Justice Department for a fine of $4.9 billion, for selling toxic mortgage-backed securities in the US. This settlement was seen as a "major milestone" in the bank's recovery, paving the way for the UK government to prepare to sell the bank back to the private sector.[8]

"The banking crisis was most acute in the US and Europe, including the UK," wrote Darling, "but the downturn had spread much further, hitting both Asian and developing economies, including China, India and those in

7   https://www.thebalance.com/dodd-frank-wall-street-reform-act-3305688
8   Harry Wilson, *The Times*, 11 May 2018

South America. The sub-prime crisis had shown how a problem in one part of the world could infect the entire system within months or even weeks, not years as in the past."

Information technology had also played a major part in exacerbating the crash, with "high-frequency" share trading by computers triggering rapid sales of investors' stocks in minutes, even micro-seconds, like lemmings over a cliff. Just how driven Wall Street traders were to make a fast buck is well exposed in Michael Lewis's book *Flash Boys* (2014). By shaving a microsecond off the speed of a purchase or sales trade they could pre-empt orders and beat them. One company even installed a fibre-optic cable as straight as was physically possible between Chicago and New Jersey, the sites of two exchanges, just to shave off three milliseconds. On the day that Lewis's book was published it emerged that the FBI was investigating high-frequency trading.

The rot continued long after the crash of 2008. Scandal piled on top of scandal. Bradford and Bingley, once a reputable UK mortgage lender, was found to have customers who had "self-certified" their circumstances, no questions asked, prompting the phrase "liar loans". Bank employees were then discovered to have rigged LIBOR, the London Inter-Bank Offered Rate, a key interest rate which sets the value of credit card interests and people's borrowing to finance purchases such as cars. In September 2013, Barclays, RBS and UBS of Switzerland were reported to have paid a combined fine of £2.5 billion for their role in rigging LIBOR.[9]

Then it was found that UK banks had been selling Payment Protection Insurance (PPI) to their customers without their knowledge, going back over decades. PPI was supposed to protect customers' incomes should they lose their jobs and become unemployed. Yet many found that they could not benefit from the insurance despite being charged for it. Banking staff were paid under an incentive scheme that depended on the number of products they sold to customers. Stewardship and care for customers' interests were thus overruled by banks' drive for profits. The sums were, again, staggering. British banks set aside £23 billion in compensation to customers. Lloyds Banking Group alone set aside over £11 billion. RBS set aside £4 billion.

Elsewhere, HSBC, once one of the world's most reputable banks, was fined $1.9 billion by the US authorities after discovering that its Mexico banking had been involved in money laundering, believed to be on behalf of drugs barons. Then in February 2015 a scandal broke concerning HSBC's Geneva private banking branch. It was accused of advising wealthy clients on how to avoid paying taxes by setting up "black" accounts for them in the years from 2005 to 2007. Once again, a tawdry culture, whether or not it was strictly within the law, added fuel to the public's cynicism towards the banking sector. Since then HSBC has aimed to clean up its act. The bank sent me, through one of its senior executives involved in the clean-up, a statement that HSBC was now "adopting the highest or most effective controls against financial

---

9   Quoted by David Marquand in his book *Mammon's Kingdom* (2014)

crime and deploying them everywhere they operate. These global standards are in the form of global Anti-Money Laundering and Sanctions policies which set out the requirements to manage financial crime risk."

The succession of scandals added up to a colossal collapse of trust in banking and bankers. Public fury focussed not only on loss of savings and public investment but on a bonus culture, amongst investment bankers in particular, which bore no relation to the appalling losses still being reported by their banks, and the perception that no one at senior levels was being held accountable or prosecuted. The popular phrase circulated that the banks and bankers, bailed out by tax payers, were "too big to fail, too big to nail and too big to jail". In fact, by 2014 nearly 6,000 London banking and financial services staff had been dismissed since 2008 because of corruption, dishonesty or excessive risk-taking.

By August 2012, the UK's public trust in bankers had collapsed to an all-time low. Research by Which?, the consumer association, found that 71 per cent of the UK public believed banking culture had not improved since the crash of 2008. The Chief Executive of Which?, Peter Vicary-Smith, said, "Five years on from the beginning of the financial crisis, public confidence in the banking industry is at an all-time low, with a series of scandals exposing mismanagement and corruption that have cost UK consumers dear."[10]

By 2014, the levels of trust in financial institutions had hardly changed or had declined even further since 2009, according to the Edelman Trust Barometer Annual Global Survey 2014. In the US, trust in banks had gone up from 35 per cent to 45 per cent; in the UK it stayed the same at just over 30 per cent; in the Netherlands there was a dramatic decline in trust from over 50 per cent of the population to 25 per cent; and in Ireland, where banks had invested in disastrous commercial property deals, the trust factor had declined from 25 per cent to 15 per cent.

Public regulatory bodies such as the USA's Security and Exchange Commission and the UK's Financial Services Authority (since replaced by the Financial Conduct Authority and the Prudential Regulatory Authority) were seen to have failed in their duty of oversight, and credit rating agencies were equally criticized for having given strong ratings to weak asset-backed securities.

The banking crisis led to disillusionment with the whole capitalist edifice, particularly among the young. The celebrated author John Lanchester, writing ten years after the crash, believed that for those who turned 20 following the crash, "the idea of capitalism being thought of as morally superior elicits something between an eye roll and a hollow laugh. Their view of capitalism has been formed by austerity, increasing inequality, the impunity and imperviousness of finance and big technology companies, and the spectacle of increasing corporate profits and a rocketing stock market combined with declining real pay and a huge growth in the new phenomenon of in-work poverty"—the kind of work that doesn't pay enough to live on.[11]

10 *Evening Standard*, London, 9 August 2012
11 *The Sunday Times* magazine, 9 September 2018

Those who advocate the capitalist system as the only show in town have a great deal of work to do in recovering the public's trust. Regaining the public's trust is essential to the good performance of banking and financial services. "Restoration of trust within the financial industry is a prerequisite for the restoration of trust between financial institutions and society", wrote Andreas Suchanek and Christina Kleinau in an article asserting "how trust is a valuable commodity that has been neglected by banks" and "why investment in it can bring benefits not just to the financial sector but society as a whole".[12]

"Systemic stability is a common good", they wrote, concluding, "If banks could be trusted to be prudent, they should be able to access interbank lending whatever the health of their respective sovereign. Banks know a lot about managing assets. It is high time that they once again come to understand that trust is an asset that needs and deserves investment and one that offers a return."

References

Brummer, Alex, *Bad Banks: greed, incompetence and the next global crisis*, Random House Business, 2015

Darling, Alistair, *Back from the Brink: 1,000 days at No 11*, Atlantic Books, 2011

Lewis, Michael, *Flashboys: cracking the money code*, Penguin, 2015

Marquand, David, *Mammon's Kingdom: an essay on Britain now*, Penguin, 2015

Moore, Paul, *Crash, Bank, Wallop*, New Wilberforce Media, 2015

12   *Financial World* magazine, London, August/September 2014

5   Banking on change

Not all banks were culprits, of course, and there are outstanding examples of best practice amongst smaller banks, such as Handelsbanken of Sweden—which maintained a culture of prudence—and Triodos, the green bank founded in the Netherlands, whose mission is to "make money work for positive social, environmental and cultural change". Banks in Australia and Canada also remained relatively unscathed from the crash.

In the UK, Nationwide is the world's largest mutual building society, serving the interests of its customers or "members", and retaining a reputation for trustworthy banking.

Joe Garner, Nationwide's Chief Executive since April 2016, emphasizes character as being an essential ingredient of good banking and business practice. He highlights "the importance of character in a transparent world".

I first met Garner in 2013 when Professor Roger Steare of Cass Business School in the City of London took me to meet him in his office, high up in the HSBC headquarters at Canary Wharf in the City of London. Garner was at that time Head of HSBC UK's retail banking, including its Internet bank First Direct. It turned out that we lived near each other in Wimbledon and so we kept in touch.

The financial crisis had resulted in a drastic erosion of trust, increasing corporate scandals, and "a massive pressure for change" in business, he said.[1] Old management tricks couldn't work anymore. The economy has changed and customers are much better informed thanks to the Internet. "We are at the beginning of the impact of technology. The search engine will turn out to be more revolutionary than the steam engine." Employees needed to be inspired by their supervisors rather than simply obeying rules. In such a world, how could managers succeed?

Garner's solution at HSBC had been to gather his new team and have everyone share "what they love, what they fear, and what they have in their pocket". It led to a great deal of personal discussion, even heart-searching. They realized they could deal with all the tough issues of life as human

1   Garner gave the opening address at the 2013 business conference in Caux, Switzerland. See Chapter 6.

beings. "We concluded that we could deal with anything, but that the business world had frozen us. As long as we keep our humanity, things pass." It was paramount to create work environments "where people can be themselves, where people can be people first, and bankers second", and where they do not overly rely on rules and processes.

Garner has introduced a similar approach at Nationwide, developing what he calls a "significant leadership development programme" called Leading for Mutual Good.[2] This annual three-and-a-half-day offsite gathering brings together 40 to 50 senior managers and other influential leaders. It aims to instil the values of mutuality, care, inclusive leadership and a people-centred approach throughout Nationwide—"not drawbridge up but drawbridge down", as Garner likes to quote Stephen Shakespeare, the CEO of YouGov. Garner immerses himself in the event, setting the scene with an introductory talk each day. Other external participants from big UK organizations are also invited to give talks.

Striking the right balance between rules and trust depends on good management, he says. Quoting General Norman Schwarzkopf, Garner asserts that "leadership is a potent combination of strategy and character. But if you must be without one, be without strategy."

Emmanuel de Lutzel from Paris tells how he persuaded the top management of his bank, BNP Paribas, to invest in microfinance and social business schemes.[3] In 2004 he began a volunteer initiative which started with ten people and now has over 1,000 engaged in supporting small, community projects and organizations around the world.

In 2005, he came to the idea that microfinance, more than just volunteering, could become a business for the bank: not just a classical business, but business with a social purpose. "I presented the idea to 40 colleagues in different departments. Everybody was supportive, saying that the top management should decide but no one was ready to present the case to the top management. So I asked for an appointment with the No 2 of the bank, who after ten minutes told me: next month you will present the subject to the Executive Committee." The Committee was very supportive. They asked De Lutzel to develop a business plan and to launch the activity.

Since then the microfinance team at BNP Paribas has financed 40 microfinance institutions in 15 developing countries and four countries in Europe. In 2013, the scheme scaled up to finance social entrepreneurs in Belgium, Italy and France, reaching more than 200 social businesses in those three countries.

"I didn't know that what I was doing was called social entrepreneurship", De Lutzel says. "I started to be interviewed by newspapers such as the French magazine *L'Express* and I was fascinated by this subject. I have started writing a book about entrepreneurship, based on my own experience and that of

2   Email to the author, 15 June 2018
3   De Lutzel told his story to the 2014 Caux business conference.

another entrapreneur, to provide tools to those interested in changing their companies from the inside."

Microfinance had first taken off in the 1970s when economist Muhammad Yunus lent $25 to a group of women in Bangladesh. When he was repaid, he decided to expand the initiative. Thirty years later, the microfinance sector was lending to an estimated 150 million borrowers which in turn directly impacted the lives of a billion people.

In 2009, De Lutzel told a London audience how he had become involved with microfinance. He had worked in the banking sector for 25 years but, alongside this, he had been involved in business ethics at a national level. He was a member of the board of Transparency International France, the anti-corruption organization, and a member of the board of Initiatives of Change in France. Despite being socially active, he thought that he should be doing something more and in 2005 his calling clarified while reading *The Economist* magazine. That was the Year of Microfinance and while BNP Paribas was involved in funding microfinance initiatives in France, as part of its Corporate Social Responsibility (CSR) policy, it was supporting only two small microfinance pilot projects abroad, in Guinea and Morocco. These have since been replicated in ten other countries.

De Lutzel was inspired by what he had read about microfinance's potential to make a social impact. He started as a field volunteer for Adie, a French microfinance organization, and proposed that colleagues from the bank might join Adie as volunteers. The response was overwhelming. "I was really surprised at the number of people who turned up", De Lutzel said. He transformed his "hobby" into a job, to work full time for microfinance, starting with his proposition to the bank's Executive Committee to launch a global initiative to invest in microfinance internationally. As his previous banking experience had been in corporate banking and cash management and not microfinance, he faced a challenge to demonstrate his expertise behind his conviction that microfinance could be a tool to reduce poverty and make a social impact whilst not losing the bank any money. The executive committee agreed and the project was given the green light. "Big banks are not just bureaucratic monsters; they are made up of people and I knew I just had to reach the people individually", commented De Lutzel, who in 2018 was appointed Vice President Volunteering at BNP Paribas.

Another microfinance lender was the south Indian banker J S Parthibhan. A native of Tamil Nadu, India's southernmost state, he arranged microloans for local village communities near his bank branch in Salem, all from the back of his small, black Honda motorcycle.

"When you begin a new venture, don't think only of yourself and your family. It should benefit the community, the village, and the surroundings", he told the 2014 Caux business conference. He has always believed that banking should be a service-orientated, holistic business, rather than one where customer service is only part of the profit strategy. Indeed, such community-based banking has little in common with risk-based financial speculation.

Parthibhan's banking journey began in 1998 when he became the manager in a branch of the government-owned Indian Bank in Connaught Circus, New Delhi. "I used my position to help beggars and street vendors to manage their money intelligently and live a life of dignity." There were no bank schemes for them and Parthibhan was astonished to find that they earned 500–600 rupees ($10–12) a day, which not even a government official earned. But they had to pay bribes to allow them to operate on the streets. They were street smart and took their work seriously but were ignorant about money management. Most came from nearby states with a lot of dreams, leaving their families behind, Parthibhan explained. "But the reality in Delhi was different; there were no steady jobs and their earnings were never enough to make ends meet. They would borrow money from lenders, at high interest rates, to get over their immediate problem. They never earned or saved enough to clear their debts. The interest rates charged by money lenders kept them in the debt trap. Yet they were totally ignorant of the role that a bank could play in managing their earnings."

Parthibhan wanted them to get out of debt, so he took the initiative to educate them. This took time and patience to earn their confidence. "I showed genuine concern to understand their lives and businesses. Seeing my sincerity, they began talking but they rejected my suggestion of saving in the bank." A common complaint was that they had no money to save when they didn't even have enough to make ends meet. But Parthibhan's persistence convinced them to give it a try, with small savings to begin with.

"They had no idea how to go about it; it was difficult to open a bank account; you needed many documents, such as proof of residence. I made sure that my staff made them comfortable and that they understood how to open a savings account." In a few cases, he even took their personal guarantee. "Their need was genuine and I took the risk."

The bank opened almost 500 savings accounts and 300 deposit accounts for beggars, newspaper vendors, tea-wallahs, shoe-shine boys, restaurant waiters, auto-rickshaw drivers and housewives—everyone opening an account for the first time in their lives. "I remember a man who sold water for half a rupee per glass. He would earn 600–700 rupees ($12–14) per day and would have 20,000–25,000 rupees ($405–505) in his pocket and did not know where to keep it. The idea of a savings account clicked with him. By the time I moved [back to Tamil Nadu] in 2002, he had 200,000 rupees or $4,050 in his account and he had repaid his loans. He was free from worry and started spending quality time with his family."

For Parthibhan, solving problems, including economic ones, is ultimately about cultivating healthy communities. Changing broken systems is important but the real work is with people, he says. "If you help them change their attitude toward life—what they are doing, why they are doing it—if you can help them find an answer to these things, I think we have found an answer to all the big headlines in the newspapers. It gives me great satisfaction to bring happiness to so many poor individuals and their families."

Parthibhan's journey of personal honesty and integrity had begun when he was a student. His "inner voice" of conscience had told him to return 200 "borrowed" library books when he was the student president at Madras Christian College in the 1960s. The principal told him to tell a college assembly what he had done. He did so with great embarrassment, a humbling experience for him.

The result was that hundreds of books were returned by other students in the following days. This was a transformative turning point in Parthibhan's life. Now retired from banking, he has served as the Manager of the Asia Plateau centre in Panchgani.[4]

Professor Hiroshi Ishida from Japan told his story when he spoke on the same platform as De Lutzel and Parthibhan in Caux in 2014. After graduating, he joined the Industrial Bank of Japan where he became a speculator with a hedge fund. "At that time my interest was not in peace," he said. "Whenever there were conflicts they were seen as a big business chance. That's banking. Everybody panics and then we jump into that market. If it was in the Middle East we'd go to the City of London. If it was South America, we'd go to New York City." Ishida commented: "People called me Darth Vader."

After four years the bank moved him to risk management. "There I learned something very strange. They told me problems had occurred concerning cooperation. They said, 'Please don't speak out, hide it.'" So over ten years of his career, he learned how to "manipulate things".

"A big question came up in my mind; am I doing right or wrong? Then when my daughter was three years old, she asked me, 'Papa, what are you doing?' 'I'm a banker.' A few months later she asked, 'What is a banker?' 'A banker collects the money and invests somewhere to increase the asset.' She kept asking me all these questions and I found out she's truly my daughter: she has half my DNA. By the time she grew up I wouldn't know how to explain my career and my work to her."

His daughter's questions acted as a spur to Ishida quitting banking in 2000. He continued:

> This decision was very simple, but it was really tough for me to change my career after ten years in banking. Fortunately I found this (IofC) organization of many influential people. I joined IofC Japan and the Caux Round Table Japan.
>
> What I have learned about "banking on purpose" is that, in the long run, banking is how to increase and enhance the assets effectively and invest efficiently. Money is very important but it's just like the blood in our body; if it circulates well it means you're very healthy, but if it doesn't go well the economy starts to decline.

---

4 Parthibhan's story is told in the short, award-winning documentary film *Banking on Change* by Andrew Hinton: https://www.youtube.com/watch?v=jTF094ZBbXc and https://in.iofc.org/Asia-Plateau

The second point is how to evaluate. When I was in banking, I was only evaluating the money to invest, how to measure the asset. That was how I measured my performance. But the traditional way is both tangible and intangible. The tangible is the balance sheet and the profit and loss account. It's easy to find out what is risk and what is not. But my challenge now was how to measure the intangible asset, which is really important for the future of corporations. This is more like potential risk—but it is not the only knowledge you need. You need a passion and wisdom.

Finally, the third point is risk management. In banking I learned that when a problem occurs you need to mitigate it. But you don't have any activities of prevention. You can only do mitigation. So, how do you have prevention before something goes wrong? That was the topic I started to learn.

My journey is still going on; how to enhance corporate value, not only the tangible but also this intangible asset. I think it's building on trust— not just globalization or diversification. Redistributive justice is win/lose, where only one party can get what they want. But for the future of the 21st century, we need to think about restrictive justice so that we can have win/win, where both parties get what they want.

This is just the start of my journey. Sustainability and CSR, corporate social responsibility, is one answer. But I use two words: CSR and PSR which is personal social responsibility. Companies are not made of machines. They are human beings. We make companies. That is why the personality is very important, in order to increase the value of companies. This is difficult to evaluate, how to increase this intangible asset.

When I first came to Caux in 2001, I learnt the simple words which are very difficult to challenge: whenever you need to be decisive, the phrase "not who is right but what is right" is very important. Three key words I also always tell myself are integrity, fairness and honesty. Banking on purpose is a new field; not only the tangibles but also these intangibles that we need to apply in our companies. This is how to increase the value of the corporation.

Like Ishida, Sam Palk tells how he walked away from a lucrative banking career in Wall Street. He might have sympathized with John D. Rockefeller's remark who, when asked "How much is enough?", is said to have replied, "Just a little more." The appetite for great wealth becomes insatiable. It cuts to the very heart of what we truly desire in life—and where the roots of satisfaction really lie.

This was Polk's experience. A typical wolf of Wall Street, he was a senior bonds trader at Pateras Capital, one of the world's largest hedge funds, in the "distressed" market—dealing with companies in or near bankruptcy. He had been tempted there from a high-flying career at Bank of America—where he had traded credit default swaps (CDS)—by a million dollar offer from Pateras' head of trading.

At first Polk loved Pateras. The library-quiet trading floor was "like a church, but for the worship of money" and he had wanted to work on a trading floor after reading Michael Lewis's exposé of Wall Street, *Liar's Poker.*

Aged 30, Polk's annual bonus was $3.6m. But it was much less than some of his colleagues and he felt angry. "I was devastated because my enormous bonus wasn't bigger. What was wrong with me? How had I become like this?" he writes in his book *For the Love of Money* (2016), a seeringly honest account of his personal journey.

He had no children, no debts and no philanthropic goal in mind. Yet he wanted more money "for exactly the same reason an alcoholic needs another drink: I was addicted", he wrote in *The New York Times.*[5]

He had been brought up by his Dad to believe that money would solve all his problems. Competitive and ambitious, he was a daily drinker, pot smoker and regular user of cocaine, Ritalin and ecstasy. With such a propensity for self-destruction he was suspended from Columbia University for burglary, arrested twice and fired from an Internet company for fist-fighting. He regarded it as a miracle that he got a job in Wall Street at all.

Four years after he started at Bank of America, Citibank offered him a "1.75 by 2"—$1.75 million per year for two years. He started dating a pretty blonde and rented a loft apartment for $6,000 a month. At 25, he could go to any restaurant in Manhattan—Per Se, Le Bernardin—just by picking up the phone and calling one of his brokers. Yet he was nagged by envy. "When the guy next to you makes $10 million, $1 million or $2 million doesn't look so sweet." Working elbow to elbow with billionaires he became, in his own words, a "fireball of greed".

Following his life of college wrestling championships, alcohol, drugs, chasing girls, obesity and bulimia, Polk eventually quit drinking while making the grade in Wall Street. His work ethic became prodigious: "I was the first on the desk in the morning, arriving at 5.00am." Yet the money simply didn't satisfy. His girlfriend dumps him, declaring: "I don't like who you have become."

Nor did he himself. "I was tired. Tired of lying. Tired of hurting other people. Tired of ruining everything that was important to me. Mostly, I was tired of myself. I wanted to be a different person. I wanted to live a different kind of life." He lacked any sense of self-worth.

He had sessions with a spiritual counsellor who told him: "What you need is not to achieve the fantasy but to heal the wound." He needed to reconcile with his estranged twin brother. His bulimia, he realised, was not about hunger for food, but for love.

In the end, it was his "absurdly wealthy" bosses who helped him to see the limitations of unlimited wealth.

I was in a meeting with one of them, and a few other traders, and they were talking about the new hedge-fund regulations. Most everyone on

5   First published in *The New York Times*, 18 January 2014. The full article can be read on his website: www.samuelpolk.com

Wall Street thought they were a bad idea. "But isn't it better for the system as a whole?" I asked. The room went quiet, and my boss shot me a withering look. I remember his saying, "I don't have the brain capacity to think about the system as a whole. All I'm concerned with is how this affects our company." I felt as if I'd been punched in the gut. He was afraid of losing money, despite all that he had.

From that moment on, I started to see Wall Street with new eyes. I'd always looked enviously at the people who earned more than I did; now, for the first time, I was embarrassed for them, and for me. I made in a single year more than my mom made her whole life. I knew that wasn't fair; that wasn't right. I was a derivatives trader, and it occurred to me the world would hardly change at all if credit derivatives ceased to exist. Not so nurse practitioners. What had seemed normal now seemed deeply distorted.

In 2010, in a final paroxysm of his withering wealth addiction, he demanded $8 million instead of $3.6 million. His bosses even said they'd raise his bonus if he agreed to stay several more years. Instead, he walked away.

Wall Street, he reflects in his book, "wasn't a talent-based meritocracy; it was more like an addiction. Doing whatever you had to do—rationalizing, lying—to get money to fill that empty hole inside." Polk's book delves into the very heart of the psychology of Wall Street: what drives the young and ambitious to take enormous trading risks? And what, ultimately, satisfies: acquisition of wealth and a hedonistic lifestyle or contribution to others' wellbeing? "Even on Wall Street people live lives of quiet desperation.... Our obsessive accumulation of money had led to the widest inequalities in centuries."

In the three years after he left Wall Street, he married, spoke in jails and juvenile detention centres about getting sober, taught a writing class to girls in the foster system, and started the non-profit Groceryships in Los Angeles to help poor families struggling with obesity and food addiction. It teaches poor families about nutrition and healthy cooking. "I am much happier. I feel as if I'm making a real contribution. And as time passes, the distortion lessens. I see Wall Street's mantra—'We're smarter and work harder than everyone else, so we deserve all this money'—for what it is: the rationalization of addicts."

Groceryships gives nutritional guidance and financial support to impoverished families. His second start-up, Everytable, is a for-profit social enterprise which sells healthy, ready-to-eat meals in low income neighbourhoods.

The Los Angeles Times reported: "The program provides each participant family $100 a week on a Food 4 Less gift card for six months. Each family also receives a high-end blender for juicing. The group watches films, gets hand-outs about nutrition and learns to cook several dozen healthful dishes." The families find they spend less on more healthy food than they were accustomed to. Groceryships, says Yohana Funes, changed her life. "Before, my children were my circle of life. Now I realize it's all of us together." And, she enthuses, "They have made me physically, mentally and emotionally beautiful."[6]

While these stories personify the struggle for integrity in banking at a personal level, has the culture of banking sufficiently changed at the corporate level, particularly in the big clearing banks, to avert another crash?

Under the banking industry's international Basel rules, banks now have to hold far greater reserves to set against bad debt on unrecoverable loans. As we saw in the previous chapter, the biggest US banks have to hold $250 billion in reserve, under the Frank Dodd Act.

Such "fractional reserve banking" is still regarded by some as a chimera, a gamble, given that a run of withdrawals could, in theory, lead to catastrophic failures, even if that is an unlikely scenario. Tighter corporate legislation also means that bankers, including non-executive directors, are much more likely to be prosecuted for wrongdoing or for failing in their fiduciary duties.

Just how much the culture in banking still needed to change was highlighted by a scandal that came to light in November 2014. A coterie of City traders had been rigging the foreign exchange currency markets over a five year period, reported the UK's Financial Conduct Authority (FCA). The dealers had behaved "like sniggering schoolboys doing naughty things", said the FCA, in order to line their pockets while they cheated clients out of millions of pounds. High street banks, including HSBC, Royal Bank of Scotland, UBS of Switzerland and the US banks JP Morgan Chase and Citibank, were fined more than £2 billion by British and American watchdogs. London is the global centre for foreign exchange trading, accounting for 40 per cent of the £3.3 trillion traded every day. The FCA commented that "the failings at these banks undermine confidence in the UK financial system and put its integrity at risk." Ross McEwan, chief executive of RBS, said: "To say I am angry would be an understatement. We had people working at this bank who did not know the difference between right and wrong. I apologize to all our customers and our 100,000 staff."[7]

In 2018, the US Justice Department came to a settlement with the Royal Bank of Scotland, imposing a fine of $4.9 billion for its selling of toxic, so called mortgage-backed securities. It was almost a decade since the bank's rescue by British tax payers in December 2008. The bank had set aside a comparable sum for such a settlement, which was seen as a major milestone in the bank's road to recovery. The UK government could now prepare for the sale of its 71 per cent stake still in public ownership, back to the private sector.[8]

Ironically, following the Big Bang of deregulation of financial services in the UK in October 1986, today the pendulum has swung in the opposite

6 "South LA women changed their lives, and it started with food", by Mary Mac-Vean, *Los Angeles Times*, 28 August 2014
7 *Evening Standard*, London, 12 November 2014
8 Harry Wilson, *The Times*, 11 May 2018

direction. The industry is now burdened with 10,000 pages of rules and regulations following the collapse of 2008, as a senior economist at the Financial Conduct Authority told me. And, he said, no one is going to know them all. But this won't stop people trying to find ways of getting around them. The consequence of a loss of self-discipline, or any sense of a moral perspective, is over-regulation by law. There is the continuing need to address the culture of organizations and, at the structural level, the sheer size of governments' debts.

Ten years on from the collapse of Lehman Brothers, Nail Ferguson wrote: "The thing to worry about—as in 2008—is the sheer size of the debt mountain. Relative to global GDP, the financial sector has reduced debt and households have held steady, but the debts of governments and non-financial firms have soared. Total debt is up from 280 per cent of GDP in 2008 to 320 per cent."

Ferguson warns that

> it does not take great prophetic gifts to predict another crisis. Financial history has not ended any more than political history ended with the fall of the Berlin Wall. The next crisis will not be like the last one. History teaches us not to expend too much energy trying to prevent the last crisis from happening again, but instead to ask the broad question: which borrowers around the world have overextended themselves to the point where they will begin to fail in the event of rising real interest rates? And which lenders or investors will be in trouble if the defaults exceed their expectations?[9]

At the personal level, Ken Costa, the former Chairman of Lazard International investment bank, emphasizes the need for "consciences of practitioners" in banking.

"During the past five years, post-crash, there has been a significant shift in the attitude and practice of the City [of London]. And it has been values driven", he claimed. "No one is immune from the values vacuum which characterized the previous era.... Even before Adam Smith's *The Theory of Moral Sentiments*, Judeo-Christian tradition stressed the importance of having a set of overarching values embedded within the financial system if we wish to have a sustainable market economy. This cannot be codified in the hope that controls will compel wider ethical behaviour. It won't. Ethics have to be taught as well as caught.... But as we go forward, hopefully having seen the ethical bear market bottom out, we can look, if not to an ethical bull market—that would be nirvana—then to a new base founded on fundamental values. These values are in part already written into laws, but these are just skeletons and require all practitioners to buy into the belief that a vital market will always require good values, judgment, discernment and shrewdness from its leaders.... Codes of practice and consciences of practitioners fit hand-in-glove."[10]

9　*The Sunday Times*, 16 September 2018
10　*Evening Standard*, London, 17 April 2014

Alex Brummer, City Editor of the British paper the *Daily Mail*, concludes his book, *Bad Banks* (2014), by quoting the Archbishop of Canterbury, Justin Welby. He had reflected on the financial system from the pulpit of St Paul's Cathedral in the summer of 2013: "The biggest weakness of all in the analysis of the failure of banks to be good banks has been around understanding human beings", he said.

Welby, who spent 11 years as an oil executive before joining the Church of England, "listened to months of testimony from the bankers responsible for Libor rigging, the wrongful selling of PPI (Payment Protection Insurance) and the collapse of HBOS", writes Brummer. "He had heard nothing to convince him that the bankers were contrite, that the institutions they served had truly changed their nature, or that there had been a revolution in banking practice. On that much there still seems to be widespread agreement among moral leaders, politicians, regulators, investors and the more thoughtful bankers. That there is still so much unfinished business, after the trauma of the worst financial crisis for a century, must be an enormous cause for concern. The era of bad banks is a long way from being fixed."

At the heart of the crash of 2008 and its aftermath—regarded by many as a fundamental crisis of capitalism—lay a deep-seated materialism, a misplaced faith in the pursuit and power of wealth, a belief that acquisition is more important than contribution, and a loss of integrity and nurturing of the soul.

As Archbishop Welby concluded in his St Paul's sermon: "At the heart of good banks have to be good people."

References

Brummer, Alex, *Bad Banks: greed, incompetence and the next global crisis*, Random House Business, 2015
Costa, Ken, *God at Work: living every day with purpose*, Alpha International, 2013
Lewis, Michael, *Liar's Poker*, Hodder Paperbacks, 2006
Palk, Sam, *For the Love of Money: a memoir*, Scribner, 2017
Smith, Adam, *The Theory of Moral Sentiments*, Penguin Classics, 2010

Part 2

So what works? Leading with integrity

6   Creative connections—person to person

Take a twisting journey through pine trees up the side of a Swiss mountain above Montreux and you arrive in the Alpine village of Caux. A thousand metres high, it offers a panoramic view over the Lake of Geneva to the West and towards the Dent du Midi mountain range to the East. It is one of the most breathtaking views in the whole of Europe. Towering 2,000 metres high over Caux are the Roches de Naye, a mountain from which hang-gliders launch themselves into the swirling air currents and towards the lake below.

Caux stands on the border between French and German speaking Switzerland. It is the location for a splendid *Belle Epoque* building that, before World War II, was known as the Caux Palace Hotel. Now more prosaically known in English as Mountain House, the building was used as a refugee camp for German Jewish citizens fleeing from the Nazis during the war. The building fell into disrepair. As a hotel it had never been a profitable concern and by 1946 was in the hands of a Montreux bank who were considering demolishing it.

Immediately after the war, some 100 Swiss families clubbed together to buy the building, to convert it into a centre for post-war reconciliation. This was the vision of a senior Swiss diplomat, Philippe Mottu, who believed that if Switzerland was spared the horror of war, she should provide a centre for reconciliation in the world. Mottu in turn had been encouraged to buy the building by Frank Buchman, a Pennsylvanian American with Swiss German ancestry who knew the building from his prewar travels in Europe. Hundreds of German, French, British, Scandinavian, Italian, Japanese and other world citizens flocked there in the post-war years. Here, motivations and decision-making are transformed towards constructive ends.

As visitors take the steep mountain railway up from Montreux to the Caux station, the two-coach train passes through the Valmont Tunnel. For first-time travellers, it offers an unexpected, perhaps unsettling, experience. Emerging from the tunnel, all that was on your right hand side now appears on your left. The Lake of Geneva below seems to have shifted position. The train, in fact, has passed through a semi-circle inside the tunnel, without the traveller realizing. Our perspectives have been changed. Things have been turned around. The train journey acts as a metaphor for the Caux experience, where participants are, likely as not, to find a change of perspective on their lives and on the world as a whole. People are turned around on their journey in life.

From 2006 till 2016, the centre, run by Initiatives of Change, hosted a decade of global annual forums on Trust and Integrity in the Global Economy (TIGE) which each year attracted participants from some 30 countries. Since 2017 these forums have been called Ethical Leadership in Business. Their Managing Director is Annika Hartmann de Meuron, a Swiss-Swedish-German who studied international relations and gained her Masters in international history and politics at the Graduate Institute of Geneva. "We are living in times of extreme challenges, like climate change, pollution and mass migration," she says. "Our mission is to equip people to lead in times of extremes. Companies have the means and the interests to contribute to the solutions to these problems. It is part of our identity to go to work. So business is crucial to our society and to us as individuals."

The forums built on previous conferences addressing industrial relations, going back to the post-war period of the 1950s and 1960s, and were given a particular fillip and relevance following the banking crash of 2007–2008.

In 2013 one of the keynote speakers was Kofi Annan, the 7th Secretary-General of the United Nations from 1997 to 2006, Nobel Peace Prize laureate, and Chair of the Kofi Annan Foundation before his death aged 80 in August 2018. António Guterres, the current UN Secretary General at the time of Annan's death, described him as "a guiding force for good".

2013 was Annan's second visit to Caux. As he entered the main hall of Mountain House, the conference audience broke into spontaneous applause. The platform speaker, Lawrence Bloom, who was well into his speech, wondered what he had said to have prompted such a warm response, before realizing that they were not clapping him.

Annan settled into his reserved seat and Bloom continued his talk. Bloom had the audience in the palm of his hand as he told his extraordinary story of a change of direction in his business life—personal transformation as he prefers to call it. Such personal transformations amongst business leaders and other economic players, leading to organizational, economic and global changes, is a hallmark of the Caux conferences.

Bloom's story is remarkable by any standards. The grandson of East European émigré Jews to London, who had escaped the anti-Semitic pogroms of the late 19th century, he had made his fortune by his early thirties as a chartered surveyor in the commercial property market in the City of London. In 1974 he bought his seven-bedroom mansion in Hampstead Garden suburb, north London. One evening, as he sat outside in his 500 SEL Mercedes, he asked himself, "Is this it? Is this all there is to life?"

"I have arrived at the place where everybody aspires to be, and they're a little bit anxious because they haven't got there yet", he tells the conference. "Now I'm here and I'm still as anxious as I ever was. I realized that anxiety was like a coat hanger and the clothing I had hung on it, up to the moment I had bought the mansion, was, 'Will I ever make it?' and the clothing I hung on it after I made it was, 'Will I ever keep it?' That was a trauma for me because I realized something very deep about human nature, that there's a part of us—the ego—that is continuously feeling unsafe."

At first, to compensate for this hollowness, he went on a binge drinking spree which lasted for three years. "It wasn't very efficient or effective—nearly ruined my liver—but it brought me to a few home truths", he says. "And the home truths were that there's a part of me that wasn't being nourished. I call it my soul. Other people can call it what they like. But it's something deep inside us that needs to be nourished. I realized that this reality is a dance between the material and the spiritual. So what was my soul asking me to do? It was much less concerned with me being unsafe as it was with me being in right action. And, ever since the alcohol haze of the three years cleared, that's how I've intended to live my life."

Switching his career from property agent to a multinational, and still totally committed to "right action", he joined the Executive Committee of the InterContinental Hotels group, at that time Japanese-owned, where he sat from 1988 till 1993. There he was in charge of their $3 billion global real estate portfolio. Whilst there, with the support of the tech services department, he created their three-volume environmental manual.

Just three paragraphs in the manual were to have a profound impact on the global hotel industry. It offered hotel guests the choice of having a clean towel every day, or keeping the same towel. Such a simple idea revolutionized the hotel industry, cutting its laundry bill, detergent and water use, and the environmental impact. It is now standard practice in over five million hotel bedrooms world-wide. As Bloom tells this story there is more spontaneous applause. But he adds that the board's decision was not an easy one. He had to fight it through in the teeth of fierce opposition from fellow board members.

"It was a huge opportunity but the idea wasn't very popular", he explains. "We're talking about 1992. The Chief Financial Officer would say, 'Lawrence, shareholder value. Don't talk to us about this fluffy sustainability nonsense: shareholder value.' And the Chief Operating Officer would say, 'Quarterly bottom line, Lawrence, talk to me about quarterly bottom line; you're here to increase the value of our properties, not to come up with fluffy ideas.' But I knew an environmental manual was needed and I was sick every morning into the sink when I woke up, knowing how they were trying to marginalize me on the main board to stop me pushing this through. I could lose my position on the board and my job. For three months every morning I got up feeling terribly unsafe but knowing that it was the right action. Gradually the CEO was supportive and, after three months of me being sick in the basin, we created the manual which we then offered to all the other hotel companies, much again to the anger of the remainder of the board."

Bloom later explains in more detail what actually happened. At first other hotel chains were not interested. No thanks, we'll write our own, they said. Fearing that this would undermine the environmental impact, the CEO of

InterContinental approached Prince Charles, who promptly invited the CEOs of half a dozen five-star hotel chains to meet with him at Highgrove, his country home in Gloucestershire. He presented to them what became known as the Prince's Manual and they could hardly refuse. This initiative then spawned the International Hotels Environmental Initiative which continues to this day.

Another unique outcome of the initiative is the standard plastic door key, inserted into the bedroom wall to connect the electricity, thus preventing guests accidentally leaving their lights on when they leave their rooms.

In 2013, Bloom was staying in the Novotel Beijing, owned by the French Accor hotel group, when he was delighted to read about Accor's environmental initiative. The company has a commitment to plant trees in agroforestry projects, to support sustainable agriculture. "AccorHotels encourages every guest staying more than one night to reuse their towel," explains Baptiste Hetreau, Project Manager for Sustainable Development at Accor. If the guest accepts this commitment, "the hotel will give half of the savings (water, energy, detergent, etc.) to our partner, Pur Projet, which is in charge of tree plantation. We currently have 375 different projects in 25 countries, supported directly by Pur Projet or a local NGO. In every country where we have a local project, the money collected by the hotel stays in the country. So far, we have planted almost six million trees, and we plan to have 10 million trees planted by 2021."[1]

For its part, InterContinental Hotels has introduced its "Greener Stay" initiative, which allows guests staying for more than one night to opt out of housekeeping services in return for additional InterContinental Hotels Group (IHG) Rewards Club Points. "This helps our guests to make more environmentally conscious decisions when travelling and allows our hotels to reduce their energy and water usage", says Kate Gibson, Vice President, Corporate Responsibility, for IHG. "As of year-end 2016, there were 1,400 IHG hotels participating in the programme in our Americas Region."[2]

Bloom continues his environmental campaigning as Secretary General of the Be Earth Foundation, a UN intergovernmental organization, and is Chair of Be Energy a green energy company specialising in the conversion of waste and plantation timber to sustainable energy projects. His next big project is in Mexico where he and colleagues hope to develop a hotel complex that will support the local economy, providing a market for locally grown food and other products.

Bloom asserts:

> This is not an age of change; it is a change of age. What I mean by this is that the rules, the cultures, the understandings of the last 400 years won't serve us anymore. They've served us very well up till now. They've been like the booster rocket of a spaceship. The booster has a function. The

1   Email to the author, 15 March 2018
2   Email to the author, 24 October 2017

function is to reach the escape velocity of 17,500 miles an hour and then its job is done. The skill in a space shot is to blow the explosive bolts and to enable the booster to fall back to earth, otherwise it will jeopardize the mission. The last 400 years has given levels of wealth and freedom to over a billion and a half people whose parents, let alone grandparents, couldn't imagine. But it won't take us any further. And so on a billion and a half of us rests a great responsibility for the future.

Bloom's story and convictions, told from the platform in Caux, delighted Kofi Annan, who said that in the spirit of the previous speaker he would put aside his prepared notes and speak from the heart. He immediately had the audience in stitches of laughter as he told what happened when he retired from the UN. Annan and his wife, the Swedish lawyer Nane Lagergren, who lived in Geneva, desperately needed a long rest and a holiday. In a remote village in the northern Italian lakes district, they were spotted by tourists. One of them approached him with great enthusiasm, and asked for his autograph: "Please, Mr Freeman". Evidently, the autograph hunter had mistaken Annan for the Hollywood actor Morgan Freeman. Annan didn't let on and obligingly signed his name "M Freeman", knowing that he couldn't and shouldn't forge the actor's full name!

In his wide-ranging keynote speech, Annan emphasized that healthy democracies needed three pillars: peace, economic development, and respect for human rights. He told a story of his initiative, when at the UN, that has saved millions of lives blighted by HIV/AIDS and other diseases:

We established the global fund to fight HIV/AIDS, malaria and tuberculosis. When I signed off on the fund, I had hoped that we'd get contributions from governments, from individuals. In fact the first contribution came from me. I had been given an award by a group, so I gave the cheque to start the fund, hoping it would encourage others. In the end most of our money came from governments. Believe it or not the first cheque given to me came from George W Bush's Administration. He gave me $200 million for the fund. The American NGOs were very upset saying that the President should have added a few zeroes. There should have been two billion instead of $200 million. A week before I went to George Bush to ask for the money, I explained to Bill Clinton why we were setting up the fund, with millions dying and the medication available but which the poor couldn't afford. Without batting an eyelid, Bill Clinton said, "You know what, this may be one of the most important things George Bush does throughout his time, so I hope he listens." George got it; he was the first to give us a cheque.

At that point the medication per person cost $15,000 a year. There was no way people in Africa, Asia, and Latin America could afford it. So Dr Gro Brundtland and Professor Peter Piot, who was then Head of UNAIDS, and I convened a meeting in Amsterdam where I brought together the chairmen of the seven largest pharmaceutical companies, to urge them to make it possible for the medication to reach the poor. It was a fascinating discussion. The first chairman who spoke said, "I don't even know why I'm here, I could be taken to court." I said, "For what?" He said, "For price fixing." I said, "Price fixing is when companies collude to maximize profits. I've invited you here to lose money, to reduce your prices, which will cost you money, and to do good and to help the poor." Another one said, "Well my lawyer is not here, I don't know whether we should." At that time they were suing [Nelson] Mandela in a South African court because Mandela had threatened to use compulsory licensing to produce a generic version of the medication for his people. So I told them, "I am not a public relations expert but when you sue Mandela in a South African court on an issue like HIV/AIDS, if you win, you lose and lose and lose and if you lose of course you lose. You'd better take the case out of court and settle privately", which they did.

But what was interesting was that they responded, despite the argument that if they sell cheaper in Africa it would undermine a different package in Europe and America. But they responded. Today the medication is $150 per person and at that point they were even giving away Naverapine which was to prevent mother-to-child HIV transmission, the cruellest of all transmissions. So the things they started by saying couldn't be done, they did. They saved millions of lives and the operations are still profitable. None of them has gone bankrupt as they feared.

In his speech, Annan expressed his deep concern for the over 70 million young people, often graduates, around the world who are unemployed at a time of economic recession:

How have the governments used their revenues to ensure that they improve the livelihood and well-being of people? Have we invested the revenues in education, in health, in infrastructure, in areas that will really benefit the people? And of course when I look over the financial crisis, as you may have guessed, I'm not worried for the banks, I'm worried for the impact on the people and governments and individuals. I travelled the world and I talked to people. And people are angry. I have been quite pleasantly surprised that we haven't had more social conflict in societies around the world. We've seen demonstrations in Spain, Greece, Italy, in other parts but it's been reasonably peaceful. It's not been violent, it has not been aggressive.

But the situation is something to be worried about. He appreciated the conference's emphasis on new models of integral and inclusive economics and ownership—from social enterprises and employee owned companies to benefit corporations—as being "extremely important and something that has to be pursued".

Following Annan's speech, it later emerged that an incident when he was a young schoolboy in Ghana had left a lasting impression on him. A British diplomat, Bill Peters, had addressed the school, urging them that they could achieve anything in life they set out to do. Years later, Annan, by then the UN Secretary General, told Peters that he still remembered his stirring talk.[3]

I first met Lawrence Bloom across a boardroom table in the City of London in March 2013. We were there with 15 others for a morning's Mindfulness exercise, invited by the practitioner and trainer Rohan Narse. A few days later, Bloom phoned me to ask if he would be allowed to take part in the Caux TIGE conference that summer. Not really knowing him, I invited him for lunch in a Turkish restaurant near Victoria Station. I feared that he was a typical corporate, bottom line player. I couldn't have been more wrong. As he told his story, I said to him, "Lawrence, this is what you need to tell the Caux conference. Share your story. It is exactly the ethos of Caux." He was surprised and said that he hadn't expected that response from me. He would speak from his heart. It was this that so touched the audience, including Kofi Annan.

Narse had acted as an unwitting intermediary. His story is equally intriguing. Narse comes from a humble background in the Mumbai suburb of Chembur. He graduated in engineering in 1987 and gained his MBA from the prestigious Indian Institute of Management in Bangalore. By sheer hard work and thanks to a capable mind, he spent 23 years in such firms as the Tata Group, KPMG, PwC and Goldman Sachs, where he became an investment banker. Successful at the material level, he brought his family to live in the salubrious suburb of Putney in South-West London.

But he was burning the proverbial candle at both ends. He had been exploring different forms of meditation for many years as a way of dealing with the angst of "a life unlived". While returning late at night from one such camp in Dorset in 2009, he fell asleep at the wheel of his BMW as he drove along the M25 London orbital motorway. As he drifted onto the hard shoulder and into a head-on collision with the edge of it, a passing truck missed him by centimetres. It would have surely killed him.

That was a wake-up call for Narse as he looked at his crumpled BMW and the deep blue sky above. He reflected that the drive for greater wealth and prestige was not giving him satisfaction, happiness or fulfilment in life. He was running an investment advisory firm by then, for investors from the UK and the USA, and was in the midst of expanding the investor base. His relationship with his business seemed untenable and he decided at that very moment to leave the corporate world. He was already on a personal quest to find lasting peace, which the accident highlighted as being "time-dependent"—and as one that had a safety net tied to its exploration. He decided to drop all that he knew as his own, his past, and venture out, without the need to return to the safe climes of his home.

---

3   Obituary of Bill Peters, *The Independent*, 18 June 2014

During the months and years that followed, Narse visited Varanasi (also known as Benares), one of India's oldest cities and a famed place of pilgrimage on the river Ganges. There he found the time and space for deeply reflective moments to ponder the direction of his life. He subsequently wrote an engaging book, *In Search of Silence* (2011), and trained in the practice of Mindfulness. He now runs Rhythm Meditations and has added, in 2018, a second company, Shining Darkness. "The focus of both", he says, "is to work with CEOs only and the quest is to work, one-to-one, towards what it means to be real". He offers this service internationally, mostly in the UK and the USA.

One of Narse's school classmates, Satej Kulkarni, had become a chief cook at Asia Plateau, the Initiatives of Change centre in the hill resort of Panchgani, south of Pune in India. Kulkarni invited Narse to visit there. Impressed and intrigued by what he saw, Narse took up a suggestion to visit one of the engineers who had helped to build the centre in the 1960s and 1970s, David Young, now an elderly man living in retirement in Brighton. After meeting Narse, Young phoned me to say that I really should meet him. And so we met in London and got to know each other.

Narse is a courteous man in his late forties, with a centredness and calm to his life that is very appealing. He practises what he preaches. And he takes a real interest in people. He lives in the "now" moment with his full attention on the person he is meeting. He is also a great networker, and I find myself pleasantly encouraged by the range of business leaders he knows and who hold him in the highest regard.

Part of his pursuit of personal integrity was to admit to himself that his arranged marriage to his wife was unworkable. They are now divorced and share their time with their daughter, in her early twenties, and teenage son. He and his ex-wife remain "very good friends and, in fact, are on even better terms than ever before", he says.

Narse has found kindred spirits in the networks of Initiatives of Change, not least thanks to its emphasis on the need to take time out each day for silent reflection in order to connect with our true selves and the sources of spiritual wisdom within.

Another of Narse's friends is Anita Hoffmann, a highly regarded personal coach to top business executives. She is the founding Managing Director of Executiva, a leadership search company which works alongside organizations to attract and develop socially, ethically and economically aware global leaders in the energy, infrastructure and sustainability sectors. Her book, *Purpose and Impact: how executives are creating meaningful second careers* (2018), is an encouragement to senior executives and professionals "to rethink and even relaunch careers that align with wider purpose and societal impact".[4] Hoffmann is Swedish by birth, Danish by passport and a Londoner by residence for over 30 years. Narse describes Hoffmann as his "soul sister".

4   Routledge/Greenleaf, 2018

My wife and I first meet her at a dinner party given by Narse, then living in south Wimbledon. We meet someone with a cheerful disposition and a ready laugh. Hoffmann, in turn, agrees to be the chair of a plenary session during the 2014 Caux TIGE conference. She also has a forgiving nature, as a communications gap between the conference organizers means that no one confers with her about her conference role till it is almost too late. As it turns out, she chairs an engaging plenary session of a potpourri of speakers.

Such creative connections, person-to-person links in the chain of events, in the great scheme of things, are what IofC's founder Frank Buchman saw, from his faith perspective, as being the workings of the spirit of God. "People", he would urge his colleagues "are your strategy."

Of course you have to know what your strategic objectives are, what you want to achieve in the world, whether it is organizational and environmental sustainability and tackling climate change, or job creation and greater economic fairness in society, or addressing social exclusion and inhuman deprivation, or the social purpose of business in a world of great disparities. But justice in economic relationships and structures, and human wellbeing, are built on human relationships, person by person. Have a deep care, indeed love, for individuals and your strategies for changing the world will emerge.

This sometimes leads to the kind of profound changes of direction in life that Lawrence Bloom, Rohan Narse and countless others have experienced.

Bloom urges the Caux conference organizers not to lose sight of this experience, this "magic of Caux" which those who have been there talk about: the unique atmosphere and spirit in its human relationships. It is a platform for all stakeholders in the global economy who wish to inspire, connect and encourage businesses and individuals to act according to their core values, and contribute to an equitable society and humane world.

References

Hoffmann, Anita, *Purpose and Impact: how executives are creating meaningful second careers*, Routledge, 2018

Narse, Rohan, *In Search of Silence: dropping the baggage, discovering what's real*, Ecademy Press, UK, 2011

7 Conscience capitalism

Nudging towards change

I met Scott Allshouse when he addressed marketing students at the University of Virginia in Richmond, VA, about ten years ago. He is the Mid-Atlantic Regional President of Whole Foods Market, the up-market US and international grocery chain, now owned by Amazon, which promotes organic foods. Amazon paid $13.7 billion to acquire Whole Foods' 487 stores in 2017. It was Amazon's largest acquisition.

Allshouse spoke to the students about "conscious capitalism", advocated by John Mackey, Whole Foods Market's Co-Founder, and Raj Sisodia.[1] The Conscious Capitalism movement advocates a clearly articulated purpose for businesses and organizations—their contribution to society—other than just making a profit: "purpose maximization" rather than profit maximization leading to "firms of endearment", as Allshouse puts it.

Mackey and Sisodia make great claims for the Conscious Capitalism movement. "Conscious Capitalism", they write, "is an evolving paradigm for business that simultaneously creates multiple kinds of value and wellbeing for all stakeholders: financial, intellectual, physical, ecological, social, cultural, emotional, ethical, and even spiritual". Businesses can thus "bring themselves into close harmony with the interests of society as a whole." This demands a "higher purpose" for business than just the bottom line, including a culture of many traits "such as trust, accountability, transparency, integrity, loyalty, egalitarianism, fairness, personal growth, love and care".

We look at some of these values in this book, which have become even more critical since the Western capitalist edifice was called into question following the global financial crisis of 2007–2008. The Western economic model seemed to have triumphed in the struggle for supremacy following the collapse of Soviet-style communism in 1989. Yet the *laissez-faire* free market model all too easily carries the seeds of its own destruction if it is infected by materialist motivations of acquisition, greed, corruption, injustice and polarization between rich and poor. In all this, human motivations play a vital role, for good or ill.

---

1   *Conscious Capitalism: liberating the heroic spirit of business*, John Mackey and Rajendra Sisodia (2014)

Professors Richard Thaler, winner of the 2017 Nobel Prize for Economics, understands this. Famed for his "nudge" theory,[2] Thaler recognises that small incremental changes in human behaviour have great accumulative consequences. The challenge, therefore, is to see how to encourage "nudges" in behaviour to make a real difference. As the old saying goes, "Big doors swing on little hinges."

How does this work in practice? Sometimes it is a simple matter of communication and presentation. The UK workplace pensions scheme, or Nest, for instance automatically enrols employees in a workplace pension, while giving them the opportunity to opt out. This has resulted in a greater take-up than when employees were required to opt in, which took more time and effort.[3]

Nudge, known in the UK as the Behavioural Insights Team, has also helped to recover taxes, according to a BBC report.[4] In one six-week exercise, 140,000 people were sent a variety of letters by the UK's Revenue and Customs. One was a standard communication stressing the need to pay outstanding taxes while others contained statements such as "nine out of ten people in Britain pay their tax on time" or stressed other people living in the same area had already complied. Letters emphasizing such "social norms" produced a 15 per cent higher response rate than the standard letter. Revenue and Customs believed this could help it to collect £160m extra tax revenues a year if carried out across the country.

Thaler, Professor of Behavioural Science and Economics at the University of Chicago, has shown that economics has to take into account the vagaries of human nature. Economics is not a precise science with predictable outcomes, however much some economists would like us to think so. Thaler told the *Financial Times*: "The mantra I always give is that you have to make it easy. I think of nudging as like giving people GPS. I get to put into the GPS where I want to go, but I don't have to follow her instructions."[5]

Following his Nobel Prize award, Prof Thaler said that his most important contribution to economics "was the recognition that economic agents are human, and that economic models have to incorporate that." The Nobel committee stated that Prof Thaler had "built a bridge between the economic and psychological analyses of individual decision-making". It added that his efforts to explore the consequences of limited rationality, social preferences, and lack of self-control, had shown how these traits systematically affect individual decisions, as well as market outcomes.[6]

The sum total of individual decision-making has a profound effect. All the more, then, the world needs a conscience-based market economy, what I

2   *Nudge: improving decisions about health, wealth and happiness*, Richard H Thaler and Cass R Sunstein (2009)
3   Delia Bradshaw, *Financial Times*, 15 November 2015, https://www.ft.com/content/e98e2018-70ca-11e5-ad6d-f4ed76f0900a
4   BBC, 8 February 2012, https://www.bbc.co.uk/news/uk-politics-16943729
5   Delia Bradshaw, ibid.
6   *The Independent*, 9 October 2017

would call a considerate capitalism—considerate of the needs of others and not just self-interest as owners, producers and service providers; an economy that is fuelled by empathy for others and for human wellbeing. The world needs considerate, conscience-based decision-making in business and economic life. In a globalized world, the need is to globalize such ethical considerations.

Adam Smith, the founding father of modern economic thought, recognized this aspect of human nature. His philosophy went far deeper than the "invisible hand" of the market—the notion that the common good would be served if we each pursued our own self-interest. As Smith wrote in his seminal book *The Wealth of Nations* (1776, republished frequently): "By pursuing his own interest he frequently promotes that of the society more effectively than when he intends to promote it."

Seventeen years before *The Wealth of Nations*, Smith wrote *The Theory of Moral Sentiments* (1759), when he was Professor of Moral Philosophy at Glasgow University (1752–1764). In it he spoke about the Impartial Spectator—an imagined outside, objective viewpoint—which he described as "the great judge and arbiter of our conduct" and a "demi-god within the breast". It encouraged the human emotions of sympathy and compassion. He believed that if, in the pursuit of wealth, injustice is done then the Impartial Spectator changes sides from support to disapproval. In other words the pursuit of wealth could not be condoned if it led to greed and social injustice. Smith also talked about the "man within" which acts like the "vice-regent of the deity"—in today's language the conscience. "By acting according to the dictates of our moral faculties", he wrote, "we necessarily pursue the most effectual means for promoting the happiness of mankind and may, therefore, be said, in some sense, to cooperate with the Deity, and to advance as far as is in our power the Plan of Providence."[7]

In the opening words of *The Theory of Moral Sentiments*, Smith wrote: "How selfish so ever man may be supposed, there are evidently some principles in his nature which interest him in the fortune of others, and render their happiness necessary to him, though he derives nothing from it except the pleasure of seeing it." Smith's use of the word sympathy throughout his book, in the context of the provision of goods and services, is better understood today as empathy—the ability to live into the other person's shoes and needs, including towards those operating in the supply chain and the division of labour. In other words, what do I need to do to fulfil the other person's interests?

"Compassion is thus a basic principle of human nature for Adam Smith", writes Jesse Norman. "Yet it quickly becomes clear that the key idea here is not so much compassion in the sense of pity, but rather compassion as empathy or fellow feeling."

Norman continues: "Thanks to sympathy and the impartial spectator, human beings have the capacity for self-conscious moral introspection; they

---

7   For an interesting exposition of Adam Smith's moral philosophy read *The Rescue of Capitalism: getting Adam Smith* right by Dr James Dyce (1990)

know the difference between honest ambition and a yearning for an undeserved approbation, and that shows itself in their moral judgements of themselves and others."

Norman adds: "This idea is the foundation stone of Smith's analysis of moral and social psychology—and it is specifically framed in terms of sympathy and in opposition to theories of self-interest." Smith's book "specifically rejects the idea of selfishness as the only source of human motivation". Moreover, "the key idea of the impartial spectator functions as a kind of moral conscience, offering an explanation of the duties imposed by justice and the feelings of resentment that accompany injustice, and lifting the treatment of these ideas above the purely conventional".

Norman gives an excellent evaluation of Smith's moral philosophy and to what extent it was derived from, or dependent on, a sense of a divine impulse. He also insists that Smith "was not a market fundamentalist, an economic libertarian, or in that strong sense a *laissez-faire* economist. He was not an advocate of selfishness, pro-rich or a misogynist, the creator of *homo economicus* or the founder of predatory capitalism." Rather, Norman writes, "Smith is the father of behavioural economics".[8]

In fact, the word capitalism never appears in Smith's writing. Yet for journalist Edward Lucas of *The Economist*, writing in *The Times*, "Capitalism is a bad name for a good thing. For all its flaws, our economic system fosters creativity, freedom and innovation; happiness as well as prosperity. Global trade lets risk-takers find new customers and suppliers, benefiting both and pulling a billion people out of poverty in the past 25 years."[9]

On 17 July 1990, the bicentenary of Adam Smith's death, Alan Ryan, then Professor of Politics at Princeton University, wrote that Smith "was an important figure in the history of moral philosophy. His *Theory of Moral Sentiments* was—to the extent such a thing is possible—a breakthrough in the subject. It steered a delicate course between reducing morality to mere feeling, and making moral judgment an implausibly rational business." Smith's moral philosophy, Ryan wrote, "relied on the thought that sympathy is a key emotion in restraining selfishness," even if it was "robust and sensible about the limits of any such mechanism: he noted, for instance, that no man has much intuitive sense of the pains of childbirth."[10]

Smith's philosophy—his belief in a "vice-regent of the deity" and a "demi-God within the breast"—suggests that, "there's a divinity which shapes our ends, rough-hew them how we will", as Shakespeare's Hamlet puts it.

In their book *Conscious Capitalism*, Mackey and Sisodia write that "Smith's views on ethics were largely ignored, and capitalism developed in a stunted way, missing the more human half of its identity."[11] Stephen Young,

8   Jesse Norman, *Adam Smith: What he thought and why it matters*, p 165 (2018)
9   *The Times*, London, 6 October 2017
10 *The Times*, London, 17 July 1990
11 Mackey and Sisodia, ibid.

author of *Moral Capitalism* (2003), makes the same point. "The separation of Smith's two texts has left us with a distorted notion of how the capitalist system should work", he told me.

Following the financial crisis of 2007–2008, it was more than ever clear that capitalism, the market economy and business in general needed a moral basis. David Cameron told the 2009 World Economic Forum in Davos: "It is time to place the market economy in a moral framework." The last chapter of Gordon Brown's book, *Beyond the Crash* (2010) is headlined "Markets need morals". Pope Francis called, in the summer of 2014, for a "moral capitalism" to serve the common good. George W Bush even told Wall Street, after the collapse of Enron in 2002, that "In the end, there is no capitalism without conscience, no wealth without character."[12] The consensus was coming from both right and left of the political spectrum.

It is one thing to say so. It is another to put such sentiment into practice, especially when organizational and economic structures all too easily militate against "doing the right thing". It also begs the question: From where do individuals draw their sense of conscience?

Of course people don't have to have a religious affiliation to have a sense of personal or social conscience. What are the well-springs of inner motivation, which can vary from self-interest to altruism? Motivation, say psychologists, is concerned with exploring what underlies our actions. Motive comes from the Latin word *movere*, meaning to move, and denotes that which energizes and gives direction to people's behaviour. The psychologist G A Miller said: "The study of motivation is the study of all those pushes and prods—biological, social and psychological—that defeat our laziness and move us, either eagerly or reluctantly, to action."[13]

I would also add to those "pushes and prods" the words "ethical" and "spiritual". In other words, motivation results not just from personal need but also from altruism and an informed conscience—about the state of the world, the state of people in it, and the state of ourselves. This begs the question: How is conscience informed? To which I would suggest by information and knowledge, an awareness or consciousness of the true state of things, by listening to others, by empathy and "emotional intelligence at work", by objective moral standards, by turning the searchlight in on ourselves, by silent reflection and, for those of religious persuasion, a sense of the divine will. Thus, inner motivation can spring from a deep personal spiritual or religious experience or conviction and can determine our behaviours at a personal level, with profound results.

The late Nottingham businessman Richard Hawthorne told how a travelling theatre group from India called *India Arise*, which visited London in the late 1960s, had a profound impact on his life. One particular song, *Will we have rice tomorrow, Dad?*, made a deep impression on him. Sitting in his car

12 CNNMoney, 9 July 2002, http://money.cnn.com/2002/07/09/news/bush/index.htm
13 Richard Gross, *Psychology—the science of mind and behaviour*, 2015, p 118.

on the Thames Embankment the next day, he felt an inner call to "open my heart to people whom I had kept at arm's length and to newcomers to Britain who were treated as second class citizens". An Anglican, Hawthorne felt he was being urged to "the biggest task that God was asking of me and not to restrict myself to things I felt I could undertake without making a fool of myself". It meant conquering his innate shyness. This inner experience affected the direction of Hawthorne's life's work. He began to reach out to people in the Afro-Caribbean, Asian and Muslim communities.[14]

He joined Nottingham's Commonwealth citizen's consultative committee, which became the city's Race Relations Board. He was a founder member and Chairman of an independent Partnership Council in Nottingham which, from the late 1990s, brought together community and local government leaders in four deprived inner city neighbourhoods. Hawthorne was decorated with the MBE by the Queen in 2002 for his services to community relations. In 2004, the Nottingham Partnership Council initiated a series of annual demonstrations called "Holding hands around St Ann's", one of the poorest areas, repeated every year since then. The day brings everyone in the community together in a demonstration of solidarity. It was the brainchild and inspiration of Maxine Cockett, a West Indian community leader and single mother, who had lived through real poverty and hardship in her youth, including homelessness. The day aims to counter the gun violence that had blighted St Ann's, with Cockett and Hawthorne making an unlikely but compelling team. Speaking at his funeral in 2018, Cockett said that Hawthorne had been a father figure to her and they were "ebony and ivory".[15]

Like Hawthorne, others also derive their conscience values from their faith tradition. Richard Higginson and Kina Robertshaw, in their book *A Voice to be Heard* (2017), highlight how entrepreneurship can be an expression of the Christian faith of individual business people, in providing the goods and services the world needs rather than just making money. They urge the churches to understand this constructive role of entrepreneurship at a time when too many Christians regard entrepreneurs with suspicion, believing they are driven only by the profit motive.

Reviewing the book in *The Sunday Times*, Luke Johnson wrote: "Most of the more impressive entrepreneurs I have known, whether religious or not, don't really do it for the money. They build businesses to provide the world with their products and services, to generate jobs and taxes, to contribute productively to society, and to make full use of their God-given abilities. A little like those who have a religious faith, entrepreneurs often see their work as a calling, rather than just work." Johnson goes on to highlight the role of Quakers for their "remarkable impact on the industrial landscape of Britain".

14 "Game Plan" by Michael Smith, *The Guardian*, 17 January 2001.
15 Richard Hawthorne died, aged 86, in April 2018 after suffering a stroke. Obituary, *The Guardian* online edition, 17 May 2018: https://www.theguardian.com/uk-news/2018/may/17/richard-hawthorne-obituary

He writes: "Not only did Quakers found the original Lloyds and Barclays banks, but they also started Cadbury's confectionary and Clark's shoes."[16]

Another person motivated by his faith is former British Army officer Peter Neville Lewis, founder of Principled Consulting and visiting lecturer at the University of Buckingham, who comes from a Roman Catholic background. He emphasizes the need for the cardinal virtues of prudence (or wisdom), justice (fairness), temperance (restraint) and fortitude (courage) in the business and organizational context.

I was travelling with Lewis in Switzerland when his briefcase, containing his laptop, was stolen from the platform at Montreux Station. Several years earlier, my family's large suitcase was taken off the train at Lausanne station without us knowing. I reported this to the police at Geneva Airport and duly put in a claim for £700 to our travel insurance company. Several weeks later, I took a phone call from Swiss National Railways who said, to my astonishment, that they had found our suitcase on the platform in Lausanne. What should they do with it? Evidently it had been taken off the train by another group of travellers by mistake. Swiss Railways agreed to get it to Swiss Air at Geneva Airport, who delivered the lost suitcase to our home in London without charge. That very same day, we received a cheque for £700 from the insurance company. I phoned them to thank for the cheque and told them that I was returning it. The woman on the phone laughed and said that many would have simply cashed the cheque. They would have been none the wiser. Not long afterwards I read an article reporting that, at that time, one in seven insurance claims in the UK was fraudulent, which meant that insurance companies had to push up their premiums. More recently the figure has been as high as one in four. There is a cost to society of the collective accumulation of individual dishonesty. Sadly Lewis never retrieved his briefcase and laptop.

Of course motivations to do the right thing can equally come from a secular or commercial imperative. Ecover, the environmentally friendly cleaning products company, for instance, boldly states on its website:

> CLEAN. It's the five-letter word we've lived by for the best part of 40 years. You see, clean means much more to us than washing the dishes or doing the laundry. We like to think of it as an attitude. A philosophy. A way of thinking, feeling... and yes, living clean. In fact, we're on a mission to lead a clean world revolution—for the sake of ourselves, our homes, our communities and our world. Bit feisty coming from a cleaning brand, we'll admit. But how else do you think we're going to save the planet and still make it home in time for tea?

For such a mission, customers are prepared to pay a premium price for its products.[17]

16 *The Sunday Times*, 26 March 2017
17 https://www.ecover.com/

Adam Smith's values, it turns out, are as relevant today as when he first articulated them, and the capitalist system lost something by overlooking his moral vision.

The notion of "trust and integrity in the global economy", advocated by the Caux conferences, implied a process, a means rather than an end, an emphasis on values rather than outcomes: the *how* rather than the *what*. This was deliberate. In stressing the values of integrity which build trust in society, the TIGE conferences stood on its head the old Machiavellian notion that the ends justify the means. They stressed that the means determine the ends. The way we do things is as important as what we do, as this often determines outcomes. This was patently the case in the lead up to the financial crash of 2008: dishonest, hubristic and materialistic means, aided by the opportunities given by complex instruments and technologies, led to disastrous outcomes. Its nadir was the collapse of Lehman Brothers, then the USA's largest corporate failure, on 15 September 2008, and the near collapse of Royal Bank of Scotland following its disastrous take-over of the Dutch bank ABN Amro.

Since then reservoirs of trust in public institutions have been seriously drained: the public's loss of trust in politicians, in the UK through the scandal of corrupt expenses claims and elsewhere through adversarial politics, corruption and the notion of "fake news"; in the media through illegal phone hacking, leading to the closure of the Murdoch-owned Sunday newspaper the *News of the World*; in big business due to corruption scandals and huge boardroom pay rewards and bonuses, regardless of the performance of their organizations; in banks and financial institutions since the crash of 2008, leading to an all-time low in the public's trust of banking; and in historical conflicts between nations, ethnic groups and religious perspectives, where each side feels to be the victim of the other side. Such loss of trust breeds a deep-seated cynicism.

The roots of trust, and trustworthiness, lying in the values—the virtues—by which people live and act, are a key emphasis of the global Initiatives of Change movement, highlighted by its strap line: "Building trust across the world's divides". The ethos of integrity which builds trust is embedded in its business programmes and conferences, like the lettering through a stick of seaside candy rock.

References

Brown, Gordon, *Beyond the Crash: overcoming the first crisis of globalization*, Simon & Schuster, 2010

Dyce, Dr James, *The Rescue of Capitalism: getting Adam Smith right*, Stress Publications, 1990

Gross, Richard, *Psychology—the science of mind and behaviour*, Hodder Education, seventh edition 2015

Higginson, Richard and Robertshaw, Kina, *A Voice to be Heard: Christian entrepreneurs living out their faith*, IVP, 2017

Mackey, John and Sisodia, Rajendra, *Conscious Capitalism: liberating the heroic spirit of business*, Harvard Business Review Press, 2014

Norman, Jesse, *Adam Smith: what he thought and why it matters*, Allen Lane, 2018

Smith, Adam, *The Theory of Moral Sentiments*, Penguin Classics, anniversary edition, 2010

Smith, Adam, *The Wealth of Nations*, Penguin Classics, fourth edition, 1999

Thaler, Richard H and Sunstein, Cass R *Nudge: improving decisions about health, wealth and happiness*, Penguin, 2009

Young, Stephen, *Moral Capitalism: reconciling private interest with the public good*, Berrett-Koehler Publishers, 2003

8   Pillars of trust for a leadership of integrity

For a leadership of integrity there has to be a culture of trust. Integrity builds trust; and a culture of trust is an indicator of integrity at the workplace and throughout organizations. Researching the case stories for this book, five pillars of trust emerged as being essential for effectiveness in business and the economy: integrity, sustainability, purpose, stewardship and cooperation. We shall look at each of them in turn.

Integrity

When I spoke to 500 business students in a huge auditorium in Pune, India, in January 2016, I asked them what they understood by the word integrity. After some hesitation, a single hand went up. "It's doing the right thing when no one else is looking", the young man replied. It was an excellent answer.[1] The notion was originally coined by Henry Ford in relation not to integrity but to quality: he implied that if you did the right thing when no one else was looking you didn't need supervising on the assembly line.

I put the same question to 200 business lecturers at a Businet forum in Portugal in November 2017, inviting them to role play as if they were students. One person replied that it meant walking the talk: doing what you say you are going to do.[2]

The word integrity implies honesty, soundness, wholeness—an integer is a whole number—and that we live by the same values in both our personal and professional lives. We are not divided personalities; we don't hang up our values when we hang up our coats at our workplaces. We should not be expected to compromise on our integrity in our working careers.

Mumbai businessman Vivek Asrani tells how he runs his company, Kaymo Fasteners, on the basis of integrity, not expediency. At one point he turned

1   The Sri Balaji Society and Management Institute, Pune. https://uk.iofc.org/ tige-uk-delivers-pillars-trust-and-integrity-presentation-500-mba-students-india
2   The conference was organized by Businet, a global business education network with over 100 member organizations. https://uk.iofc.org/five-pillars-trust-advoca ted-200-business-educators

down a contract that would have doubled the company's sales, because the purchasing contractor wanted kickbacks.

Established in 1959, Kaymo is India's leading manufacturer, distributor and service provider for a range of staplers and fastening tools. Asrani, who is the Managing Director, is also a trustee of the Asia Plateau centre in Panchgani. He tells his story:[3]

> We had a small scale industry which my father and grandfather set up, which was doing well, taking care of the family. We had a good market share but after 42 years of existence the company was near closure.
>
> One of the big challenges we faced was competing with the unorganized sector. People had started manufacturing our products and selling them without invoices, giving less quantity in boxes, and we suddenly found that our market share was plummeting. It reached a point where the business was on the verge of closure. This was a year before I was going to get married.
>
> We had two decisions in front of us; one was that we could go down the same path and do whatever it took to continue being in business. We would have been able to legitimize it by saying, "Look we didn't set the rules, the market dynamics have changed. We are just doing what the market is doing. If the market cleans itself up, we will be happy to be clean. We've just got to do what it takes to be in business." Or move up the value chain and make our principles non-negotiable.
>
> We took the second decision and moved into a new industrial range of products which had not been introduced in India.
>
> When we started the new company, about 15 years ago, one of the first decisions I made was that we would build it rooted in principles, and we would make those principles non-negotiable. We came up with four principles on which we founded the company: integrity, win-win, customer delight and excellence. For us integrity isn't just being honest with money; it's the respect and care with which we work with people. Win-win is a paradigm I learnt from my grandfather and father that everyone sitting at the table must benefit. Customer delight was an obvious value for us: we put the customer at the centre of all discussions and decisions. I tell my people it's not me or the company who pays your salary, it's the customer. If we take care of the customer, he takes care of the company. And finally excellence. We have a young team and I keep telling them that we spend the best years of our life, 25 to 65, and the best time of the day, 9:30 to 6:30, at work. So, make it the best experience for yourself. The company will take care of itself. Excellence is a value we cherish because the quality of our life is dependent on how we work.

3   Asrani first told his story to the 2013 Caux TIGE conference from which this account has been updated.

It is all very well to start this off. I was soon challenged in the second year of the company's existence when we were still very small. I was negotiating an order which was equal to the turnover of the company at that time. It meant we could have potentially doubled the size of the company with that one order. It was one of the most corrupt purchase departments I have ever come across—private sector, not government. We walked away from their order. I came back to the office—we were a team of five or six people—and I said we're not taking this order. Having said that, what would it take for us to be market leaders? It's not good enough to say that we are good, therefore we are losing. We have to say that we are good and therefore we win. And I said to the team, "What does it take for us to be market leaders and win the game out there?"

That was 10 years ago when we had only eight products, no distributors, no dealers, no service centre. Today we run a portfolio of more than 400 products, a distribution network in 90 cities in India, managing about 200 distributers and 800 end customers. We have India's largest service centre and we've set up 67 authorized service centres all across the country. We've built a supply chain network of more than 20 suppliers around the world who supply products to us.

I'm not saying this to impress anyone, but the beauty was that, because we chose not to take that order, it forced us to go down a creative path. That was one of my first learnings in my business: that when we are committed to our principles in challenging situations, it leads to growth and development. Today I look back and I bless that corrupt purchasing officer because honestly I think he kicked us in the right direction and we've moved to a different level altogether.

Business has its challenges and I had a very interesting situation with the tax department. During one of our assessments, our accounts department had given a wrong stock statement. We were running a new software and by mistake they had taken the print out from the wrong software. The assessing officer refused to accept the correct stock statement. He said, "Now I have found the discrepancy I am going to penalize you." It was a very substantial amount. I remember my accounts manager came looking very worried saying this is what's happened. So I said, "It's not a problem, take the chartered accountant and go meet the officer." He said, "I've taken the CA, but this guy is just not listening." So, I went and met the officer and said, "Look this is what has happened. We're running a new software and through an oversight they've taken a print out from this new software and I'm giving it to you in writing that, yes, we have made a genuine error and here is the correct stock statement."

I went on to tell him, "If you think that we have actually committed a fraud and, now that you have seen the difference in figures, you think we are trying to cover it up, then you must penalize us and penalize us double. But if after having met me, heard me and understood the whole situation, if you come to the conclusion that, yes, this was a genuine oversight and this was a human error, which any human being can make, then the right thing for you to do would be to accept my correct stock statement. If you think I'm lying then penalize me."

He looked at me and said something very interesting: "A dishonest person will never have the courage to sit in front of me and talk like this. Go, your work is done." That's when I learnt a very important lesson. People say it takes courage to be ethical. According to me, being ethical makes you courageous. When I met the officer I had no fear because at the back of my mind I knew that we had done nothing wrong. We had simply made a mistake. That's what I learnt, that when we drop our fear, our ability to solve a problem becomes bigger than the problem.

I was negotiating with a Canadian company who wanted to ship us some goods. We'd never met them and they said they wanted to start. I was telling them on the phone: "We'll start provided you give us 90 days credit." They said, "Look, we don't know each other. When we come to India we'll meet you, we'll talk about it." I said to him over the phone: "You know, my company is named after my great grandfather. His name was K Motiram", from which we have the name Kaymo, and I said, "For me the value of the good-will far exceeds any financial gain." There was silence on the phone and after a few seconds he said, "Ninety days' credit is approved", never having met the company. This is when I realized that being ethical has been one of the best business strategies that we have ever adopted.

Six years ago I was negotiating the largest transaction of my life. I met this person, we transacted and we shook hands.

Then he tells me, "But I need a down payment in the next 10 days." I agreed. He then said "We'll make a kind of temporary agreement but the final documents will be after 18 months because I need it to span across two financial years." I said, "Done." Over the next 18 months I developed a deep friendship with this astute businessman, 20 years my senior. Closer to the end of the transaction, when I went to him, I said, "Look, I'm travelling to America; I'm going for a month. I still owe you about 10 per cent of the money. I would like to somehow close this transaction. It is wrong for me to ask you but this was on my mind. I've just come to share this with you." He looked at me and said, "Draw up the documents." He signed, sealed and delivered the transaction to me without having received his final payment. Honestly he couldn't have done anything if we had decided not to pay. But I told him, "It's going to take me four to six months." He said, "No problem."

After four months, I went back to him and paid the last instalment. I said, "Mr Somani, you didn't know me, I just came to you as a buyer for this property. It was a huge transaction, the last 10 per cent you allowed me the facility with no collateral in your hand. You signed, sealed and delivered with the property. Why did you do it?" He looked at me and said, "You remember the first day you came to me and I said I needed x amount in the next 10 days and you gave it to me? The moment you trusted me and I needed the money at that time, for me that established your credibility."

The big learning for me after that transaction—of course he was a wonderful person to deal with—was that my ability to trust people comes from my own faith in trust. There's a lot to be said about a handshake, of looking someone in the eye, getting an instinct and saying I think I can trust the person. The largest transaction of my life was based on just the look in the eye, the handshake and instinct.

Of course trust can be broken. People will take advantage. Fourteen people left our company to join a competitor. Eleven of them left the competitor. One of them has come back asking for a job. Two of them are still there. It was a very difficult period for us, about three years ago. But one of the things I realized—and from then till today we've grown about 40 per cent in spite of having lost so many people—is that an organization that is deeply rooted in its principles has a better chance of weathering a storm. This is when I realized the value of the principles in challenges. Something beautiful my mother taught me was: "Never ask, why me? Always say, now what?"

Once the business started to grow with a bit of momentum, I started saying to myself that there has to be a purpose beyond profit. For us profit is like petrol or gas in a car. Without the petrol you cannot run the car, but you do not drive the car for the petrol. You drive the car to reach a destination in life. Similarly, the company has to be built for a higher purpose.

For us, the ethos of what we do came to me in the word that we exist to "Give": to give to the nation a responsible company that generates employment and wealth with integrity. To give to industry, suppliers and customers a reliable and trustworthy partner giving the highest standards of service and quality. To give to our team a better quality life and an opportunity to maximize our potential and, more importantly, to give to society a caring citizen.

One of our junior accountants went on maternity leave. She came back saying that she would not be able to come back for a year because her child was unwell and in need of a few surgeries. We told her that her job was secured: take as long as you want, the job is not going anywhere. We give our men one month paternity leave, because when I became a father I had to take a lot of time off. I didn't have to ask anyone, after all the company belongs to me. I told them, "You guys are no less a father than I am. Your wife and child need you as much. So the company will pay you a month's salary to stay at home to take care. Your family is a stakeholder in our company." So that's our small investment. When we give at every level with a certain amount of love, it compels us to do our best. For us the growth in the company has been through giving.

We understand that the results are a function of our effort and circumstances. Circumstances are not in our control. So results are not in our control. Therefore the only place we really focus, as an organization, is in the effort. It's really all about the "how" to live each experience with integrity and excellence. For me personally success lies in doing a job really well and knowing that I and we as an organization give it our 100 per cent, irrespective of what the outcome might be. For us the journey is the goal.

Like Asrani, Vinal Shah, Chairman of the BIDCO Group, a multi-award winning agribusiness in Kenya, tells how he runs the business on the basis of integrity and "customer-centricity". The aim is to "do the right thing from day one—don't cheat anyone", he says. A "fork in the road" came when the company could make a lot of money if they were unethical. Instead, he decided to shut down an IT company when politicians wanted kick-backs for awarding contracts. "We lost $20 million by not being corrupt", he says. But now the business is sustainable. The group opened a new $20 million plant in Madagascar "without paying a single bribe", despite pressure from politicians to do so. Shah sees "winds of change in the next years" for the private sector, thanks to Kenya's Anti-Bribery Act passed in 2017.[4]

Genevieve Boast is another person of courageous integrity. Her story illustrates how a personal change of motivation leads to organizational change. She risked her career when, in her early twenties, she exposed theft in the logistics company in Sheffield where she worked. It was supplying electronic equipment to a renowned satellite broadcasting company.

I first met Boast, a vivacious woman, then in her thirties, when we shared a speaking platform in the City of London in 2012. Her story was so compelling I urged her to tell it to a Caux TIGE conference.

Born in Colorado, Boast grew up in England when her parents moved to Cambridge, UK, when she was six. Her father, an archaeologist, was studying for his PhD there. For Genevieve, the culture shock, moving away from the wide open spaces of Colorado, was little short of traumatic.

She had a rollercoaster ride as a teenager. Aged 17 she was caught up in a sex and drugs culture and was arrested for shoplifting at a shop where she was working in Cambridge. She was driven off in a police car and put into a cell. "It takes panic to a different level", she says. Yet she recalls the police treating her with surprising kindness and politeness. A tall police officer came to her cell and sat next to her. He made a single remark to her: "Gen, you are worth so much more than this." Then he left. Boast has never met him since then and to this day does not know his name. But his remark completely turned her life around. From then on, she says, she determined to live a life of personal integrity. With her criminal record, blowing the whistle in the logistics company was all the more risky as she wondered who on earth would ever employer her. She takes up the story:[5]

4   Shah was speaking at the February 2018 Caux Initiatives for Business conference in Panchgani, India.
5   Boast told it to the 2013 Caux TIGE conference.

I fell into a job, working nights, at a logistics company in Sheffield, where I had studied at university. It was a horrific shift: four in the afternoon to four in the morning. It was one of those places where it was an incredibly traditional, male-dominated environment. It was a warehouse, so it was pretty much all guys. It was run on fear and the dictatorial management style of the people at the top. But it was also a place where anybody who had a spark, passion and enthusiasm got promoted very quickly. Within a year, at the age of 21, I was running a team of 17 people, all older than me, not having a clue about leadership, but finding my way having jumped into the deep end.

My team was responsible for all of the stock in the warehouse that belonged to our customer, a major entertainment company in the UK.

One thing I discovered that I loved about leadership was forming real human connections with people. Not only did I do that with my team but I also formed an incredibly close friendship with my counterpart at our customer. About a year into this I was doing some investigation in the warehouse, looking at stock, and I started to discover that, where it was saying on the system we should have lots of electronic stock belonging to our customer, there were just big gaping empty holes. So I started asking questions: "Where is this stuff?" I was told by the warehouse, "Oh it's just a system problem, don't look at it." But it was my job to look at it. So, I started asking questions higher up: "Where is this stuff?" I'm going to get asked by the customer, "Where is it?" They said, "Oh, no, just don't look at it, it's an audit fault."

But the more I looked into it, the more I found that many items of the equipment were showing up in places where they shouldn't be. Through my investigation over a couple of months, I found that the company had lost, stolen or misappropriated about £1 million worth of our customer's stock.

So I was faced with the decision, at a very young age, of what do I do? And I was scared. I had pretty much been told to shut up by the company. I knew what the right thing was. But I agonized over it for about three days.

The stories I created in my head, from the basis of fear, overruled that quiet voice of my intuition, knowing what the right thing to do would be. I made up every story in the book: you'll lose your job, no one will give you a reference, you'll have no credibility, you'll have to go back to digging in the field and make no money (I used to be an archaeologist).... It sounds very biblical now when I tell it, but for three nights I agonized over this decision. On the morning of the fourth day I walked back into the office, took my phone and locked myself in the computer server cabinet. I called my friend, our customer, and said, "I've got something to tell you." And I did! There was silence at the end of the phone. Then he said, "Wow, Gen, thank you so much for that. You know I'm going to have to have this conversation but I'll try and protect you." And I was thinking, "Thanks... but you're not going to be able to protect me."

I'd been asking questions for months. Everybody knew it had to be me but couldn't prove it. My life at work became a living hell. I felt alienated, I felt victimized. Every meeting was painful. It got to the point where it was almost unbearable. I thought, "Okay, so now I'm faced with another decision. I know I've done the right thing, I can sleep at night. My conscience is clear, so now what do I do?" I was going to leave. It was the only thing I could do. At best, maybe I could get a reference.

I started looking around and got some interviews. I called up my friend at our customer and I said, "Look, I'm going. I can't stand this anymore." He said, "Don't move, someone will call you back in half an hour." I starting thinking okay, fine, intrigued. In half an hour somebody did call me back. It was the newly appointed Head of Supply Chain at the customer, a guy called Euan Smith. He said, "Gen, I'm so impressed with what you did, I want to create a job for you with us. I'm going to pay you more money. I want you to come up and head our entire stock division, and I want to call you Stock Integrity Manager!"

That call opened the door to my career in the media. For the next seven years I had several different jobs there. The positive ripples of that into my career spread wider and wider.

The story gets better still. Five years after joining the entertainment company, Genevieve found she wanted to work more in leadership with people and on environmental concerns. So she moved into the corporate social responsibility team.

There she found herself on a flight from Scotland to London "with Euan in the seat behind me, laughing and joking and pulling my hair like two kids". They were both going through divorces, following youthful, unfulfilling marriages. By now Genevieve had trained in psychology and said to Euan, "Why don't I coach you and you coach me and we'll see where we get to?" In June 2013, they made their sacred vows to each other on the side of a volcano in Hawaii. They are now formally married. Genevieve comments: "I honestly cannot believe the magic that has happened in my life as a result of that one decision to stay in integrity."

In 2014, Boast returned to Caux with Euan, who had since moved companies and was based in Germany. In a platform interview he confirmed that the logistics company contract had been quickly terminated. The company had since been bought out. He told the TIGE conference why he had decided to hire Boast:

There was this little beam of sunshine in the corner (in Sheffield). That was the first time I met Gen. It was a two-second interaction before I got back in my car and wondered how I was going to change this whole logistics operation. It was a big amount of stuff to lose—over a period about ten articulated lorries full of kit. You don't lose that amount easily. For me, it was a natural no-brainer (to hire Genevieve). Most people would run away from a whistleblower. I chose to run towards her, because if there is one thing you need it is somebody who, first, was the only positive, smiling face in an otherwise very disappointing day for me, but, second, you are trying to make sure that you've got on your team someone who cares where every single piece of stock is and lives with it passionately. The person who is prepared to put their entire career on the line because they have that principle—that is the person I needed on my team. You can train the skill. You are looking for the spark—the spark that says, "I care about doing the right thing."

[For more on the stance against corruption see Chapter 9, "Beheading the snake of corruption".]

The Anglo-Swiss businesswoman Jane Royston tells how she walked away from a lucrative career with a multinational corporation rather than compromise on her personal integrity.[6] She remembers vividly the moment when her career took a dramatic turn. It followed a champagne buffet party in Paris in September 1986. She was 28 years old and head of IT in France for the US chemicals multinational DuPont. Originally from England, she had been with the company for six years following her graduation in pure maths from the London School of Economics. She was being fast-tracked for the top—one of those with CEO potential.

The evening party was being thrown by DuPont's European chief, who congratulated the staff for record growth and record profits. In order to achieve such continuing success in the following year, he remarked casually that 20 per cent of the global workforce were going to be sacked. Others at the party hardly demurred, Royston recalls. She felt incensed. Whether or not the threat would actually be carried out, the mere fact that he had said it was enough to enrage her.

She went home and that night had a vivid dream, about setting up a company that worked on the basis of fairness. "I woke up and said to myself I can't stay in DuPont anymore." That day she resigned.

She returned to her parents' home in Geneva. There she set up her own IT company, NatSoft SA, to provide IT solutions for big companies in Switzerland and elsewhere. It would be a fair company with consensual or inclusive decision-making, where management involved staff in the decision-making processes.

For the first six months she visited IT managers all over Switzerland with hardly any response.

Then in March 1987 she took a phone call, in her parents' basement, from the Social Security Department of the Swiss government. They asked if her company could update their entire IT systems. "Yes, we can", she replied

6   Royston told this story to the June 2015 business conference in Caux, Switzerland. https://www.caux.ch/swiss-business-woman-year-and-kenyan-entrepreneur-speak-tige

immediately. She set about frantically recruiting skilled staff. "It turned out to be a massive contract, installing mainframe computers and database systems", she recalls.

Following that initial contract other clients followed: Roche, Nestlé, Dow, private banks, the World Health Organization, and even for Vietnamese boat people under the auspices of the United Nations High Commission for Refugees.

The company grew to be the largest IT provider in French-speaking Switzerland, with 120 employees representing 27 nationalities, and a turn-over of SwFr 15 million. Fifty per cent of profits went to the employees in bonuses. She was voted the Veuve Clicquot Swiss Business Woman of the Year, 1993–1994. In 1995 NatSoft received the Strategis award as the best managed SME (small and medium sized enterprise) in Switzerland, given by the financial monthly magazine *Bilan*, the Swiss equivalent of *Fortune*.

"I set out to do good and I ended up doing well", she comments. One of her commitments to doing good was to take on staff from the long-term unemployed. With Royston at the helm, the company received 3,000 CVs from job seekers each year, interviewed 300 of them and took on 30 per year. Five of these had been out of work for as many as two years or more. She found that they were highly motivated. Once they had secured a job they were keen to retain it. They were the ones who would be at work promptly by 7am. She needed people with good IT skills but also with EQ or emotional intelligence—"those who were good at understanding people's spoken and unspoken needs".

"It was not only the decision making that made NatSoft different", Royston says. "It was also that we kept our word with everyone, and never took advantage of anyone. For example, many other companies pay new immigrants less because they don't know any better. We were transparent in all aspects including salaries. They were common knowledge because I felt that if I couldn't justify why one person was getting more than another then they probably shouldn't be!"

Royston asserts that "it makes good business sense to do the right thing: by treating employees right, you save money because you have a much lower employee turn-over, which is one of the plagues of the IT industry; by taking decisions consensually, you get immediate buy-in and save time persuading people to reluctantly do what you say; by being on time and on budget each time, you save money on marketing and client acquisition because of all the repeat business you get."

The company's reputation for excellence of service meant that NatSoft achieved 95 per cent client retention from one year to the next. "We never let a client down. We were always on time and within budget, even if it meant working through the night or at weekends. When you get a reputation like that you retain customers."

Nonetheless, after her husband left her she sold the company in 1996 to Cambridge Technology Partners in Boston. She had two pre-school children and couldn't look after them and the company.

"I had to make a choice and chose the children." Cambridge paid "turn-over times one", she quips. She had run NatSoft for ten years and ten days. At first she stayed on at their request. But "it was like rearranging a house you have lived in. I couldn't stand it."

She left and for six months did nothing whilst she thought "long and hard about what I enjoyed doing: people, selling, strategy and projects for clients but not operations."

At first she helped people on a pro bono basis to start up their own businesses. Then the Swiss President asked her to go to Bern to advise him and the government on the new economy, based on the Internet.

In 1999 she was appointed the chair of entrepreneurship and innovation at the Federal Institute of Technology in Lausanne. She held the post of professor there till 2005. "It was a brand new chair, first of its kind in Switzerland."

Within four years she was teaching at other major universities in Switzerland: Zurich, Basle, St Gallen and Geneva. At the same time she set up a European Task Force for Entrepreneurship. Then in 2004 the federal government's department of economy asked her to design and set up a National Entrepreneurship Centre in Berne.

She now sits on the boards of several companies and foundations, including being the chair of PRO (Private Social Enterprise foundation) which employs over 250 handicapped people in Geneva. Royston says they are particularly skilled at doing repetitive work that requires zero per cent defaults, such as packaging cosmetics and assembling electronic devices.

Royston says that her proudest achievement at the macro level was to build up NatSoft. And at the micro level she was glad "to act very quickly" to abort a *coup d'état* within the company when her business partner tried to set up a rival company pinching her customers and employees. "He made the strategic mistake of resigning. Our employees' best interest was to stay with us."

Like the English Quaker industrial pioneers, whom she trumpets, she affirms that businesses can thrive by doing the right thing for employees and customers alike.

Sustainability

"Creating a desirable, sustainable future is the leadership challenge of our time", says the Swedish businessman Göran Carstedt. He means the sustainability of the planet as much as organizations. As a senior executive of Volvo and then board member of Ikea (1990–1997), including President of Ikea North America (1990–1995), Carstedt implemented sustainability policies as part of the business plan in both those companies. He went on to chair the Swedish non-profit sustainability organization, Natural Step International.

"Something old is dying and something new is trying to be born", Carstedt told the August 2011 Caux business conference.[7] The old was the industrial,

---

7   https://www.caux.ch/node/1802

mechanical worldview, where "we, humanity, thought we were in charge—in charge of other people, in charge of nature. And of course that was an illusion. The new is borderless, global, digital—and brutal in many ways. It is interconnected in a completely new, radical complexity."

The challenge, he said, was how to create a "transformational change in our institutions". This was more than environmental sustainability, important as that is. Many nations have also become worried by the sustainability of their school and healthcare systems. Organizations were simply not capable of dealing with the complexities of today's situations on their own.

Change, Carstedt asserted, is "less about reorganizing, structuring and re-engineering and more about reconceiving. That is what leadership is about." And learning, he continued, is dependent on "becoming part of a meaningful community". That is what he saw Caux trying to create. The future, he told Caux, "is not a road to be discovered; it is a road to be created. And isn't that very hopeful? So what future do we like to be a part of creating?" What could be more meaningful and desirable than "co-creating a sustainable future? To develop products and processes and services that are in harmony with nature, and by liberating human creativity. To give their best, people need a meaningful cause to believe in that will bring forth the passion needed."

Afterwards, he told a documentary film interviewer that "everything happens in conversations. We have to create space for that kind of very honest, open conversation. Of course bring in bright ideas and bright people for that journey. That is why I am not afraid at all of staying in questions."

Sustainability is not just a private sector issue, either. Emma Ihre, who was Special Advisor to the Sustainable Business Department for Sweden's Ministry of Finance, asserts that the nation's 50 state-owned businesses are driving a sustainable business approach.[8] And it works, she says. The state sector is Sweden's largest employer and supports a business perspective of risks and opportunities, with a focus on seven key areas of sustainability: diversity, environment, human rights, labour conditions, anti-corruption, business ethics and gender equality.

The Ministry recruits directors who have strong ethical values and a corresponding attitude. "We dare to have high expectations and a focus on transparency and cooperation", Ihre said. The state is a proud owner of its companies, setting high expectations and levels of transparency. Ihre explained that "sustainability within business isn't something that is a side aspect of otherwise more important matters. First on the agenda when the state meets with the boards of directors is to review its implementation."

The need for "open, honest conversation" that Carstedt talks about is advocated by the political philosopher David Marquand in his book *Mammon's Kingdom* (2014). In it he gives a robust call for a public debate on how to create a "moral economy". We live in a more unequal society than ever, he argues. London has more billionaires than any city on earth. Yet the poorest

8   Irhe was speaking to the 2014 Caux TIGE conference.

fifth of Britain's population are among the poorest of all the EU countries, he claims. The benefits of growth are not evenly distributed. The UK is mammon's kingdom and "no large Western democracy has been more devoted to money worship than Britain". We have lost what Adam Smith called "the bonds of sympathy" and we need to create a "decent society" that doesn't humiliate people through unemployment, zero-hours contracts, lack of housing, alienation and poverty.

The Northern Irish businessman Peter Brew, who ran the Asia-Pacific regional arm of the International Business Leaders Forum from Hong Kong (2008–2011), speaks, like Goran Carstedt, of the need for sustainability. Brew emphasizes four pillars of sustainability: economic, environmental, human and ethical.[9]

"Business has no divine right to exist", he says.

> It will only exist and be sustained if it meets the needs and plays its part in society. It's not enough just to be pious and talk the talk. Business has got to walk the talk in terms of sustainability. The sustainability agenda is not just about the environment. Companies have to be economically sustainable. I'm the first to say if you're not profitable you won't survive. Profits are important and vital.
>
> There is an environmental dimension as well. There's a human dimension. Companies have to be concerned about their employees, about the employees down the supply chain, about the communities in which they're operating, and they must make sure they are making a positive contribution to the well-being of their colleagues. And there has to be an ethical dimension. We have got to do what's right. As business people, we have got to say there is a moral dimension and we believe in a moral dimension.

He calls for business, governments, civil society and academia to work together on the sustainability agenda and to create the space for dialogue.

R. Gopalakrishnan, popularly known as Gopal, a former Group Executive Board member of Tata Sons in India, emphasizes how the notion of sustainability benefits all stakeholders. "When a business is run with the sole purpose of serving society", he says, "it encompasses all the elements of sustainability and ensures that all stakeholders benefit from its operations. Thoughts on sustainability, triple bottom line [financial, environmental and social] are written about frequently in contemporary management journals as new wave thinking, but they are not."[10]

Based on his many years of experience with Tata, and drawing on other examples of industries from East and West, Gopalakrishnan claims that if

9 Brew gave the July 2013 public Caux Lecture: https://www.caux.ch/%E2%80% 98west-not-best-%E2%80%93-we-do-not-dominate-world%E2%80%99

10 Gopalakrishnan gave the keynote address to the August 2010 Caux business conference. https://www.caux.ch/node/1645

firms focus on stakeholder value, profits follow. "Some of the most profitable firms do not sport direct profit-orientation", he says. "They simply do the right things and end up being nicely profitable." A company "is an organic part of society. When businesses put social responsibility at the core of their activities, other 'lag' measures like profits will automatically follow." The central purpose of business is to serve society, he asserts.

When it comes to environmental sustainability, Pradeep Bhargava, a leading figure in the Confederation of Indian Industry (CII), who is Director of Cummins India Ltd, argues that "the business case for going green is so strong". The CII's GreenCo initiative rates companies for their environmental performance. Bhargava insists that it is a myth that companies have to choose between market share or quality, or between financial performance and going green. Tata Motors in Jamshedpur, for instance, has steadily reduced its energy costs since 2002, year on year. The company has also planted hundreds of thousands of trees. And Delhi Airport has a strategy to go carbon neutral, including installing solar panels between runways. The payback for the cost of their installation is only two years, Bhargava says. Companies need to be pro-active and not just legally compliant. The need now is to make the trend fashionable amongst small and medium sized enterprises.[11]

Rajeev Dubey, member of the Group Management Board of the Mahindra & Mahindra automotive and tractor company, tells how the leading Indian corporation has been "going green" to meet environmental and climate change challenges. "Sustainability and corporate social responsibility are embedded in the group's DNA and form an integral part of its core values and vision", claims Dubey, who is Mahindra group's President of Human Resources for after-market and corporate services.[12]

M&M is the leading farm equipment manufacturer in India, with a 42 per cent market share, and the world's largest tractor manufacturer. The $8 billion company, with 108,000 employees in 47 countries, had recently taken over the scandal-hit Satyam IT company, after Satyam's founder and CEO was charged with falsifying the company's profits. Dubey saw Mahindra Satyam as "a litmus test in our commitment to trust and integrity", in pulling the company back to profitability.

"A sharp focus on sustainability is in line with customer and community sensitivities across the globe", Dubey said, claiming that the Mahindra group "had a unique and compelling story to tell", particularly in its environmental policies. The company sought to "create new standards in natural resource conservation". It was one of the earliest companies in India to set-up, in 2001, a bio-diesel plant, as part of its alternative fuel and propulsion technologies programme. Since then, the company has introduced tractors which use five

---

11 Bhargya addressed the 7th biennial Caux Initiatives for Business conference in Panchgani, Maharashtra, on 7 February 2018.
12 Dubey gave the public Caux Lecture on "Transforming capitalism with trust and integrity" in July 2009. https://www.caux.ch/node/1458

per cent and 10 per cent bio-diesel and was field testing vehicles that are 20 per cent and 100 per cent biodiesel, "in the most challenging conditions, from the deserts of Rajasthan to Himalayan terrains".

The company had also made the world's first hydrogen powered three-wheeler, with near zero emissions, and was developing with other partners a hydrogen powered internal combustion engine vehicle "as part of our vision of making hydrogen an important fuel of tomorrow". Meanwhile its electric three-wheelers were launched in 1999. And the company showcased its first hybrid electric vehicle at the Delhi motor show in 2006.

The company is also pioneering "green buildings", as the first residential building developer in India to receive the LEED (Leadership in Energy and Environmental Design) pre-certification. The same focus, including water and energy efficiency, is incorporated into the company's new factories and at its "Mahindra World City" R&D plant in Chennai, which opened in 2010. This includes rain water harvesting, waste-heat recovery, solar panels and turbine air ventilation replacing electric ventilators.

All this is reflected in the company's Mahindra Rise branding and marketing, as it aims to meet the challenges of the rising new India, and as a "provider of profitable and affordable improvements in the quality of life", as Dubey put it. "We dare to dream that we can make a positive difference to the communities and nations we live in and operate in, while achieving sustainable business growth and profitability. We are determined to do this with *satya, prem* and *seva*—truth, compassion and service in our daily actions at a personal and professional level." This is reflected, for instance, in the group's commitment to the education of disadvantaged children, particularly, girls, as part of its social commitment.

Tania Ellis, the Anglo-Danish author of *The New Pioneers* (2010), shifts the emphasis of CSR, Corporate Social Responsibility, towards Corporate Sustainability and Responsibility. The financial downturn had "widened the trust gap between business and people", she asserted at a forum in London, in May 2011.[13] Bridging this gap had encouraged companies to invest more in their social dimension, "allying sustainability and meaning", she said. Changes in mentalities had evolved to create a critical mass of people who put values such as ethics, responsibility, sustainability and meaning at the centre-stage, she believed. This social megatrend—a global consciousness movement—has triggered big changes in business and elsewhere. "A lot of people want to make a difference, get involved in NGOs (Non-Governmental Organizations) and voluntary work or simply change their buying habits." These changes put pressure on companies to act responsibly, thanks to increasing numbers of conscious consumers and investors. "Companies realize they need to operate with more than one bottom line and integrate social and environmental issues as part of their business strategies", Ellis said.

13 Greencoat Forum, Initiatives of Change centre, London, 17 May 2011.

Ellis cites the case of an IT consultancy in Norway which, she said, works with "zero financial goals" and bases all its activities on two core values: competence and empathy. Even during the financial crisis it had grown by 20 per cent each year despite its refusal to set financial goals. She also told about her friend who had transformed a Danish island into a carbon neutral community which exports 20 per cent of its green energy. When he talked to an Arab the latter laughed, saying, "This is two housing blocks in Dubai." His immediate reply had been, "Well this is probably where you need to start."[14]

Purpose

The Scottish philosopher and author Thomas Carlyle said that "someone without purpose is like a ship without a rudder". The same could be said of organizations, though of course their purpose, beyond profit, can change over time. Aaron Hurst, CEO of Imperative, argues that the world has moved through the agrarian, industrial and information economies to "the purpose economy"—the title of his book (2014). His book's subtitle spells out what he means: "How your desire for impact, personal growth and community is changing the world".

Anita Hoffmann of Executiva, quoted in Chapter 2, develops this further in *Purpose and Impact* (2018) arguing that terminologies for the purpose economy include "just capitalism, inclusive capitalism, capitalism for the long term, and compassionate capitalism. They all make the same point: it is time for business to play a different role in society, providing value for all stakeholders." Her book aims to make a link between "societal, business and individual motivations". Moreover, as we all live longer lives, there is a primary need and opportunity for those living between the ages of 50 and 80 to redefine their roles with new careers based on contribution to society which enhances personal fulfilment. But, she says, don't wait till your senior years. Now, she says, is the time to pursue a purpose-driven career.

Hoffman finds herself a confidante to senior executives who want to rethink their contribution to society, especially when they have reached the age when most executives leave their mainstream corporate employers but still have some 30 active years ahead of them. She describes her role as "helping executives find purpose and develop their careers to express this, especially at mid/later careers, and thereby helping to change how we do business in the world".

She quotes a 2016 study by EY (Ernst & Young) and Harvard Business Review Analytic Services, entitled *The Business Case for Purpose*, which links purpose with company growth: "Of the 474 global executives surveyed, of those who reported their organization was actively pursuing Purpose, 58 per cent reported growth in the previous three years to over 10 per cent, versus

---

14 Ellis addressed the 2012 Caux TIGE conference, https://www.caux.ch/busi ness-integrity-challenges-solutions

51 per cent that were developing a Purpose-driven direction and 42 per cent for 'laggards'—companies that are not actively pursuing Purpose.

A forum on "corporate governance for a changing world" was hosted by Cass Business School in the City of London in September 2014. It kicked off a series of round-tables around the world on the purpose of corporations in the 21st century. The forum was initiated by Frank Bold, the public interest law firm, one of whose lawyers, Filip Gregor from the Czech Republic, had taken part in the 2014 Caux TIGE conference two months earlier. One of the aims of the forums is to reform company law in the UK and the European Union.

Its forum report states boldly:

The popular conception that corporations exist principally for the purpose of maximizing shareholder value has become so enmeshed with the narrative of business that the issue is rarely given serious consideration. This popular conception is based on a model of the corporation which bears very little relationship to the reality of 21st century corporate activity and is implicated in a range of unintended consequences including an inappropriate focus on the short-term, potentially (and paradoxically) sub-optimal returns to share-holders, excessive executive pay and a range of negative social and environ-mental externalities. There is also significant evidence that it is fundamentally inconsistent with sustainability. Mounting empirical evidence suggests that shareholder primacy and the overarching goal of maximizing shareholder values contribute to short-termism, inequality, and limit companies' ability to address social and environmental damage.[15]

The report continues:

From a company law perspective, the question of for whom the organi-zation operates is paramount. The popular perception amongst business leaders is that the purpose of the corporation is to maximize shareholder value. Yet this is based on a fundamental misinterpretation of company law. The Panel agrees that such a narrow interpretation of corporate purpose is not embedded in company law, but it is rather a result of market forces and an inadequate structure of incentives—both on the demand and supply sides of equity capital. If we step away from the myth of maximizing shareholder value, we must ask what purpose to put in its place to restore social trust in business.

What makes a good company? The Panel agrees that it is one that provides goods or services that are socially and economically respon-sible, while generating sustainable profits. It is clear that business must return a profit to survive, but there must be a balance between making a return and a company's responsibility to broader environmental and social concerns. Great businesses exist to provide goods, services and

15 http://en.frankbold.org/our-work/campaign/purpose-corporation; http://www.purp oseofcorporation.org/corporate-governance-for-a-changing-world_report.pdf

employment. If a business sets out to help people then it is more likely to be successful, both in terms of achieving its mission and generating profit.

So, essentially, companies need a purpose beyond profit. As the young eponymous hero in the film *Hugo* puts it: "If you lose your purpose it's like you're broken." Like machines, everyone, every organization needs a purpose.

At the corporate level, Unilever aims to define a purpose other than profit for all the products it sells. The company believes that "Doing well by doing good is good for business." Unilever announced its Sustainable Living Plan in 2010.[16] It redefined the company's purpose and vision: to help a billion people, to improve their health and well-being, whilst doubling the size of the business. The company would half its environmental footprint and enhance suppliers' livelihoods. Unilever's Sustainable Living Plan, and the company's commitment to its implementation, established Unilever's then CEO Paul Polman as a leader in the movement to connect business to society. He asked that every brand should have a social mission, linked inextricably to its product mission and economic mission.

This is well illustrated by the "sustainable purpose" of one product, Lifebuoy soap, which is to promote hygiene particularly among young children—to "help a child to be ill less often" and so not miss school, as Malaysian advertising executive Bharat Avalani, puts it, speaking about his previous 24-year career with Unilever.[17] Hygiene was essential at a time when 6.6 million children die before their fifth birthday each year, due to malnutrition and preventable diseases. The Lifebuoy soap brand has thus taken on a whole new significance for employees, customers, NGOs and governments, combining commercial and social objectives. Brand managers are on track to educate a billion people in over 100 countries about the benefits of handwashing. The soap has become "a movement to improve lives".

The notion of good company purpose is also well illustrated by James Miller, Chairman and Chief Executive of Abermed occupational health company from 2001 to 2011.[18] He had joined the company in 1999 and took over its leadership in 2001. It was a small business employing 12 people. Turnover was about £800,000 ($1.2 million at that time). He says:

> There's a lot of oil in the North Sea. There are platforms and rigs with people living on them. The role of the business was looking after the health of those people; making sure people were healthy and able to work, and

---

16   https://www.unilever.co.uk/sustainable-living/the-unilever-sustainable-living-plan/
17   Avalani addressed the 2018 Caux Initiatives for Business conference, Panchgani, India, on 6 February.
18   Miller addressed the 2013 Caux business conference, Switzerland.

caring for them if they were ill or injured. We had medics on the rigs running a sick bay and doctors on call for emergencies. Over ten years, the business grew so that by 2011 the turnover was about £22 million ($33 million). In the world's terms that would have been seen as its success. But that's just money. But what about the application of the purpose and working to its core values?

In the early days, when there were 12 people, we got together to talk about our purpose and core values. We wanted to make a positive contribution to society, always to behave with honesty and integrity and complete openness, to promote creativity, learning and personal development. We worked out what the business was about: to protect, maintain and improve the physical, psychological and social well-being in the workplace, reflecting the World Health Organization's definition of health. So, that was embedded in the business and we believe that was a very important factor in the growth of the business in those years. It's what we believed and did, and we explained that to everybody who subsequently joined us. It was also what we talked about to our clients. That was very important because we were working with an industry that can be hard-nosed and money orientated, but was becoming concerned with the health and safety of its people. So, developing trust was really vital. We had to live what we said. We had to demonstrate integrity. As a team we worked out our core values:

We should be the best at what we do best.

(It wasn't about being the best at everything we do because that's impossible but we focused on what we were good at and then we focused on excelling at it.)

We should serve our customers and patients with unconditional integrity.

We would demonstrate empathy and respect for all people—staff, patients and our customers.

We wanted to make a positive contribution to society. We would care for one another.

[See more from James Miller in Chapter 13]

Stewardship

"Wise stewardship, good governance and concern for the common good need to be core values of any market economy", says the Caux Round Table group of senior business executives in their "Bangkok Agenda" on "reshaping capitalism to ensure sustainability". "In other words", their statement says, "a rich set of ethical principles for doing business should underpin all business activity." This means managing their "off balance sheet risks and opportunities, as well as those on the balance sheet" and the current value of a company "depends on its future intangible advantages in customer loyalty, employee productivity, supplier quality, credit worthiness and community approval".[19] The CRT's Principles for Responsible Business were first published in 1994, and quickly became a standard for global business.

Mark Goyder, Founding Director and CEO of the agenda-setting think-tank Tomorrow's Company, also emphasizes the notion of stewardship as essential to business success and longevity.[20] "We have been working with institutional investors and challenging government and regulators", he says. "We have now achieved a 'stewardship code' which is officially recognized. Institutional investors sign up to the code to say, 'We will be good stewards'."

Goyder quotes Tomorrow's Company's definition of stewardship in his book *Living Tomorrow's Company* (2013, p 107) as: "The active and responsible management of entrusted resources now and in the longer term, so as to hand them on in better condition." There is a role here for both directors and investors/owners:

> The rights and duties of shareholders give them the stewardship role alongside that of directors in protecting the long-term health of the company and promoting the long-term value of the investment. Directors are the effective controllers of companies. They are entrusted by share-holders with the management of the company on a day-to-day basis and are accountable—and can be influenced by—shareholders. This idea that the core responsibility for stewardship is shared between shareholders and directors is, we believe, very important.

Goyder illustrates stewardship from the Japanese experience: 20,000 Japanese companies have existed for more than 100 years; 600 companies have continued for more than 300 years; 30 companies have lived more than 500 years and five companies have survived for more than 1,000 years. What did they have in common? "Leadership driven by clear values, vision, mission, strong sense of legacy, vision of the long term, emphasis on the value of people, commitment to society, customer orientation, innovation and continuous improvement", Goyder says. His statistics come from the book *Timeless Ventures* by Haruo Funabashi (2009).

Goyder says that stewardship needs to be promoted by legal frameworks as well as people's behaviours. He outlines four principles of stewardship:

Setting the course for an organization, with a clarity of purpose [which also reflects Conscious Capitalism's emphasis on purpose];

---

19 Published October 2013. http://www.cauxroundtable.org/ The 20th anniversary of the CRT's Principles for Business was marked in a talk given by Robert Mac-Gregor from Minneapolis, one of the original authors, during the 2014 Caux business conference.
20 Goyder gave a keynote talk to the 2014 Caux business conference

Attention to continuous improvement [also reflected in the Japanese concept of *kaizen* or "good change"];
Sensing and shaping the landscape [by which Goyder means "looking outwards" to the world around in order to build trust with customers and communities];
Planting for the future with coherence over time [by which he means striking the right balance between the short and long term; the implication is that quarterly reporting should not trump longer-term interests].

Goyder launched the Indian edition of his book, subtitled *Rediscovering the human purpose of business*, at a business conference in Panchgani, India, in November 2013. In it he writes about the Indian concepts of *Niti* (codes of conduct, instruments of law and normal behaviour), *Nyaya* (delivery of justice), and *Niyat* (voluntary standards and behaviour, the outcome of inner convictions). "The Bhagavad-Gita concept of leadership", writes Goyder, "emphasizes reflectiveness, selflessness and service. Confucian philosophy too is holistic, rather than linear. The Daoist tradition speaks of harmony with the environment, and balance with integration with nature."

Goyder cites an heroic example of stewardship and trusteeship applied in practice, when staff at the Tata-owned Taj Mahal Hotel in Mumbai protected hotel guests, saving their lives, during a terrorist attack on the hotel on the night of 26 November 2008. Thirty-one people were killed in the attack, half of whom were hotel staff. One hotel guest said afterwards: "Over the period of 11 hours, the staff saved my life several times." They chose to put themselves in harm's way, for their guests, and in so doing made the ultimate sacrifice.

Goyder emphasises that business needs to be seen as a "force for good" in society. Those companies that "do good" have a positive consequence on their performance. "One recent study of 50,000 brands across the world found that companies that put people's lives at the centre of all they did outperformed the stock market average by 400 per cent over 10 years", he said.[21]

David Marquand, the political philosopher and former Labour MP, also argues for an "ethic of stewardship". "The question is no longer, 'What's in it for me?' It is, 'How can I best honour the generations that have gone before me and discharge my duty to distant generations that I will never know?'" This includes the environmental legacy for future generations: "The imperative is sustainability."[22]

Marquand says the need is "to master capitalism". In his view, "the decent society [he borrows the phrase from the Israeli moral philosopher Avishai Margalit] is incompatible with today's untamed capitalism and the proliferating humiliations that are its hallmark". He writes: "The old elites tamed the capitalism of the 19th century in the name of an overriding public

21 Goyder was speaking at an event to launch his book in the Initiatives of Change centre, London, 24 April 2014.
22 Marquand launched the paperback edition of his book *Mammon's Kingdom*, in the London centre of Initiatives of Change on 5 May 2015.

morality. In the last 30 years their achievements have been undone." And "capitalism's helter-skelter untaming in the last 30 years has made it indecent". He hardly needs to reference Margaret Thatcher's big-bang deregulation and all its untamed, if unforeseen, consequences.

Marquand acknowledges the role of the Abrahamic faiths in promoting the private and public virtues needed to master capitalism: "Good capitalism is impossible without good people living good lives."

Cooperation

Cooperation in business seems counter-intuitive. The received wisdom is that a competitive free market drives down costs and fuels efficiencies; it encourages quality and the pursuit of excellence; it offers consumer choice. All this is true. But taken to extremes, the competitive market can have negative consequences.

Margaret Heffernan, the Texan businesswoman and best-selling business author, gives a devastating critique of excessive competition—in education, sport, scientific research, factory farming and business—in her book *A Bigger Prize* (2014). Her earlier best-selling book *Wilful Blindness* (2011) was shortlisted by the *Financial Times* and Goldman Sachs as one of the world's six best business books of 2011.

Ruthless competitiveness can be bad for the body and the soul, from sport to education to pharmaceutical and scientific research, Heffernan argues. The win-at-all-costs mentality in sport from childhood, rather than the sheer joy of playing, fuels a largely undetected drug-abuse culture and turns American football from a contact sport to a collision sport, with long-term detrimental health consequences. Competition in science leads to excessive secrecy, fraud and plagiarism, to prevent competitors getting there first. Employees' competition for success within large corporations prevents sharing of information and leads to a climate of fear that militates against the very creativity for which they have been originally recruited. No one dares step out of line. Competition drives down wages to exploitation levels and destroys trust.

Competition creates a culture of cost cutting that turns out to be deadly dangerous, as BP found to its great detriment in Texas and the Gulf of Mexico. Competition to be the biggest in the world, fuelled by an overweening hubris, led to the debacle that was the Royal Bank of Scotland's takeover of ABN Amro, for which UK tax payers are still paying the price. Banks are simply too big. Competing for size has led to factory farming of pigs and other animals which creates unforeseen health hazards, including MRSA.

We do better not by competing but by cooperating, Heffernan argues. This leads to the bigger prize which should be the world's new paradigm. Heffernan tells engaging stories to support her thesis. Ocean Spray cranberry sauce and juice—good for health—has become a global brand because New England farmers decided they would cooperate together, sharing information about their crops and weather patterns, rather than competing against each other. This and other cooperatives and employee-owned companies have consistently outperformed the economy as a whole. They reward "mutual assistance and support, openness and honesty". Another fine example of this is Gripple, the prize-winning international, inventive company founded by Yorkshire businessman Hugh Facey, where everyone owns shares in the company and a spirit of inventiveness is positively nurtured.

Mapping the human genome has depended on thousands of scientists collaborating together, though even here a profit-driven science firm, Celera, became a fly in the ointment, patenting 6,500 genes. Even Adele's massive hit album *21* depended on a team of 100 creative people who each had an input into its success.

Perhaps the most inane competitive league table is that of nations' GDP, which, Heffernan points out, simply measures all economic outputs, whether they are healthy or detrimental to nations' well-being. It is farcical, for instance, that the proceeds of prostitution and drug dealing are included in measuring Britain's GDP, yet the vast contribution of volunteering isn't. And anyway, says Heffernan, economic growth is far too often unevenly distributed within nations. Instead what is needed is the Boston-pioneered Sustainable Economic Development Assessment (SEDA);[23] and "trickle up" by which employees are paid a fair, living wage which helps to stimulate the economy as a whole.

It is, of course, hard to see how business organizations can move beyond the competitive spirit which drives efficiencies, cuts costs and offers consumer choice. But Heffernan redresses the balance. As she argues, "Trust is valued more highly than secrets because giving away ideas is what makes them proliferate."

Heffernan is keen not to promote herself as a paragon of virtue. Nonetheless, she resisted a corrupt practice when she was a young, junior employee at the BBC. Submitting her taxi and other expenses claims one day she was told by the accounts department that she should inflate her claim. Everyone else did. The implication was that if she didn't then others' malpractice would be exposed. Aghast, she realized that there was a rip-off culture going on amongst BBC staff. "I just couldn't do it", she said. She still has her taxi receipts as a reminder. I tell her that she couldn't write the books she does now with any sense of moral authority if she had compromised at that point.

Another strong advocate of cooperation is Professor John Carlisle of Sheffield Business School, who was an advisor to the UK government on large-scale infrastructure projects. He spells out the need to bring all contractors together around the table in a spirit of cooperation at the very beginning of such large investment projects, especially in the construction industry which is, notoriously, one of the world's most corrupt business sectors. His company, the John Carlisle Partnership, renamed Cooperation Works, was able to help

23 Developed by the Boston Consultancy Group: https://www.bcg.com/industries/public-sector/sustainable-economic-development-assessment.aspx

deliver the Hong Kong rapid transport system at 30 per cent under a reduced budget, saving $1.5 billion, and completing it four months early. His company also helped to relocate the Johannesburg stock exchange on time and within budget. Carlisle told a one-day TIGERoadshow, on trust and integrity in the global economy, held at Sheffield Business School:[24] "The best business model is not to cut the cost but to improve the quality. The new order can be established straight up through working with your suppliers."

John Place, the founder and CEO of American Slate from 1978 to 2006, one of the world's largest slate mining companies, based in Santa Fe Springs, California, also has a strong sense of "doing the right thing" based on trust. Now retired and living in Melbourne, Australia, he tells how he built cooperation and trust in doing business with the Chinese:

> In 1980 I received a call from the office of the US Secretary of Commerce. President Nixon had opened up trade links with China. They had a delegation from China interested to know about the construction products business. I decided this would be a good test of getting to know people and setting up trust. I met with them at San Francisco Airport and decided to tell them that we were going to spend two days sightseeing. I thought this was the best way to get to know them. It would give us a chance to talk casually while we looked at the Golden Gate Bridge and other places of interest and give them a chance to relax and get over jetlag. We spent ten days seeing products and after a week they started to talk together and with me and it seemed to open a door of communication.
>
> Months later, I received an invitation to visit the People's Republic of China as a guest of the government. On arrival at Beijing Airport, two officers of the People's Liberation Army picked me up. I was taken to meetings and visited many plants. I met with the Vice-Minister of Trade and many officials.
>
> One of the managers stated to the Vice-Minister that I was impressed with the visits and should place an order of a hundred 20-ton shipping containers of product to commence the trade. I was asked to reply. I stated that the visits had been very helpful to understanding the potential which I believed could be very large. However, at present the quarries and plants were not producing the quality of products that would sell in the US without training and introduction of modern practices.
>
> The interpreter would not translate. Nothing negative could be stated to the Vice-Minister. Amidst the silence, the Vice-Minister turned to me and stated, "It is fortunate for both of us that I do speak English." He stated that, with what I had said to them at the meeting and my reply, he knew it to be the truth and he would have trust in what we were going to do together.
>
> At a meeting in 1985 the Minister of Trade, with others from the Ministries of Rail, Foreign Trade, and Metals and Minerals, stated that the trade I

had established was worth more than other trade. He advised that my company be given exclusive long term rights to all main quarries in China for North America, which was later extended to include the United Kingdom.

Last June, one of the managers in the government I had worked with in Beijing came to California; they had a problem with a company in Kentucky and would like my assistance to try to resolve it. He stated that they had worked with my companies for 28 years with trust and friendship. They wanted to continue with larger business now with the United States and Australia into Asia-Pacific.

I have five degrees hanging in my office and the one that is vital to success is not there, namely the contact with Initiatives of Change, outlining moral standards, a daily "quiet time" way of living and the truth of integrity guidelines. As my friend in China stated, the success over 28 years in the business was based on our trust and friendship.

John Place had developed his sense of personal integrity growing up in South Africa, the son of a Methodist minister, before moving to live in California.

The five pillars of trust outlined in this chapter are by no means comprehensive in building the whole temple of trust in the business world. One might add, for instance, "character"—an enigmatic word which we shall look at again in Chapter 14.

What is clear is that these pillars of trust—integrity, sustainability, purpose, stewardship and cooperation—are essential to a leadership of integrity. And they all make sound business sense. They pay dividends, even though that is not their primary purpose.

References

Boast, Genevieve, *Tough Bliss: restorying life*, Create Space Independent Publishing, 2018

Brooks, David, *The Road to Character*, Penguin, 2016

Ellis, Tania, *The New Pioneers: sustainable business success through social innovation and social entrepreneurship*, John Wiley and Sons, 2010

Funabashi, Haruo, *Timeless Ventures*, Tata McGraw-Hill, 2009

Goyder, Mark, *Living Tomorrow's Company: rediscovering the human purpose of business*, Gower Publishing, 1998

Heffernan, Margaret, *A Bigger Prize: when no one wins unless everyone wins*, Simon & Schuster, 2014

Heffernan, Margaret, *Wilful Blindness: why we ignore the obvious at our peril*, Simon & Schuster, 2011

Hoffmann, Anita, *Purpose and Impact: how executives are creating meaningful second careers*, Routledge, 2018

Hurst, Aaron, *The Purpose Economy: how your desire for impact, personal growth and community is changing the world*, Elevate, 2014

Marquand, David, *Mammon's Kingdom: an essay on Britain now*, Penguin, 2015

9 Beheading the snake of corruption

Buildings and bridges shouldn't be deathtraps. Yet, in too many cases, the construction industry is seen as being corrupt. Buildings collapse in earthquakes often because of shoddy or illegal construction, killing the occupants. On 14 August 2018, 42 people lost their lives when a 200-metre section of the Morandi road bridge collapsed in Genoa, plunging vehicles' occupants to their death.

On the night of 14 June 2017, 72 people lost their lives when the Grenfell Tower residential block in west London went up in flames. Visiting the site to see the black, charred skeleton of the building, as I have done, is a visceral experience: a punch in the gut. Reading the hundreds of tributes posted with flowers in the nearby streets brings a tear to the eye. The fire spread quickly upwards because banned flammable panels were used to renovate the outside of the building. The flames engulfed the whole tower after a kitchen appliance caught fire in a flat on a lower floor. The disaster revealed a construction industry driven "to cut corners and costs and get away with it", in the words of Dame Judith Hackitt, Chair of the UK's Engineering Employers Federation, who chaired an independent review into building regulations and fire safety.[1] Whether or not corruption was involved, prosecutions would be bound to follow.

Many more people—over 1,100—were killed when the Rana Plaza building collapsed in Dacca, Bangladesh, on 24 April 2013. It was this century's worst industrial disaster and the world's deadliest garment factory accident. Those who died were garment workers making clothing for Western companies such as Primark, Mango, Monsoon Accessorize, Matalan, Benetton and Walmart. The clothing industry is Bangladesh's single biggest export earner with 80 per cent of the country's production going abroad. The trade employs some four million people, earning a minimum wage of $68 a month. It is worth £15 billion a year, second only to China, and exports were growing annually at the rate of 15 per cent. Production was going at a frantic rate to meet the West's demands for cheap blouses, shirts and trousers. Shifts would work till 2am.

---

1   Profile of Dame Judith Hackitt, *The Sunday Times*, 10 June 2018

The eight-storey building, constructed originally as five storeys, would never have collapsed if the license to build the extra three floors had not been awarded, apparently corruptly, to the building's owner, Sohel Rana, a clothing boss who had influence with the ruling political party. A BBC TV documentary about the disaster commented: "The necessary licenses were a formality for a man with his connections."[2]

Power generators were installed in the new floors but the construction pillars couldn't support the extra weight. When cracks appeared in one of the concrete pillars and the reinforcing iron rods protruded from the pillar, workers refused to enter the building. Local TV reports and a newspaper article, published on the morning of the disaster, warned about its safety. A bank on the ground floor closed and kept its staff away. But the garment workers were threatened with loss of wages and their jobs if they didn't continue working. When the power generators were turned on, the building shook. It took less than 90 seconds for the building to collapse in the middle of the morning rush hour. It was a massacre. The final death toll was 1,129, while 2,515 badly injured people were pulled alive from the building. Sohel Rana, who went on the run trying to escape across the border into India, was arrested by the police. He had apparently ignored safety advice and paid bribes to add the three extra floors. Corruption, and lax building regulations, had led to devastating loss of life.

Yet Bangladesh's garment workers say, "Don't take this work away from us. It is all we have." Primark donated $9 million to the victims' families. By mid-2014, an online petition campaign was urging Matalan and Benetton to give a similar sum.[3] The disaster raised the issue about the responsibility of Western retailers in overseeing the working conditions of their supply chains' employees. Leading figures in the Bangladeshi clothing industry say that all that is needed is an extra five cents on the selling price in Western markets, to secure the lives and safety of the garment workers. Out of the ashes, a small cooperative of garment workers emerged, called *Aporajeo* (Undefeated), determined to give employment to some of the survivors. It operates in a single-storey ground-floor building in Dacca.

In May 2018, the Bangladesh Accord came into effect, addressing fire and building safety for all garment workers. Its purpose is "to enable a working environment in which no worker needs to fear fires, building collapses, or other accidents that could be prevented with reasonable health and safety measures". It is described as "an unprecedented, legally binding agreement between companies and trade unions to make factories in Bangladesh safe". The accord is supported by major retail chains including Debenhams, John Lewis, Marks & Spencer, Sainsbury's and Topshop.[4]

2   *Clothes to die for*, BBC Two, 22 July 2014
3   *The Times*, 28 July 2014
4   http://bangladeshaccord.org/

Corruption kills. And it creates poverty by stealing resources that might otherwise be invested in hospitals, schools and other vital infrastructure. It destroys reputations—such as that of FIFA, football's world governing body, where top officials were accused of taking bribes and money laundering. And it undermines trust. A leadership of integrity has to make a stance against corruption.

"Formal definitions of corruption range from the decay of society to the single act of bribery", writes the anti-corruption campaigner Laurence Cockcroft in his book *Global Corruption* (2012). Corruption always involves "the acquisition of money, assets or power in a way which escapes public view; is usually illegal; and is at the expense of society as a whole either at a 'grand' or everyday level. Personal enrichment is nearly always a key objective, although corruption may be engineered by a group with the intention of achieving or retaining political power, so that these motives can become closely entwined" (p 2).

Corruption, Cockcroft argues (p 231),

> is a force which drives poverty, inequality, dysfunctional democracy and global insecurity. Its most consistent victims are the poor who constitute a majority of the population in low-income countries; its most dramatic victims are the subjects of human trafficking. Its everyday victims are the citizens of the many countries where their voice is lost in the rush by elected politicians to pay off their backers. Corruption feeds failed states, the trade in nuclear weapons and their components, and the perpetuation of hunger even where harvests are plentiful. Unless checked, its major legacy will be an unjust and unstable world, tipping the outcome of uncertainties about the future in an ever more dangerous direction.

Corruption is endemic in countries ranging from Russia to Brazil, Colombia to China, Somalia to South Africa. It is, of course, not just a developing world problem. It is an insidious influence on a huge scale in the West, undermining Western democracies through the buying of political influence. In their book *Unmasked: corruption in the West* (2016) Cockcroft and his co-author, Anne-Christine Wegener, call this "the corruption of influence". Between 2005 and 2012, for instance, big corporations spend $5.8bn on lobbying and political donations in the US, earning them business support and tax concessions of $4.4bn, nearly a fifth of the annual GDP of the US.

The authors highlighted nine areas of the global economy suffering from corruption including: political party financing, lobbying, multinational corporations, the banking sector, tax havens, the justice system, organized crime and sport. Leaders in many walks of life need to "grasp a snake which will frequently respond with poison, and will only die with repeated attack".

Nowhere is the snake more poisonous than in the mechanism of "transfer pricing", or deliberate mispricing of products, traded through intermediaries registered in the world's "offshore" tax havens on behalf of multinational companies. This tax dodge undervalues goods in an exporting country when invoiced to a buyer in an importing country or a tax haven. The prices quoted may be less than 50 per cent of the true market price, with the difference in value being profit which can be externalized. This, says Cockcroft, gives the purchasing company the opportunity to hold its inflated profits in a low or zero tax environment, bringing them into the domicile country over time or not at all.

US and UK companies use tax havens from the British Virgin Islands and the Cayman Islands to the Channel Islands and elsewhere. The extent of the secrecy involved was exposed by the Panama Papers and the Paradise Papers leaked to the media, exposing the extent of companies' and individual celebrities' tax avoidance.

"The British Virgin Islands is the global capital for the incorporation of offshore companies", writes the British development and environmental journalist Paul Vallely. "Though it has a population of just 22,000, it has 823,502 registered companies which make vast amounts of money through the wonder of transfer pricing."[5]

Vallely argues that there is no moral case for tax havens. "The moral case against is clear enough", he writes. "Tax havens epitomize unfairness, cheating and injustice. They replace the old morality embodied in the Golden Rule of reciprocity—that we should do as we would be done by—with a new version that insists that those who have the gold make the rules."

According to Raymond Baker, founder of Global Financial Integrity (GFI) in Washington DC, the estimates of such illicit flows from developing countries to Western banks amount to at least US\$1 trillion per year. This exceeds aid flows of US\$100 billion from the West to developing countries by ten times. Thus, appallingly, the net flow of funds is from the poor world to the rich world by a factor of ten to one.

When colleagues and I met Baker in his Washington DC office in March 2014, he claimed that GFI had been able to put this issue on the media's and governments' agendas, with coverage in *The Wall Street Journal*, the *Washington Post*, the *Financial Times* and elsewhere, an issue of which they had previously been totally ignorant. David Cameron spoke out against tax havens when he was Prime Minister. But strong words don't amount to legislative action.

Meanwhile, London has become the world's money laundering capital, asserts Alexander Lebedev, the Russian-born owner of *The Independent* and the *Evening Standard* newspapers. Terrorism thrives on the back of those who fund it, he writes. "Not enough is being done to tackle their backers. Now, more than ever, we need to stop the flow of funds, to cut off their financial pipeline, to end this dirty money."[6]

Lebedev gives astonishing figures for the level of corrupt flows of funds.

5   *Evening Standard*, London, 1 September 2014
6   *The Independent on Sunday*, 28 August 2011

Between 2000 and 2011, just from China $3.97 trillion is thought to have disappeared, much of it the profits of corruption, channelled into secretive offshore financial havens. From Russia the figure is close to $1 trillion. In the EU the total lost is put at $1.2 trillion ($150 billion from Italy alone). Many of the perpetrators have been able to move abroad and draw on the expertise of what I term the "financial services oligarchy", of international banks, law firms and accountants, to ensure they can continue to live off the proceeds of their crimes. Sadly London is at the very epicentre of this web. Much of the illegal profits flows through the City.

The sheer size of offshore tax havens was exposed by what was billed as "the biggest leak in history": 11.5 million documents that were passed in 2015 to a German investigative journalist, Bastian Obermayer. They were leaked by an anonymous individual using the pseudonym John Doe. They became globally known as the Panama Papers. They blew the whistle on the Panamanian law firm Mossack Fonseca and the over 200,000 shell companies it had set up on behalf of clients, many of whom were involved in money laundering or offshore tax avoidance.[7]

Second only in size to this leak was the exposure of the Paradise Papers. They detailed the offshore holdings of over 120,000 individuals and companies in 19 tax jurisdictions. They were sent anonymously to Obermayer and a colleague who made them public in November 2017. Tax avoidance may not be illegal but it deprives governments of tax revenues and the poor suffer because of it.

Lebedev calls for a new international anti-corruption force, along the lines of Interpol, "to defeat these financial services oligarchs". He estimates it would need to be backed by $70 million a year—a small sum when set against the potential to "cut across national borders to seize people and assets". "It would have to have real teeth and at its head I would appoint someone of global credibility and stature.[8] The point would be to tackle corruption and to be seen to be tackling it—in the hope that those planning to deceive their countrymen, to steal valuable funds, would desist."

Corruption costs the European Union over 120 billion Euros or £99 billion a year, according to research by the EU Commission (2014 figures). More than three quarters of EU citizens believe that corruption is widespread in their own member states.[9] The EU's accounts have not been signed off by auditors for over two decades. This breeds a deep cynicism and Euro-scepticism amongst citizens. "Corruption undermines citizens' confidence in democratic institutions and the rule of law", says Cecilia Malmstrom, EU Commissioner for Home Affairs. "It hurts the European economy and deprives states of much-needed tax revenue. There is no 'corruption-free' zone in Europe."[10]

7   Giles Whittel, *The Times Magazine*, 18 June 2016
8   Lebedev doesn't suggest who.
9   *The Times*, 4 February 2014
10 https://www.bbc.co.uk/news/world-europe-26014387

While the worst offending states are Bulgaria, Romania and Greece, according to the research, the most common field for small bribe-paying is in the public health services of Eastern and Southern Europe. Fourteen per cent of people in Poland, Hungary and Slovakia say they have given "extra payments" and presents to medical staff.

Patrick Colquhoun, founder of the medical aid charity, Medical Support in Romania, calls this "medical terrorism". He has made nearly 80 trips to that country since 1990 from his home in Cambridge, UK. Patients, he says, too often feel "informal payments" are expected by medical staff if they are to get good treatment. One anaesthetist even threatened not to wake a patient up after an operation if he did not receive money beforehand. This is little short of terrifying. This kind of corruption, Colquhoun says, is "most horrible in health care because it threatens and terrorizes people when they are at their most vulnerable". Colquhoun was decorated with the MBE by the Queen in 2010 for his services to medical aid in Romania.[11]

Any emphasis on the integrity that builds trust in the global economy has to address the dishonesty and greed that fuels corruption. The Global Compact, the UN convention for best business practice initiated by Kofi Annan, spells out nine business commitments which cover human rights, the rights of labour, and the environment, and a tenth commitment which was added to address corruption: "Businesses should work against corruption in all its forms, including extortion and bribery."

Sir Mark Moody-Stuart, Vice-Chairman of the Global Compact till 2018, who is the former Chairman of Shell and then Anglo-American, tells how he and his colleagues fought for this tenth commitment to be added. "Corruption is at the root of many of the other evils and in many ways is the most pervasive and corrosive of all evils", he writes.[12]

Moody-Stuart says that corruption is "the biggest market failure of all". He writes:

> It is often said that climate change is the result of the biggest market failure of all time. I would argue that corruption is in fact an even greater distortion of markets and to date has done more economic damage than climate change. Corruption is a pervasive evil. While some would say that so-called facilitation payments, small payments that encourage officials to do something that is their duty, are not damaging, I would disagree.
>
> This is merely the most common form of a very infectious disease that slides readily into making a payment to encourage an official to neglect his or her duty. However, it is true that the major damage comes not from facilitation, but from the awards of contracts on the basis of corruption. In those cases, not only is the price of purchase inflated by kickbacks, but

11 https://uk.iofc.org/patrick-colquhoun-given-award-queens-birthday-honours
12 *Responsible Leadership* by Mark Moody-Stuart (2014)

also the product or service delivered is often useless or in a location designed purely to win political favours. (2014, p 170)

It was this second aspect, perpetuated by Western businesses, which incensed Peter Eigen, when he was a senior World Bank official in Kenya. He resigned and founded the global anti-corruption organization Transparency International (TI). Mark Moody-Stuart's late brother, George, (who died in 2004) was the head of TI in the UK and it was through him that I first met Sir Mark. It was thanks to TI's campaigning that the OECD, the economic and cooperation body of the world's rich industrialized countries, introduced its convention to outlaw the bribery of foreign public officials, supported in legislation by member countries. TI's annual Corruption Perception Index has become the global reference for ranking countries according to their susceptibility to corruption.

Cockcroft and Wegener call for tougher regulation and legislation and an end to "a cult of secrecy" which surrounds offshore tax havens. They argue that "individual choice and integrity is governed by ethical tradition and the strength of the law and its application". The question remains whether or not there is the political will, not least in the OECD countries, to apply the law robustly enough.

So can businesses and individuals make a stance against corruption?

Chris Weston, CEO of the FTSE 250 temporary energy supply company Aggreko, insists that the "tone at the top" has to come from him personally. The company supplies generators to events ranging from music festivals to major sports venues, such as the Olympic Games and Commonwealth Games, the Rugby World Cup and Formula One grand prix racing, as well as to whole nations. The company's reputation for integrity depends on the tone that he as CEO sets, he says. "It's a fundamental issue. We train our people in the problems about fraud and bribes. That is a message they have to hear from me." Every one of the company's 7,300 employees goes through ethics training every two years. No employee is sanctioned to give "facilitation payments"—the equivalent to bribes in most people's eyes—to customs officers or to secure a contract. Not even £10, Weston says. "If you do it once, what happens next? In Aggreko we have a reputation for being unapproachable. How I behave, day to day, how I expect people to behave is fundamental for the company. Integrity in business is absolutely essential." The company's reputation has ensured its role as the world's leading supplier of temporary energy generators. Weston has a self-effacing leadership philosophy. He likes to quote Lau Tzu: "As for the best leaders, the people barely notice their existence. When the best leaders' work is done, the people say, 'We did it ourselves'."[13]

The stance against corruption, however, can come at a personal cost—and with a great deal of courage.

---

13 Profile of Chris Weston by the author, *The Pangbournian* magazine, issue 47, 2017

The South African whistleblower Wendy Addison asks her audiences if any of them believe in the saying, "Life sucks; then you die." There was a time when she thought so herself following the traumas she went through, though she courageously bounced back. She paid a heavy personal price when in 2000 she exposed the "endemic fraud and corruption", as she puts it, of the two CEOs in the publicly listed South African fitness company LeisureNet, better known as the Health and Racquet Clubs. Her whistleblowing led to South Africa's biggest ever corporate collapse. The CEOs were colleagues and friends of hers in a company where she was the Group International Treasurer. She became known inside the company as "Wendy the wildcard" when she discovered wholesale embezzlement. Millions of rand were being secretly transferred to an offshore bank account in Jersey. The company's auditor, Deloitte, was also involved.

The CEOs ousted her from corporate and social life to become an outlier, as she puts it. But she is a rare breed with the moral fibre to speak out and report malpractice in the workplace. Wilfully refusing to turn a blind eye to corruption, Addison's whistleblowing story unfolds like a Hollywood movie, including the chilling, sociopathic behaviour of "death threats via email and anonymous calls". These forced her to uproot into self-imposed exile in the UK with her 12-year-old son; thanks to her British parents she had UK citizenship.

"I had lost my job, my career, my reputation but I wasn't prepared to lose my life", Addison says. In South Africa, where corruption is rife, "whistleblowers are shot and killed and people die for less", she states. Her parents urged her to drop the whole thing for the sake of her well-being. But she is made of stern stuff and refused to do so.

At first she was offered two high-flying jobs in London, as a senior accountant with Channel 4 television or with a renowned leisure and transport group. She chose the latter, where she received the highest appraisal in her job assessment. But then she was summarily dismissed "in a very Kafkaesque way", when it was discovered that she had been the LeisureNet whistleblower. Her new employer, it turned out, was in a bid to take over LeisureNet.

"What followed for me was an extremely dark period in my life", Addison continues. "I had no purpose anymore." With her livelihood gone and a career smeared like "mud that sticks", survival meant living in squats and begging on the streets of Kingston upon Thames, south-west London, for six months, when she had no food left in the fridge and no means of paying her rent. "You can't imagine what it is like to go from a fifth floor plush office to begging", she says.

"I found that the English love animals. So I got two dogs to increase my revenue stream!" She could also trade her accountancy skills with her fellow beggars, drug addicts and the homeless who became her friends. In the past, success for her had been defined by acquisition: Jimmy Choo shoes; a luxury holiday. Now she found that her inner sense of resilience was like "graphite in a pencil". "What had been projected onto me was that I was valueless in society. Yet I elected to like my best self, to be my best self." She refused to define herself by the particular point in time that she was enduring. She also learnt that the most difficult question in such circumstances is, "Can you help me?"—a question we all need to ask in life at one time or another.

Her begging ended when she was recalled to South Africa to act as a witness in the trial of her two former bosses. She was eventually vindicated when they were sentenced to jail after an 11-year battle. The two executives, Peter Gardener and Rodney Mitchell, were found guilty of fraud, involving six million rand each, by the Western Cape high court. They were sentenced to seven years in jail but were released in December 2012 after serving only 19 months.

Addison says:

> I am often asked about how I explained my circumstances to my son and how he accepted my explanation at that time, as a 12-year-old. I kept it simple. "Do you trust me? Have I ever let you down? Just imagine we're on a rollercoaster ride. We've been right at the top and now we're hurtling downwards. With that momentum we will be able to ride to the top again if we choose. Trust me again." Is this not what a greater power might say to us, especially when we are fearful and vulnerable? I know my son took what I said on board and had enough faith in me to move through the quagmire of despair. Although I almost faltered in my own belief at times it helped to believe in something greater than myself. Do we have that same faith in who we put our trust in?

Addison has indeed risen up again and now runs SpeakOut SpeakUp. She is a compelling public speaker. Addressing a forum on resilience in the St Ethelburga's Centre for Reconciliation and Peace in the City of London, she said, "For me resilience is like dancing in the rain." We all needed to "embrace our own metamorphoses".[14]

"Wendy is at the forefront of a major shift in business, that of being open, honest and authentic and operating with integrity", says Colin Smith, Director of *The Listener* magazine. But what means by far the most to Addison is that her son Dylan, now aged 30, says she is his hero. "My story will be his legacy", she says, rather than bricks and mortar.

So how do companies recover when they take a reputational hit, such as that suffered by Volkswagen after it emerged that the car company had been systematically cheating on tests for nitrogen oxide exhaust emissions from its diesel cars? VW could well take a leaf out of its fellow German-owned company, Siemens. In 2006, Siemens AG, the German conglomerate, was exposed to have been involved in a massive bribery scandal. The company held a web

14   www.speakout-speakup.org; see also report "The courage of whistleblowers" by Yee Liu Williams: http://www.uk.iofc.org/courage-whistleblowers?bc=node/71052; Addison and I were interviewed on BBC Radio Sussex on 2 July 2015: https://uk. iofc.org/bbc-radio-interview-mike-smith-and-wendy-addison

of secret bank accounts to hide bribery transactions. One of its accountants ran an annual bribery budget of $40 million to $50 million. The slush fund was used by corrupt managers and sales staff to bribe government officials to win contracts, particularly for its telecommunications subsidiaries, worldwide. The company paid millions of euros in bribes to cabinet ministers and other government officials in Nigeria, Libya, Russia and elsewhere in order to win contracts.

Yet Siemens was able to turn the crisis into an opportunity for fundamental, values-led change, says Sunil Mathur, CEO and Managing Director of Siemens Ltd South Asia. He tells how the parent company successfully overcame the corruption crisis which had threatened to cripple the whole organization.[15] Remarkably, Siemens is now ranked by Dow Jones as the world's number one company for best compliance.

Mathur has worked for Siemens for some 30 years and yet even he was not prepared for the revelations of large-scale corruption that hit the company in 2006. Corrupt practices involving bribes to win new business contracts were alleged to be systemic. "The news hit us straight between the eyes. We were stunned. Almost overnight, we had the [US] Securities and Exchange Commission and the German authorities against us. It was the last thing we imagined, given the size and stature of the company."

The media worldwide had a field day, reporting revelations that the company had million-dollar slush funds routinely used to bribe officials and decision-makers, and, most disturbing of all, the boardroom knew what was happening and turned a blind eye.

Ethics had always been central to Siemens' corporate philosophy, Mathur said. Over a century ago, Siemens' founder had said, "I won't sell the future for quick profits." Many of the company's projects are about improving quality of life for citizens, whether in designing more livable "smart cities" or hi-tech solutions to improve energy efficiency.

So what went so wrong?

For Mathur, it was, ironically, the proliferation of policies that played their part: "We had a guideline or procedure for everything! But, in making so many policies, we had lost our values. Our values were only on paper. They were not lived out in the fabric of the organization."

The response to the crisis from Siemens' leaders was upfront and honest: "We have made mistakes and now we will clean our house up", Mathur said. The board resigned and a new CEO was appointed, importantly an outsider, who vowed that, "Only clean business is Siemens business."

The company set to work on establishing agreements on the murky areas of client relations and expenditure. Wining and dining clients was immediately forbidden and sponsorship was stopped. "Sales forces thought we'd lost it", Mathur admitted. "How can you win client trust without taking them to dinner?" Every case was tracked and training programmes were organized to integrate the new guidelines and emphasize the values behind them.

15 Mathur was speaking at the 2015 Caux TIGE conference

The company cut back on its multitude of procedures and policies, instead putting the emphasis on individuals to make decisions based on personal integrity. The company now has questions employees can ask themselves before making a decision, "Is this the right thing for Siemens? Is it consistent with Siemens' values and mine?" and, importantly, "Is it something I am willing to be held accountable for?" Such simple but effective self-questioning builds trust in an organization and helps people act from a more ethical position.

The in-depth scrutiny and subsequent implementation of changes were painful, costly and time-consuming but incredibly effective, Mathur said. Agreements with authorities were met in a record-breaking 18 months and the company wasn't excluded from public contracts. The company paid out a massive €2.5 billion in penalties and legal fees, including the largest fine in US corporate history. But it was praised for its remediation efforts by the regulatory institutions. The real recognition externally came with its ranking in the Dow Jones Sustainability Index in 2009. Siemens was ranked number one under compliance and risk management and has proudly maintained that position since then—an astonishing turnaround for a company mired in corruption just three years before.

Siemens now shares its experiences in these areas of compliance and driving values-led change with other corporations. "It's no longer just about getting results but how you get your results that is more important", Mathur said. "Policies can only take you so far. What really counts is your values system. Individuals living their personal values in work can make significant changes within any organization, no matter how big. Large doors open on small hinges."

India, according to the annual corruption perception index published by the anti-corruption organization Transparency International, was ranked as the 78th least corrupt country out of 180 countries and territories in 2018, in the league for paying bribes in the public sector. This ranking was higher than in previous years: for India this welcome trend is in the right direction. The least corrupt countries were perceived to be New Zealand and Denmark whilst the most corrupt was Somalia.[16]

On 8 November 2016—the same day as the US presidential election that brought Donald Trump to power—India's Prime Minister Narendra Modi stunned the nation with a snap announcement that all high denomination rupee bank notes of Rs 1000 and Rs 500 would be abolished as legal tender by that midnight. His aim was to stamp out black money from the economy, in a move against corruption. It aimed to eliminate fake notes, including those used by terrorist organizations on the India–Pakistan border. The high denomination notes accounted for more than 80 per cent of all currency by value in circulation. People would have till the end of the year to trade in their high-value notes at banks. Queues quickly mounted at banks and ATM

16 https://www.transparency.org/research/cpi/overview

machines. Many small traders were left devastated and in real hardship. According to an editorial in *The Guardian*, India's demonetization "cost 100 lives, at least 1.5 million jobs and left 150 million people without pay for weeks".[17] Some expected that there would be bonfires of illegally held "black" high denomination notes, to destroy evidence. But this just didn't happen. They were simply handed in.

The issue of corruption in India came to a head on 5 April 2011 when the anti-corruption activist Anna Hazare began a hunger strike in New Delhi. The chief legislative aim of his movement was to tackle corruption in the Indian government through a proposed Jan Lokpal Bill (Citizen's Ombudsman Bill). According to *Time* magazine, it was one of the top ten global stories of 2011.[18] Successive Indian governments have declared their determination to tackle corruption with little success, hardly surprising when a third of MPs have been charged with crimes of corruption, vote rigging or violence. No wonder that civil society groups, campaigning for a bar on candidates with a criminal record standing as MPs, have found it impossible to get the necessary legislation through parliament. The Right to Information Act, passed in 2005, has given citizens the power to hold public officials accountable for their public spending. Nonetheless paying bribes remains endemic. By the summer of 2018, over 159,000 people had posted comments on the "I paid a bribe" website, detailing bribes they had been forced to pay or how they resisted paying.[19]

In the private sector, some businesses have gained a reputation for holding a line against corruption, most notably the giant Tata group of companies.

Sudhir Gogate, Executive Director of an Indo-Japanese joint venture in the automotive components industry based in Pune, tells how early on in his career he used to pay bribes to customs officials in order to release component stocks. After he became involved with the Asia Plateau centre in Panchgani, and its Heart of Effective Leadership (HEL) training programme, he decided to quit paying bribes. At an HEL course in 2009, he drew a large box on the whiteboard and divided it into four segments. One was marked "legal and ethical", the second "legal but unethical", the third "illegal but ethical", and the fourth "illegal and unethical". The participants were encouraged to shout out what examples they would put into each box. It led to a lively discussion, not least on the difference between what is allowed under law but may be totally unethical in practice.

While a corrupt tone at the top of organizations can lead to disastrous results, as Wendy Addison and Genevieve Boast found out, equally a tone at the top which sticks to integrity in decision-making is justified by the results, as the story of Mumbai businessman Suresh Vazirani illustrates.

17 *The Guardian*, 31 August 2018
18 http://content.time.com/time/specials/packages/article/0,28804,2101745_2102309_2102421,00.html
19 http://www.ipaidabribe.com

Suresh Vazirani, who I have known since he was an engineering student in the early 1970s, is the founding CEO of the multi-award-winning medical technology company Transasia Biomedicals, based in Mumbai. He grew up in a refugee camp—his parents were victims of the conflict between Pakistan and India at the time of Independence in 1947. They are part of the Sindhi community, from Sindh in Pakistan, who fled to India at the time of Partition. His wife, Mala, describes the Sindhis as "addicted to working and finding solutions without expecting too much outside help". Vazirani, a pioneering entrepreneur, fits this description well.[20]

Three considerations led him to set up Transasia, India's leading niche enterprise in manufacturing medical healthcare technology. Firstly, during his nine years of voluntary work based at the IofC centre in Panchgani, he was on the faculty for training business people in values of honesty, purity of motive and care for people. There he would urge businessmen not to be corrupt. That's all very well, they would reply, but you've never run a business. You don't know what it's like. As a result, he felt challenged to see if he could live what he preached to others. Secondly, he realized that, for demographic and economic reasons, it would be impossible to supply the healthcare needs of India through Western-produced machines and that India itself needed to make them. Thirdly, he decided that "by the time I retire, I wanted to look in the mirror, and say, 'Well done, I achieved something for my country'."

A key moment also came when, as a young man, he visited the renowned but ailing freedom fighter Jayaprakash Narayan in Jaslok Hospital in Mumbai. He was suffering from kidney disease and was on dialysis. The three dialysis machines needed to save Narayan's life had all broken down and he was within 24 hours of dying. The doctors couldn't reach the technicians as it was the weekend. A doctor turned to Vazirani and said, "You are an engineer. Can you fix it?" Vazirani was astonished but was able to do so within an hour, thus saving the freedom fighter's life. The experience opened his mind to providing such technology himself.

Vazirani began his enterprise with 250 rupees ($4), which was only enough to register the company's name. It now employs 1,500 people, a third of which are abroad, and exports to over 100 countries, mostly in emerging markets. Initially a friend offered him a loan which financed a six-month trip around the world. He visited over 40 enterprises and learned as much as possible about biomedical techniques. Returning to India, he became a successful distributor of Japanese and other machines.

A turning point came when an Italian manufacturer let Vazirani down with an order for hospitals in India. The delivery never arrived. This spurred him to start making the machines himself. With a small team he developed a prototype within three months: a blood analyzer that could test for 200 blood diseases within minutes. Such machines assist doctors with their diagnoses and save lives. It worked and they were in business. Later a supercilious

20   Suresh and Mala Vazirani told their story to the 2012 Caux TIGE conference.

German purchaser was astounded when he saw the quality of the Transasia machines.

"I don't sell you my product", he used to tell his clients, "I sell you myself"—meaning his skills and service. "If there are any troubles, this is my phone number." His approach has never changed.

Transasia sets the standard for Indian companies in other areas too. There are no strict recall rules in India, but when one Transasia product seemed not to be working properly, he recalled the product despite the cost. Customers have stayed with Transasia for 20 years, an indication of the positive effect of this kind of principle-based decision-making. The company relies on over 250 service engineers across India.

The company has become a global player with 13 overseas acquisitions in nine countries, including five in the USA, the most recent being Calbiotech in California, bought by Transasia in 2017. In Europe the company is known as Erba Mannheim.

Transasia grew eightfold in the eight years to 2017. Vazirani says that there is no need for the family-owned business to accept private equity investment through a public offering, because some 90 to 95 per cent of profits after tax are plowed back into the business, sufficient for its growth and acquisition needs. Transasia Biomedicals' objective is "to become an end-to-end diagnostics company, offering a full range of diagnostic services", writes *Business India*. "This would place them among the global giants like Roche, Abbott and Bayer."[21]

There is also a new opportunity within the Indian market, Vazirani says, following the Narendra Modi government's initiative to provide health insurance cover, of up to 500,000 rupees (£5,500), to the 500 million poorest people in India—the same population as the whole of Europe. This huge commitment was enacted on 15 August 2018. Fifty per cent of Transasia's sales, in value, is within India and 50 per cent abroad.

Vazirani's business values are revealed in his tax payments. In India, he says, it is easy to pay low taxes. Even the field agent of the tax department tried to advise him to pay less—on the condition that five per cent of the savings would go into the agent's pocket. But Vazirani insisted: "No, I want to pay my taxes. I should be happy to pay taxes to the state." It also means that he has a much better idea of the true value of the company than other companies do.

His philosophy is reflected in the way Transasia treats its employees. His company provides healthcare insurance to all family members of the employees including their parents. It also provides interest-free student loans for employees' children, to encourage them to overcome the limitations of the Indian caste system. All employees participate in an orientation programme, where they are introduced to the company's ethical values. Compared with

21 "In the major league", report by Sumit Ghoshal, *Business India* magazine, 4–17 December 2017

other companies, Transasia's employees are considered particularly reliable, willing to go "above and beyond" to serve customers. In one case, they went into a conflict zone where bullets were flying to explain to doctors how to use the machines.

Vazirani is often asked why his income isn't ten times more: "Are you not tempted to increase your salary?" "No, earning money was never my goal", he answers. According to Mahatma Gandhi, businessmen should not consider themselves as owners of their properties, but as trustees of the wealth of society, he says. He is sometimes accused of working too hard: "You have a nice living standard, sit back and relax." His reply? "My mission is far from accomplished." The Vaziranis' home, an apartment overlooking Juhu Beach in the salubrious area of north Mumbai, is open to all comers and a visitor there may find others from Europe or Japan staying with them.

Vazirani has a mission to provide affordable healthcare for all Indians. Seventy per cent of the population is without health insurance, higher than in Bangladesh or Sri Lanka. More than 20 per cent of the population earn less than one dollar a day. For them, affording European-produced technology is a fantasy. To meet this need, Transasia first set up a research department, but progress was slow. The next tactic was to buy technologies, which was not easy. So they decided to buy European and American companies close to bankruptcy in order to inherit their technology. Their companies in Germany, Italy and the USA have all survived and improved. Transasia can produce technology more cheaply due to lower labour costs, but the main difference comes through product simplification. Vazirani still sees a long way to go in improving the healthcare system in India. "This won't happen in my lifetime", he says. This doesn't deter him from putting all his efforts into the project.

Change is still needed, Vazirani notes—people and the system becoming honest. An American senator had told Vazirani that there is also corruption in America. "Last month a consul went to jail for corruption", the senator said. "Well", Vazirani replied, "this is exactly the difference: in India those people go court-free. But I have full faith that one day we will succeed in overcoming corruption. Honest business in India is possible."

It is a conviction he is putting into practice himself. What especially marks out the Vaziranis is their courageous and dogged stance against corruption. At one point he employed two lawyers full-time to fight the cases that arose. When, for instance, he wanted to install a fountain in the lunch area, two government officials demanded a $100 bribe for a license. Yet no such licenses had been issued for 20 years. It took his lawyers four years in the courts, costing $4,000, to deal with the case. But Vazirani feels it is worth making a stand on such issues, as his company's reputation for integrity is paramount.

Early in the development of the company, he risked losing a 20 million deutschmark sales contract to Germany because a customs officer wanted a bribe to release vital imported components. Rather than paying up, Vazirani left the components in the warehouse for three months. He went to the top customs officials, arguing that if Transasia didn't get this order the country would lose. "We appealed to their sense of national pride." The components were released just in time for Transasia to win the contract.

Then there was the time when a politician suggested to Vazirani that it would be "an opportunity" if they each pocketed part of the World Bank aid the politician had received to improve health care. "Yes, and is it an opportunity if we land up in hospital needing urgent care ourselves?" replied Vazirani. At this, the politician realized that Vazirani was not to be bought and hastily changed his tune. He even promised to increase state aid to hospitals. "Corruption is a big road block to progress", Vazirani says. "Because of it everything goes wrong. The intimidation leads to wrong decision-making. Transasia can be an example. But many more companies need to be."[22]

Deep vested interests perpetuate corruption, venality and greed. They are exacerbated by new technologies, leading to industrial espionage and cyber-crime. The antidote lies in a series of necessary measures, according to Laurence Cockcroft of Transparency International. They include a far tougher regulation of business to tackle the "shadow" or black market economy; the abolition of "secrecy jurisdictions", from Swiss bank accounts to tax havens, which facilitate large-scale global corruption; the abolition of corruption and the bribery of foreign officials in world trade, supported by the OECD's Anti-Bribery Convention, which now needs to include the BRIC countries of Brazil, Russia, India and China; a concerted effort to tackle organized crime; the prosecution of senior politicians, including heads of state, involved in corruption though the International Criminal Court; and the repatriation of stolen assets to their countries of origin.

Cockcroft acknowledges the "real progress in addressing corruption" made by the Extractive Industries Transparency Initiative (EITI), covering oil, gas and minerals, which makes the payment and receipt of royalties and taxes transparent in energy-rich countries.[23]

The antidote to corruption is also found in individuals such as those quoted here and countless others who have the courage and commitment to the values of personal integrity including honesty and care for people—especially the world's poorest and the disenfranchised. Businesses such as Tata, Transasia, Kaymo and many others have performed far better than they might otherwise have done had they not established a reputation for trust-worthiness. The business case for integrity and the stance against corruption is proved by the results.

---

22 Thanks to his leadership of integrity, Vazirani was elected in July 2018 as the global President of Initiatives of Change for a three-year term. In his acceptance speech he said, "If you decide to do the right thing, the Universe conspires to make it happen."

23 https://eiti.org/

References

Cockcroft, Laurence, *Global Corruption: money, power and ethics in the modern world*, I. B. Tauris, 2012

Cockcroft, Laurence, and Wegener, Anne-Christine, *Unmasked: corruption in the West*, I. B. Tauris, 2016

Moody-Stuart, Mark, *Responsible Leadership: lessons from the front line of sustainability and ethics*, Routledge, 2014

10 The silent crisis

Meeting environmental challenges

The Sahara Desert, says Yahaya Ahmed from northern Nigeria, won't ask you if you are Christian or Muslim, animist or pagan. It will encroach anyway. "We are talking about a common enemy—the desert", he says. Ahmed is one of many giving a leadership of integrity in the light of global environmental challenges.

Ahmed, Chairman and CEO of DARE (Development Association for Renewable Energies) in Kaduna, has seen at first hand the tragic consequences of religious conflict in his region: churches and mosques razed to the ground; the burnt carcasses of people caught up in violence. But religious warfare is also a conflict over resources. And that is exacerbated by deforestation and desertification, he says.

The Sahel, an area stretching across north Africa which Ahmed calls "the veranda of the desert", is now within a few miles of Kano, the Muslim heartland of northern Nigeria. As the desert expands, people are forced to migrate south. Populations from Niger and Chad have poured into Nigeria with the consequence that the country's "middle belt will be choked up", Ahmed believes.

Women inadvertently cause the southerly creep of the desert as they search for firewood for cooking. When trees are cut down, the desert sands can be blown further. If new trees are planted, they are soon stripped bare and chopped down, such is the demand for firewood.

Bulk haulage trucks bring tonnes of timber for firewood from the forests of southern Nigeria to the north. Ahmed counted 23 such trucks during a two-and-a-half-hour journey from Abuja to Kaduna. Petroleum tankers can often be seen with timber heaped on top. He fears that this shipping of timber from south to north will, in turn, cause as much deforestation in the south as in the north of the country.

The problem is that it takes eight pounds of wood to cook one family meal on an open stove using traditional cooking methods. Women have to trek up to four miles to find the firewood they need to keep their families alive. Meanwhile they are also desperate for drinking water for their children but desertification means less water to go round. No wonder Nigerian women fear the invasion of populations from other countries in the north.

What can be done about it? Ahmed, who gained his civil engineering degree in Darmstadt, Germany, in 2002, founded DARE in 2004 with the idea of developing renewable energy resources. He was especially inspired by an all-African conference he attended in Caux, Switzerland, in 2006. There he heard Cornelio Sommaruga, former head of the International Committee of the Red Cross, give a powerful speech urging Africans to find African answers to African problems. "You are the ones to solve Africa's problems", rather than relying on aid from the West, Sommaruga had said.

At that time Ahmed was working as a broadcast journalist for Deutsche Welle, the German international radio service, in Bonn. But he was well aware that the encroaching desert was coming close to his native Kano State. He returned to Nigeria determined to put his engineering skills to work.

At first he and his team developed a solar cooker, the SK14, with a parabolic dish, but the women found it difficult to adapt to it. In hazy weather it didn't work well, and their menfolk complained that the food no longer tasted smoky! "It would take a long time to get their acceptance", commented Ahmed. "But the desert doesn't wait."

Then his DARE team hit on the idea of a heat-retaining cooking stove. The portable metal box, standing about three feet tall, is made from metal sheets supplied by the German industrial company ThyssenKrupp.

This small piece of low-cost technology is called the Save 80 because it requires only 20 per cent of the normal quantity of firewood needed to boil water and cook a meal. It is described as "an initiative for climate change management". It is combined with a separate lidded Wonderbox which keeps food hot for many hours: rice, vegetables, maize porridge, potatoes, chicken, fish and flat-bread.

DARE's salaried staff and distributors—young men aged 17 to 27—tour the region marketing the stoves and Wonderboxes. Some of the men, who come from Christian and Muslim backgrounds, used to be at war with each other but have now renounced violence thanks to their new employment.

So far they have sold and distributed some 49,000 Save 80 stoves and Wonderboxes to families, mostly in the north-central and north-eastern regions of Nigeria. "But the Boko Haram insurgency almost brought our activities to a standstill over the last four years", Ahmed reports.[1] "We've lost contact with quite a considerable number of the stove users—either dead or internally displaced refugees and living somewhere else. Now that the insurgency is being contained and people are returning to their homes, we are also gradually reviving our activities again."

They have plans to distribute about 50,000 stoves in a special programme with the Government of Niger State in 2019, in their efforts to reduce the alarming rate of deforestation in the state.

Ahmed and his team have sold the cooking stoves in over two-thirds of the 36 states of Nigeria. "We have 35 salaried staff and about 180 trained youths

1   email to the author, 15 May 2018

who assemble the stoves and are paid based on the number of stoves they assemble", he says. "We also have about 20 distributors in various states who help in disseminating the stoves in their regions and are paid on a commission basis." Moreover, sales and marketing have expanded into Malawi, Rwanda and Zambia.

The UN Framework Convention on Climate Change (UNFCCC) has registered and validated the Save 80 stove. Burning less wood also means less emission of greenhouse gasses. "We applied for the CDM (Clean Development Mechanism) registration and were approved for a ten-year term. We have even been granted CERs (Certified Emission Reduction certificates) after evaluation of the project by UNFCCC auditors", Ahmed says. CDM registration brought a subsidy that allows DARE to sell the stoves at a reduced price of about 50 euros (15,000 Nigerian naira) each. Families can pay in instalments, using the money they have saved on buying firewood.

This allowed Ahmed and his team to expand from a pilot project mainly in two towns in the Guinea Savannah to the rest of Nigeria. In several villages, 80 per cent of inhabitants now use the Save 80. He calculates that 12,500 such stoves reduce carbon dioxide emissions by 30,000 tonnes a year.

But what really encourages him is the way the project is bringing together Christians and Muslims, in a region where there has been brutal bloodshed between the two communities. Some Muslims entered a Christian church to watch a presentation about the Save 80, and a Christian pastor was welcomed to the compound of the Muslim district head for the first time. Now a pastor and a Muslim village chief travel together to villages to promote the Save 80 and teach people how to use it. "It is a sort of chain reaction of cooperation", Ahmed says. "These men, who used not to have anything to do with each other, have become very good friends. At least in one community they don't see the church or mosque as a place of the enemy."

Instead, together they are fighting their common enemy: the desert.[2]

Such land degradation, the spread of deserts and the resultant water and food scarcities exacerbate extreme poverty, conflict and mass migration. Tackling desertification—its mitigation, reversal or adaptation to it—is a major priority as climate change raises global temperatures. On average, six to 10 inches of topsoil is all that separates stability from conflict. Every year agriculture loses an area three times the size of Switzerland.

The central importance of land is most obvious in the world's drylands, which used to feed about 40 per cent of the world's population. As land is lost and populations grow, conflict increases with more and more people competing for what remains. Nearly 80 per cent of the world's conflicts take place in its drylands, and countries under particular pressure risk becoming failing states.

Yet there are encouraging initiatives, such as Africa's "great green wall" of trees being planted initially across 11 sub-Saharan countries. It is 15 kilometres

2   Updated from article by Michael Smith, *Africa Today* magazine, August/September 2012

deep and 8,000 kilometres long, from West to East, beginning in Senegal. The aim is to fight the effects of climate change by reversing desertification. The roots of the acacia trees hold water in the soil and, what appears to be miraculously, former dry wells have filled up again. Women plant vegetable crops and the local economies are being transformed. The project, which began in 2007, is being funded by the African Union, the World Bank, the UN, and the UK botanical gardens.[3]

The Caux forum in Switzerland embarked on looking deeply into the root causes of conflict. One of them was environmental degradation and, in this context, a dedicated day on land degradation was held in 2012, following a passionate speech given by Luc Gnacadja, then Executive Secretary of UNCCD (United Nations Convention to Combat Desertification), from Benin. Gnacadja told Caux in 2011 that only "six to ten inches of top soil separate mankind from extinction."

In 2013, Caux launched a programme to tackle the fundamental resources issue which too often leads to conflict. Called Initiative for Land, Lives and Peace (ILLP),[4] it held its first international conference that year—the Caux Dialogue on Land and Security—in partnership with UNCCD. The annual conference has been held every year since then.

The aim, say the organizers, is "to deepen understanding of the links between land degradation and human security and to build the trust needed for effective collaboration on joint land-peace initiatives."

They add that:

More than 75 per cent of the world's conflicts occur in dryland areas, which are home to just 35 per cent of the world's population. While many people are aware of the rapid speed of desertification (one per cent of agricultural land lost each year), few understand that deserts are often man-made. And fewer still realize that by applying simple techniques, lost land can be restored to sustainable productive use, enhancing food security. On top of this, improved management of the world's land represents one third of the overall global climate change abatement potential by 2030."[5]

The Caux Dialogues aim to provide a safe environment which facilitates much-needed conversations, and to offer solutions as well as analysis. Little known outside expert circles, there are simple, effective, inexpensive and proven ways of restoring land to its full capacity to grow food, retain water and act as a natural buffer against extreme weather. This approach directly supports the most poor and vulnerable, helping them find income and employment on their own land. In addition, capturing carbon dioxide from the atmosphere in soil and vegetation through restoring and re-vegetating land could provide between one third and one half of the cost-effective

---

3   https://www.youtube.com/watch?v=4xls7K_xFBQ;   https://www.youtube.com/wa
     tch?v=JOjwJFBRFSQ; https://en.wikipedia.org/wiki/Great_Green_Wall
4   https://www.iofc.org/initiatives-land-lives-and-peace
5   http://www.iofc.org/initiatives-for-land-lives-and-peace

response to climate change, especially in the short- to medium-term, thereby gaining vital time for a low-carbon economy to emerge.

Despite all these advantages, astonishingly little land restoration is taking place. The reasons lie in divided responsibilities, and in the fact that most of the solutions exist outside the normal focus of governments and development agencies. Besides, the first priority may be unconventional, such as the need to reconcile hostile groups on the ground so that they can cooperate. The Caux conferences address these issues by including a range of stakeholders, from grassroots activists to world leaders, big business to top scientists. Land restoration practitioners also particularly value the chance to meet there to exchange best practice. They keep in touch via social media outside the formal conferences.

Luc Gnacadja of UNCCD told the 2014 ILLP conference: "Human security starts with functioning ecosystems. We must therefore address the loss of agricultural land in fragile states and work to secure ecosystems. In striving towards land degradation neutrality, human security is a key consideration."

Adam Koniuszewski, who was then Executive Director of Green Cross International, based in Geneva, said that 1.5 billion people in 168 countries were impacted by land degradation. Desertification is advancing around the world. But land degradation was not inevitable; it was the result of human activity through: 1) Overgrazing (35 per cent)—especially in Africa; 2) Deforestation (30 per cent)—especially in Asia and South America; 3) Poor agricultural practices (28 per cent)—particularly in North America.

Climate change exacerbates the problem. According to the UK Meteorological Office, climate change contributed to the 2011 East African drought that killed 100,000 people and pushed millions into starvation.

"Yet every day", Koniuszewski continued, "innovative solutions are being deployed around the world and degraded lands are being restored—often through low-tech cost-effective solutions". He cited how Tony Rinaudo [see his story on p. 108] was bringing back life to trees and vegetation with a pocket-knife and how Allan Savory uses cattle to restore degraded lands. Yacoubé Sawadogo, known as the "man who stopped the desert", has also re-greened areas of Northern Burkina Faso using such methods, where international institutions and scientists had failed to make a difference.[6]

"Our first priority", continued Koniuszewski, "should be to stop land degradation from occurring in the first place. Avoiding damage is much easier, faster and cheaper than restoration. We urgently need to stop the misguided policies that lead to deforestation, biofuels that compete with food and carry an unfavourable footprint, and the wasteful mass-irrigation techniques for crops that are not suited for local conditions."

Koniuszewski, who is the founder of the Bridge Foundation, made a gift to the Caux centre of a "trendy" compost box, to put in place a composting

---

6   See the film *The man who stopped the desert*: https://www.youtube.com/watch?v=IDgDWbQtlKI

scheme on site. This turns all the food and biodegradable waste at Caux into a resource, enriching the soil for future generations. The aim is for all who attend Caux to walk the talk and be a part of the solution, not of the problem, he says. "Solutions start at home and this is what all these gatherings are about."

ILLP chair Dr Martin Frick, then the German ambassador to the international organizations, based in Bonn, and Ian Johnson from the Club of Rome agreed that if land degradation and desertification are to be slowed down and reversed, the urgent need is to massively scale up the solutions.

Jamie Shea, Deputy Assistant Secretary General for new security challenges at NATO, told the 2014 Caux Dialogue:

> In the face of what seems to be the return of geopolitics with tendencies to become more nationalistic, more populist and less generous, the greatest challenge, above all else, is to keep the Human Security agenda alive. To ensure human security for people on the ground, land restoration is central for peace and stability. Particularly as climate change exacerbates existing vulnerabilities, land management is the crucial issue if we are to stop the vicious circle of migration, organized crime, terrorism, and the drug trade.

Earlier at the 2013 Caux Dialogue, the human rights activist Bianca Jagger had quoted Mahatma Gandhi: "The earth, the air, the land and the water are not an inheritance from our forefathers but a loan from our children."

"My generation has done a bad job in keeping Gandhi's saying", Jagger commented. "Seventy million people are now climate refugees, displaced by natural hazards since 2009...particularly indigenous and tribal peoples, who are the best guardians of the lands they live on."

Tony Rinaudo, Natural Resources Advisor to World Vision, said: "When my wife and I first moved to Maradi, Niger, we were overwhelmed by the environmental destruction and suffering. Our initial efforts met with failure, but a solution came as an answer to prayer. Our attention was drawn to desert bushes which we had ignored as useless."

Reporting this in his column in *The Daily Telegraph*, UK, Geoffrey Lean, then the paper's environment editor, wrote:

> The bushes turned out to be clusters of shoots from the buried stumps of long-felled trees, whose root systems still drew water and nutrients from far beneath the arid soil. The shoots could never grow much before being cut or eaten by livestock, but when Rinaudo pruned them down to a single stem and kept the animals away, they shot up into substantial trees within four years. As the trees grew, so did crops. And as local farmers began reaping good harvests, neighbours and visitors followed suit. Now, two decades later, some 200 million trees have been regenerated in this way, covering five million hectares of Maradi and the neighbouring

region of Zinder, enabling the growing of enough extra grain to feed 2.5 million people. Besides increasing harvests and reducing poverty, all this helps combat climate change. The Sahel's regenerated trees can take 30 tonnes of CO_2 out of the atmosphere per hectare.[7]

Development agriculturalist and film-maker Dr Alan Channer describes this development in Niger as "perhaps the most rapid, farmer-managed re-greening in human history. Over seven million hectares [2018 figure] of mosaic parkland—characterized by a range of indigenous trees, interspersed with millet fields—have been restored through the regrowth of 'underground' trees.... Millet yields in these parklands have soared without the use of chemical fertilizers.... Satellite images reveal a vast area of southern Niger that is now greener than northern Nigeria—although it has less rainfall."[8]

As with land reclamation, another area of environmental awareness and sustainability is recycling products. This is what inspires the Indian entrepreneur Rajendra Gandhi, a Gujarati living in Mumbai. He is the founder and Managing Director of GRP Ltd, India's largest rubber and polymer recycling company. It employs over 1,000 people at seven manufacturing units across India, reprocessing 70,000 tons of waste tires each year. It has customers in over 60 countries and claims to be one of the world's top four companies for recycling reclaimed rubber. GRP's corporate social responsibility statement says that the company aims to "add value to society, while reducing the impact on the Earth's resources.... The ethos of our organization is to minimize damage to human health and the environment, both locally and globally."

The notion of reducing the impact on the Earth's resources particularly appealed to Gandhi after he read a World Bank report that recycling would be an up-and-coming business in developing economies. "I was quite fired up by that thought", he says. It led him to founding GRP in 1974.[9] Rubber is non-biodegradable and so recycling it is environmentally friendly. Old tyres and tubes—from buses and bicycles, cars and coaches, tractors and trucks—as well as used latex gloves and worn hose pipes all pass through the company's plants in the states of Gujarat, Maharashtra and Tamil Nadu. GRP has grown to be one of the world's top four rubber recycling companies. It supplies reclaimed rubber to the world's major tyre companies: Apollo, Bridgestone Firestone, Ceat, Continental Tyres, Cooper, Dunlop, Good Year, Pirelli, Trelleborg and Yokohama.

But what also appealed to Gandhi was running a business without the compromises of corruption. Indira Gandhi was the prime minister when Rajendra Gandhi founded GRP. In those days the economy was much more centrally controlled than today's more liberal economy. That might have

7   Geoffrey Lean, *The Daily Telegraph*, 12 July 2013
8   http://www.oikodiplomatique.org/regreening-africa-gets-a-major-boost.html
9   The acronym, under a brand resurgence in 2012, is derived from the company's original name: Gujarat Reclaim & Rubber Products Ltd.

meant having to pay bribes, Gandhi explains. "If I had gone into any other industry I would have come under a quota system in the controlled economy. I would have needed a quota license for getting raw materials and it was customary to bribe government officials to get the maximum quota. But my raw material was scrap rubber and I didn't need to bribe anyone to get that, as it was readily available." Some 300 agents from across India are now his suppliers. Gandhi implies that a liberalized economy is potentially a less corrupt one.

Gandhi's company also pioneered the design and manufacture in India of rubber recycling machinery. Again, his motive was to avoid the corruption involved in importing technology from overseas. "To get an import license you had to pay bribes to officials in New Delhi." So Gandhi asked a rubber technologist, WG Desai, if it was possible to make the machinery themselves. "It was a big risk for me", says Gandhi, "but with his help and the support of bank loans we started to put the technology together". He needed seven million rupees (US$ 250,000 in those days) in start-up capital which came from bank and family loans as well as a public issue of shares. He eventually raised sufficient capital in 1977, after a delay due to Indira Gandhi's period of emergency rule in India, and the company went into production in 1978, four years after its founding. The company, with an annual turnover of close to US$50 million, now produces Reclaim rubber that equals to a saving of 1.5 million tyres. This in turn saves landfills and the environment.

The company might never have happened if Gandhi had not dealt with an issue in his personal life: his relationship with his father.

Vadilal Gandhi was the owner of Ashok Silk Mills in the Mumbai suburb of Ghatkopar, as well as being a local Congress politician. He had a reputation for philanthropy but at home had a fiery temper. He sent his son, Rajendra, to boarding school at the age of nine. From there Rajendra went to live in a student hostel at Mumbai's prestigious Indian Institute of Technology, where he studied metallurgy. His father remained a remote figure.

Travelling on a bus one day, the young Gandhi found himself sitting next to a Westerner who was reading a copy of a magazine called *Himmat* (the Urdu word means courage). "The fact that he was travelling on a bus amused me", recalls Gandhi, as Westerners usually travelled by taxi. He engaged him in conversation. The man, from Wales, was working on the staff of the magazine. He invited Gandhi to a film showing in a downtown apartment on Marine Drive. Rajendra thought it would be a Hollywood movie. Instead, it was very different from what he expected: a drama dealing with racial conflict in colonial Africa.

Another young Indian at the film show invited Gandhi to the ceremonial opening of a new residential block at an international centre in the hill resort of Panchgani, south of Pune. The centre was the vision and brainchild of Rajmohan Gandhi, a grandson of Mahatma Gandhi, who was at that time the editor-in-chief of *Himmat*.

"There I was challenged to look at my life", recalls Rajendra Gandhi. "I had the clear thought to share my life with my parents. I was very afraid of my father. So I wrote a letter to him in a tone of honesty and apology." Rajendra had been sending his monthly pocket money on movies and "vulgar" books whilst telling his parents it was going on text books. "This is the type of son you have had and I have decided to change my life", he wrote to his father. He gave the letter to his mother to give to his father, "because I didn't have the courage to give it to him".

When his father read it he summoned his son from the student hostel to his room at their home. For five minutes his father didn't say a word. Then he said, "I feel very sad that you have been up to all this mischief." He gave his son a piece of his mind, but Rajendra noticed that he didn't flair up into a temper. Then, to his surprise, his father began to talk about the things he had got up to in his own childhood. "As he talked, I could feel the generation gap, that wall from him, breaking. And I felt a respect for him coming out of love instead of fear."

Not long afterwards, Rajendra borrowed his father's new transistor radio without his permission, when he was away on business, in order to listen to a cricket commentary. Within a day it was stolen from his student room. He was overcome with fear of facing his father again. "In a time of quiet reflection I knew I must own up by going to him straight away. When he returned two or three days later I told him and said I was sorry. He really raised hell and said I was an irresponsible young man. I knew I had to take this with humility and face the consequences."

The surprising effect of all this on Rajendra was to remove the fear he had of his father. He found it gave him the courage to discuss and disagree with him on business matters.

Rajendra graduated in metallurgy in 1971 and, at first, joined his father's silk mill. But after reading the World Bank report on the importance of recycling to developing economies, he asked his father's permission to start his own business. "He really supported me", recalls Rajendra. "I didn't want to live in the legacy of what my father was doing. My decision to be honest with him gave me the courage to approach him. Otherwise I might have remained under his shadow and control. Instead he allowed me to use family money to start my own business."

In 2001, Rajendra's son, Harsh Gandhi, joined the business, bringing in a fresh perspective with new ideas, astute leadership, and setting up many more business units. Rajendra allowed his son to bloom under his guidance, ensuring that there is no fear or stress in their relationship.

Under the duo's acumen, GRP contributes towards environmental sustainability through the 3 Rs: Recycling—tyre re-treading and Polymer Composites units; Reusing—custom die-forms unit; and Reducing—reclaim rubber and Industrial Polymers units. The seven manufacturing units, in four locations in India, supply to over 300 customers and to over 60 countries worldwide.

As well as contributing towards environmental sustainability through recycling, what particularly satisfies them is to know that they have created jobs for over 1,000 people, "at well above the minimum wage".

Near Asia Plateau, the IofC centre in Panchgani which had such an impact on Rajendra Gandhi's early life, a group of women run a village development scheme called Grampari (Grameen and Pariyavaran Rural and Ecology Centre), established in 2008. Its mission is "to build the capacity of rural society through thoughtful, community-led programmes in livelihoods, empowerment, health and environment, and local governance".

Grampari's founder is Jayashree Rao, whose husband, Ravindra, is the Director of the Asia Plateau centre, who used to run a dental practice in Bangalore. Short in stature, Jayashree has a big heart and a real empathy for the poor.

Thirteen thousand villagers have clean drinking water, thanks to Grampari. "People get drinking water from springs", says Deepak Jadhav, who runs Grampari's governance programmes. "But open springs are often contaminated." Grampari has encouraged people in 21 villages to build boxes to cover their springs. "We also create soak pits and cover sewage canals to prevent waste water getting mixed with drinking water." This prevents diseases.

The Grampari centre employs 17 people who run residential training programmes. People from 30 neighbouring villages come on week-long residential courses, housed in old farm buildings, to be trained in the use of sewing machines, making products such as handbags, and how to repair solar powered lamps and the inner workings of cellphones. They also learn to grow organic crops. Before, when solar powered lamps or cellphones broke down they would be left unattended. Grampari is empowering villagers, especially women, in this self-help scheme, in a country where 68.8 per cent of the population—833 million people—live in rural areas, including more than 600,000 villages (2011 census).

Grampari also teaches the villagers to convert biodegradable garbage into compost and to reduce the use of plastic.

Grampari seeks to build capacity in three areas:

Livelihoods—providing opportunities for self-employment and entrepreneurship;
Leadership and governance—strengthening local institutions, developing ethical leaders and empowering the voiceless;
Health and environment—improving the quality of life through access to safe and sustainable drinking water, hygiene and sanitation and building capacity through natural resource management.

When I visited Grampari in November 2013, villagers were being shown the simple sanitation expedient of hand-washing using an ingenious piece of "intermediate technology"—a tippy-tap rain water collector.[10] This has now been extended to handwashing training in 132 schools. The Maharashtra state government asked Grampari to train teachers to take this handwashing programme to all the district's schools. It is estimated that handwashing with soap could save 1.2 million children's lives every year.

A spirit of democracy prevails at Grampari, amongst the leaders and those who are being trained on the residential courses. Groups, typically of 15 or 16 people, take time in silence to listen to their "inner voice" and then share their thoughts. "Everyone's thought is regarded as equal. Everyone's voice is important", says Archana Rao, daughter of Ravi and Jayashree.[11]

Archana Rao tells the following touching story of Grampari's impact on one rural family:

> We were less than half way up. We'd been trekking for over two hours, in the hot sun, our legs giving way, our hearts beating faster than I've ever known. None of this was remotely assuaged by the spectacular views of the valleys of the Western Ghats. It was a spring we were hiking up to look at; a spring that had a substantial year-long supply of water, and if developed could provide the relief that the desperate villagers of Kirunde needed. The sheer vertical heights we scaled finally ended with luscious green wheat fields. Nestled in the middle of these fields were two modest huts.
>
> We still had a while to trek but the temptation of food made us stop. Collapsing on the mats that were indulgently laid out for us we slowly emerged back to life eating their delicious fresh yogurt. As I took my last greedy mouthful of yogurt a little boy peeped out of the corner. I asked him the annoying yet inevitable question. Do you go to school? He nodded. Where?, I asked, looking around with a little bewilderment. He pointed all the way down to where we began our trek.
>
> Our once-in-a-lifetime-never-to-be-repeated trek was his daily commute to school. His only problem was that after school ended he had to trek back particularly fast to ensure he had enough sunlight to do his homework.
>
> Sunlight? I asked quizzically. The residents (three families) smiled benignly and kindly at us, explaining that they had not had electricity there for over 150 years. And whilst they hadn't felt the need for it, today, now, they do.
>
> My colleague and I were so moved by this that we decided that we would donate two solar lanterns to these generous, humble, undemanding residents.
>
> This was over a month back. I hadn't done anything about it apart from tell this story with much enthusiasm to all my friends. I even blogged about it, feeling a misplaced smugness. I hadn't got the lanterns to them, I only said I would.
>
> One of my criteria for giving these lanterns was that I wanted someone from those three families to be trained in the maintenance and repair of

---

11 Archana Rao, India Country Director, Global Citizen Year, told this to the Ethical Leadership in Business Forum in Caux, Switzerland, 30 June 2018

the lantern, a course that we offer at Grampari. The village being so high up and so extremely inaccessible, it was hardly surprising that they didn't make the trip down to Grampari. Who could reassure them that I would make good on my promise? These lanterns were expensive and the trip to Grampari complicated.

This story was also related to the 17 boys at the boy's residential programme we had here at Grampari. Unbeknownst to me, it resonated very deeply with one of the boys, Vinayak.

Vinayak sadly couldn't go but the course director Himanshu, Deepak, our wash programme coordinator, and four other boys from the programme resolved that if they couldn't come down for the training, they would take the training to them. And so they hiked. All the way up. But unlike me, they had the added burden of carrying two lanterns and the solar panels.

Today, thanks to the conviction, commitment and compassion of one boy and his vision to motivate others, three families are overjoyed to have been given the gift of light. Vinayak, also a trained electrician, has taken a further decision to be on hand for any issues these lanterns might have.

It's not just free solar lanterns that bring about change in people's lives; it is the compassion of thought that does. One of the reasons I firmly believe the work of Grampari is so effective is that, at its core, the most important objective of the organization is compassion. Through inner listening, personal change and following four standards—honesty, purity of heart, unselfishness and love—as part of the core of rural development we see some extraordinary acts of love. This is just one such example amongst hundreds.[12]

The cost to society of environmental indiscipline is huge. In 2015 BP was fined a record $20.8 billion by the US government for the fatal Deepwater Horizon blowout in the Gulf of Mexico in 2010. The explosion killed 11 rig workers, whose bodies have never been found. The US courts concluded that the company acted with gross negligence and wilful misconduct. BP set aside $43 billion for the cost of the clean-up of beaches, for settling lawsuits and for funerals.[13]

In India, some 25,000 people died, according to Amnesty International, as a result of a deadly gas leak from the Union Carbide plant in Bhopal, on the night of 2 December 1984. It was the world's worst industrial accident and 30 years later the site is still poisonous. Thousands of tonnes of toxic waste have seeped deep into the soil and groundwater. Efforts to clean up the site are still bogged down in a legal quagmire between the Dow Chemical Company, which bought Union Carbine in 1999, and the Madhya Pradesh state government.[14]

12 www.grampari.org, reproduced here with permission.
13 *The Times*, 23 December 2014; *The Sunday Times*, 7 September 2014
14 "Bhopal is still killing us, 30 years on" by Robin Pagnamenta, *The Times*, 2 December 2014

Yet all the evidence is that going green pays companies handsome dividends. The late Ray Anderson was described as the "greenest chief executive in America" after he committed Interface Carpets, the company he founded in Atlanta, Georgia, to recycling. His epiphany moment was reading Paul Hawkens' book *The Ecology of Commerce* (reissued 2010), which declared that industry was destroying the planet and the only people to stop this were industrialists themselves. This, said Anderson, was "like a spear to the chest". He came to realize that going green—cutting out landfill waste through recycling, cutting carbon emissions from boilers by 99.7 per cent—reduced costs and increased profits. "It's not just the right thing to do, it's the smart thing to do", he told the Houston Advanced Research Centre. He saw his company's role as pioneering "the next industrial revolution: one that is kinder and gentler to the earth".[15]

In the wider struggle to tackle climate change, Geoffrey Lean, the British doyen of environmental journalists (who is now retired), saw positive signs coming not just from the third sector or environmental campaigns such as Greenpeace or Friends of the Earth, but from the very heart of the free market system itself. For the fourth year in a row, 2013 saw "greater worldwide investment in renewable energy than in fossil fuels, as the cost of solar and wind power tumbles. The worldwide market in low carbon goods and services exceeds £3.4 trillion a year and often outperforms the rest of the global economy."[16]

According to a report published by leaders of the IMF, the Bank of England, OECD, China Development Bank, the World Bank and business leaders, Lean wrote, "Tackling climate change can help, not harm, economic growth." And, he wrote, "No country has seen the opportunity more clearly than China, now the world's biggest renewable investor. Formerly better known for rapidly building coal-fired stations, it has closed and cancelled scores of them, mainly to combat the air pollution that kills some 250,000 Chinese a year."

The challenges remain huge. As demand for consumer goods rises, particularly in the world's most populous countries of India and China, so too will the demands on the world's limited and finite natural resources and how they are shared. China and the USA alone, for instance, account for 44 per cent of the world's carbon dioxide emissions affecting climate change.[17] And the developed nations produce over five times the amount of CO_2 than the developing nations, says the World Resources Institute.[18] This will continue to fuel our inventiveness, for instance over energy supplies and agricultural processes. It also urges the better off among us to confront our comfort and ease,

15 "Business hero" by Jennifer Beck, 18 March 2009, http://myhero.com/hero.asp?hero=r_anderson
16 Geoffrey Lean, *The Daily Telegraph*, 20 September 2014
17 https://www.statista.com/statistics/271748/the-largest-emitters-of-co2-in-the-world/
18 http://pdf.wri.org/navigating_numbers_chapter4.pdf

our selfishness and materialism—especially if we are to retain any sense of common humanity. As Mahatma Gandhi is reputed to have said: "The rich must live more simply so that the poor may simply live."

Leading with integrity in the light of global environmental challenges is not only possible but is also cost effective, as shown by the stories in this chapter. Perhaps Adam Smith's "invisible hand" of the market is doing the right thing after all.

References

Chabay, Ilan; Frick, Martin; Helgeson, Jennifer, *Land Restoration: reclaiming landscapes for a sustainable future*, Academic Press, 2015

Hawkens, Paul, *The Ecology of Commerce: a declaration of sustainability*, Harper Business, revised edition 2010

Hazarka, Sanjoy, *Bhopal: the lessons of a tragedy*, Penguin Books India, 1988

11 The impact generation
"Furry animals" of social entrepreneurship

While Princess Diana campaigned for the victims of landmines in Angola, the Dutch social entrepreneur Merel Rumping is coming to the rescue of amputees in Colombia. Over 30 million people worldwide need prosthetic limbs due to landmine injuries, vehicle accidents, diabetes, other illnesses and injuries. Yet too often in developing and emerging economies they have little or no access to them.

Rumping is determined to do something about it. You could say she has gone out on a limb in her commitment to making a difference. In July 2014 she founded the social enterprise LegBank which aims to provide easy-to-fit prosthetic limbs for victims of landmines and other amputees in Colombia and elsewhere. LegBank's mission is to "increase access to affordable, qualitative prostheses for low-income amputees in upcoming economies".

Rumping gained her masters degree in international relations, which included a focus on business ethics, in The Netherlands in 2010. She studied political science in France before working in the Dutch embassy in Morocco.

Aged 20, she had worked in an orphanage in Medellín, Colombia, for three months, helping to rehabilitate former child soldiers caught up in the civil war and street children in tough neighbourhoods populated by sex workers. Many were glue sniffers and drug addicts using cheap cocaine. One of the first children Merel took from the streets to the orphanage was an 11-year-old girl, Tatiana, who was prostituting herself in order to support her seven-year-old brother. Merel worked with over 30 children. She filed stories from there for her local Dutch newspaper which helped to raise funds for the orphanage.

Three years later, in 2006, she returned to Colombia for six months, to work with a microfinancing agency, la Corporación Mundial de la Mujer (World Corporation for Women). It was the year that Mohammad Yunus was awarded the Nobel Peace Prize for his pioneer microfinance work with the Grameen Bank. Though initially sceptical, Merel had become increasingly aware of the effectiveness of supporting people from impoverished backgrounds through microfinance. She also began to take note of the sheer numbers of amputees in Colombia. And she began to realise the potential for social entrepreneurship.

Back in The Netherlands she joined ProPortion, which consults for NGOs and charities on how to create and sustain social enterprises. ProPortion has also launched its own social enterprises in emerging economies—water projects in Bangladesh and agribusiness youth enterprises in Kenya.

A regular participant in the Caux conferences in Switzerland, Rumping's inspiration to launch LegBank—under the ProPortion umbrella—emerged from conversations she had with a Colombian businessman. He connected her to a Dutchman who worked for an orthopaedic workshop in Asia. An idea grew in her mind based on her experience in the micro-financing agency: a "lease your leg-construction" which would remove upfront costs to recipients, combined with her newfound knowledge of the scale of the problem.

She reached out to industrial designers from the technical university in Delft, gaining volunteer support from six students who helped to map and research the problem. They found that diabetes, motor accidents and landmines are the main reasons for amputations in Colombia. The country has the world's second highest rate of landmine victims, following the world's longest running civil war dating back to the mid-1960s, where only recently a peace agreement has been signed.

Forty per cent of amputations worldwide are below the knee. The quality of the prosthetics is the key and current standards of the sockets are intricately linked to the production methods. The result is often as different as the people who create the socket. The barriers to access for patients are time, quality and cost. The challenge—the art—is how to create the socket uniquely suitable to the individual patient. Yet developing economies lack 40,000 suitably trained people to fit prosthetics. Furthermore, patients are sometimes not covered by healthcare insurance at all or only partly covered for the actual prosthetic and not the travel to the orthopaedic centres in the cities, which can be long and costly.

Another reason why healthcare is so centralised is because clinicians in rural areas face several obstacles to starting their own clinic. They lack seed investment and have no experience with the business side of running a clinic. Therefore they often have manual, time-consuming administration, incomplete patient data, and no clue how to make their facility compliant with the law. All this can lead to unprofessional, low quality care.

Merel and her team needed to understand the needs and desires of both rural as well as urban amputees. They found a small village in Colombia where there were some 300 landmine victims, many of them amputees in need of a prosthetic limb. It can take up to two years to get one—a factor detrimental to most rural inhabitants' livelihoods. So the aims became clear: support clinicians to create excellent care facilities and so bring the production closer to the rural areas; make the process quicker; and produce better quality prosthetics.

In cooperation with the University of Strathclyde, Glasgow, the team created the first prototype of the Majicast socket production unit in January 2015. Majicast, invented by Dr Arjan Buis and developed by the Amsterdam-based design agency Reggs, is a tubular tank filled with water. Once the casting material is applied, the clinician instructs the patient to insert the limb into the Majicast, and then to transfer his/her full body weight onto the inserted limb while remaining in a standing position. This creates a mould for a unique fit to suit the patient, thus producing a consistently high quality prosthetic product. The device reduces production time to create a bespoke, comfortable socket almost immediately.

Following the initial successful production of Majicast prosthetics, Merel and her team mapped where to provide orthopaedic services, based on a large amount of collected data, to the areas most in need.

In order to be able to expand the operation, they now needed capital investment. Merel pitched LegBank to Bill Gates when he visited the Netherlands. However it was Google which invested \$1 million in this innovative solution, through its Google Impact Challenge awards. The project was off to a flying start.

This investment has helped LegBank to fund three initiatives: an App, tested by three orthopaedic clinics in Colombia, which guides clinicians in treatment protocols, eases data collection, stores patient information safely and monitors patient satisfaction; secondly, the Majicast itself; and, thirdly, a franchise formula to drive the quality, sustainability, compliance and efficiency of a clinic in a rural area.

The latest version of the Majicast, patented by Strathclyde University, is still being tested. The aim is to sell them worldwide, whilst creating three more orthopaedic services in rural areas in Colombia, with the first one opening in the small city of Tunja in 2019. "We have also been looking to collaborate with three large orthopaedic centres in Bogotá, who have promised to send us the clients in rural areas that they usually treat", says Rumping.

She is gaining the backing of the Red Cross in Colombia: "I visited the Red Cross who said that, on the condition that we open another clinic in a tough post-conflict area, they would want to help us with components, train our prosthetist and send us clients."[1]

Rumping's "exit strategy" from Colombia, in order to work elsewhere, is to have four of these rural orthopaedic centres up and running, and sell 20 Majicasts. To do this, she needs to raise a further half a million dollars. Meanwhile the Colombian government has undertaken a nationwide landmine clearance programme, aiming to clear all landmines by 2021.[2]

Rumping's story is typical of the millennial generation's determination to make a difference—and, while about it, live an adventurous life. Yet there is nothing typical about Rumping. She was chosen by her Dutch university, the distinguished Rijksuniversiteit in Groningen, as the 2016 alumnus of the year out of 30,000 students. She attributes her motivation to her family upbringing: her grandfather had worked with refugees, her father worked with children with learning disabilities, and her mother is a nurse. So the "caring" aspect, she says, is in her DNA. Her initial experiences in Colombia gave her

1   Email to the author, 11 June 2018
2   Trust Talk by Merel Rumping, Initiatives of Change centre, London, 20 February 2018

a strong sense of justice issues. And, she adds, she really enjoys her work. "So maybe it is also artistic." She likes to quote the former President of Liberia, Ellen Johnson Sirleaf, who said: "The size of your dreams must always exceed your current capacity to achieve them. If your dreams do not scare you they are not big enough."

While Rumping dreams big, she also has an enchanting voice, singing Portuguese Fado music with her guitarists Ralph Bijvoet and Antonio Carlos Costa, who formed the ensemble group Palpita.

Social enterprises, says Tony Bradley, are the "furry animals in the undergrowth", scurrying around under the feet of "dinosaur corporations". Bradley is the Senior Professional Tutor in Social Enterprise and SEARCH Research Associate at the Social & Economic Activity Research Centre, Liverpool Hope University. SEARCH is one of only a few institutes in the world which combine an emphasis on both social enterprise and ethical business models.

He and his colleagues have been researching the rise of ethical markets over the past two decades, amidst turbulent economic times. From their findings Bradley points to the ways in which the old model of "dino-capitalism" is changing, away from global-scale, inflexible corporations towards smaller, more agile and "ethical market-sensitive" modes of businesses.

A "serial entrepreneur" himself, Bradley has run a range of businesses in TV and multi-media, training, education and Fairtrade hospitality. As a former producer/director for Sky TV, he says he is "committed to communication that is fun, friendly and effective". But, more significantly his Christian faith—he is an Anglican priest—challenges him to follow the Gandhian dictum, "Be the change you wish to see in the world", in all that he does.

This has inevitably led him towards a conviction that "the future evolution belongs to social enterprises and ethical businesses. These new companies are making a profit whilst, at the same time, tackling the disruptions caused by four "Ss"—size (of global population growth); scale (of the middle classes in emergent economies); sources (of rapidly depleting raw materials); sinks (of natural systems increasingly stretched to cope with pollution and other externalities); and responding to the challenge of meeting the needs of a social media generation.

So what are social enterprises? How are they defined? Essentially, they offer an altruistic form of entrepreneurship that focuses on the benefits to society rather than to shareholders. They become a social endeavour when they transform social capital in a way that affects society positively. The success of social entrepreneurship depends on factors related to social impact that traditional corporate businesses do not prioritize.

Social entrepreneurs recognize immediate social problems, but they also seek to understand the broader context of an issue across disciplines, fields and theories. Ashoka Fellows, for instance, recognized by the Washington DC-based Ashoka social enterprise network, have to prove that their models have been scaled up to have a national or global impact.[3] Gaining a larger

3   https://www.ashoka.org/en

understanding of how an issue relates to society allows social entrepreneurs to develop innovative solutions and mobilize available resources to impact the greater good. Unlike traditional corporate businesses, social entrepreneurship ventures focus on maximizing gains in social satisfaction, rather than maximizing profit.

Bradley is one of many campaigners advocating this direction towards increasing solidarity amongst businesses in pursuit of a sustainable social economy.

Green spending in the UK in 1999, he says, was worth £9.6bn; by 2016 it was worth £86bn, a nine-fold increase over the period. Green hot-spots such as Brighton (where the UK's only Green Party MP, Caroline Lucas, won her seat in 2010), Bristol, Edinburgh, the West Country and East London show the fastest growth in ethical markets and consumption.

Social enterprises that are scaled up to have national or global impacts are celebrated at the annual Skoll World Forum on Social Entrepreneurship, held at Said Business School, Oxford University. The forum was founded by the Canadian entrepreneur Jeff Skoll, the first President of eBay. It brings together nearly 1,000 people to Oxford each year.

They are also celebrated by Ashoka: Innovators for the Public, the largest network of social entrepreneurs in the world, with nearly 3,000 Ashoka Fellows in 70 countries. Ashoka was founded by Bill Drayton in Arlington, VA, in 1981 and has as its motto "Everyone a changemaker".When I interviewed him at the Skoll World Forum in Oxford he emphasized that the number one quality for good business leadership is empathy. He means that businesses and enterprises exist to meet human needs rather than just serving the bottom line and shareholder value. Empathy encourages us to live into other people's situations—to step into their shoes.

Social entrepreneurship now needs to take the next leap forward, Bradley says, into what he calls "societal entrepreneurship". This is already happening in places across the world. Leading examples include the Mondragon cooperatives in the Basque region of Spain, Muhammad Yunus' Grameen microfinancing unions, pioneered in Bangladesh, the Ubuntu drive to the feeding miracle of Chinyika in Zimbabwe and throughout South Africa, Sekem in Egypt, the Sarvodaya movement in Sri Lanka, Enova in Mexico and many more.

Bradley enthuses:

> In each of these regions social and ethical businesses are coalescing to create social economies that are changing the life chances and societies for thousands of people. Capitalism is the only game in town, but it's evolving, becoming smaller, greener, more ethical and collaborative. And just as the dinosaurs evolved into the birds we see all around us, so these businesses will one day fly and dino-capitalism will be gone.[4]

4   Quoted by the author in his book Great Company (2015, p 121)

Social enterprises sometimes benefit from impact investors who want to make a difference as well as a return on their capital. The US impact investors Lisa and Charly Kleissner from California speak about their vision as "impact people".[5] They attract like-minded people who are "trying to make the world better with their investments", Charly Kleissner says. They describe themselves as "hundred-percenters", as they go "all in" with impact investment, to build, step by step, a revolution in the way money is used and invested for good.

They see that philanthropy is changing: "Investors want impact as well as return on their investments." It is like a rising tide, Lisa suggests. "It doesn't necessarily require epiphany tsunami-like realizations to move in a new direction, but rather it comes out of constant movement towards trust, integrity, joy and partnership." "I've never had an 'ah-ha' moment in my life", she insists, "but I've always realized that my consciousness is very present in me".

Growing up in rural Hawaii, she gained from an early age a strong sense of preserving scarce resources. Following a Hawaiian ancestor's myth of consciousness and doing good, she knew she wanted to impact the world.

Yet she has also been through a crisis in her life. In 2009 she was diagnosed with a brain tumour. "I went into shock. My husband said to me, 'Don't worry. We'll figure this out.' And we did." Despite the risk, they eventually found a doctor who carried out the operation successfully. Afterwards, she reflected for a year on her good fortune, "believing we were going to find a path for our skills".

Returning to Silicon Valley, they brought together their peers and launched what is today Toniic, a global action-oriented community for impact investors.[6] They have always seen their wealth as a responsibility and something they were given to steward rather than something signalling prestige. The couple has had the fortunate opportunity to put capital and resources together.

Charly Kleissner stresses that integrity is to act according to one's life goals and values. "How can we as individuals be doers of justice in the economy?" he asks. "Our life is the expression of what we are; we therefore have a responsibility to commit ourselves to what we believe." Or, as Lisa Kleissner puts it, "It is up to us and each individual across the globe to raise the integrity of our world; to raise it out of this current failing and unequal global economy."

One person who is doing so is Bob Doherty, Professor of Marketing at the York Management School, University of York. He was the first marketing director of Divine Chocolate, an international Fairtrade social enterprise which partners with the cocoa-growing farmers' cooperative, Kuapa Kokoo, in Ghana.[7]

---

5   Speaking at the 2014 Caux TIGE conference
6   www.toniic.com
7   He told their story at the 2012 Caux TIGE conference.

Ghana liberalized its cocoa production in 1993, and a group of small-production cocoa farmers formed the cooperative. Kuapa Kokoo, which means Good Cocoa Farming, earned its Fairtrade certification in 1995.

With the help of partners and investors, Kuapa Kokoo launched Divine Chocolate, a UK-based company, in 1998. The cooperative was already earning a Fairtrade price, selling their cocoa to other companies when they decided to make Divine Chocolate from *Papa paa*, meaning the best of the best, of their cocoa beans. Kuapa Kokoo farmers own 45 per cent of the company and occasionally represent Divine in meetings with potential buyers in the UK. Two representatives are board directors, and a quarter of the board meetings take place in Ghana.

Being a Fairtrade company means that not only are the cocoa beans Fairtrade, but so too is the sugar used in making the chocolate. In the first 14 years of production, Divine Chocolate opened an office in Washington DC. It was voted the UK's Best Social Enterprise in 2007 and The Observer Best Ethical Business in 2008.

Doherty sees big companies such as Nestlé as his "Goliath". One of the many challenges associated with the Fairtrade industry is meeting demand at a respectable price. Fairtrade prices are, on average, 25 to 30 per cent higher than competitive market prices, and rely almost entirely upon an ethics-driven customer clientele. The trend of mainstream brands meeting the minimal standards of Fairtrade has split the industry; Divine, which is entirely Fairtrade, has to compete with larger companies that only use some Fairtrade cocoa, meaning that a bar of milk chocolate may only use 25 per cent Fairtrade products, and thus can be produced much more competitively.

Doherty's first visit to a remote farm in Ghana had a profound effect on him, showing him how he could make a difference in the world.[8]

Divine Chocolate, he said, works in partnership with London-based Twin Trading. Its unique ownership structure allows the farmers to be involved in decision-making and marketing. "The farmers can see themselves in the product and they are proud of it." It was a "bean-to-bar" story.

Profits are invested in development projects including community infrastructure, healthcare, and clean water. There were other benefits too: Ghana's population is composed mainly of small farm holders living in village communities; young people try to escape their fate of becoming cocoa farmers by migrating to cities. The development of the cocoa market in a fairer way encourages them to stay.

Doherty had also worked with Liberation Nuts, which is 42 per cent owned by nut producing cooperatives on three continents. This wide network of partners gives the enterprise a strong position on the supply chain, he said. It also allows the people involved to exchange information about pricing and product quality. And their partnership with Twin Trading encourages them to work further on quality. This had two consequences: first, the whole sector is

8   As he told a forum at the IofC centre in London in May 2011.

changed, including the behaviour of consumers, raising the level of quality that they expect; secondly, the added value generated by the brand itself goes to the farmers as share owners in the enterprise.

Doherty emphasised the need for "getting the investors right". Food retail was concentrated in a few mainstream supermarkets, which already had market leaders in the products that Divine and Liberation were offering. It was hard for Fairtrade companies to get bank loans due to the highly competitive nature of these markets. Fairtrade social enterprises therefore needed to develop quality brands that appealed to consumers. It was important to work with investors who shared the mission of trade justice, such as Comic Relief and Twin Trading, which are ready to back this process.

While social enterprises had to be commercially sustainable, Doherty highlighted the importance of consumer activists and campaign organizations such as Christian Aid in promoting fair trade.

Another African initiative which has been scaled up to have a national impact comes from Duncan Nduhiu of the Nyala Milk collection scheme in Nyakururu, Kenya, known to many as Maziwa Mingi (Much Milk). In 2000 he was troubled by the lack of milk marketing facilities for the many small farmers in his area. He met with friends to discuss the matter. The first meeting ended in disagreement. He met again with ten close friends and they each decided to find ten more, each person selling a goat to raise funds to found what became the Nyala Milk collection scheme. They started with 240 members, and have grown to over 30,000 members—the largest milk collection scheme in Kenya. It provides a secure income for farmers with as little as one cow. The regular income has transformed the economy of the area: young men can get a loan to buy a bicycle to collect the milk from the farms, and there are improved facilities in the villages. Buyers come to the area for produce, because they see what the local farmers have to offer. Local employment has thus been created for many young people who would otherwise migrate to the towns.[9]

Jewellery, it could be said, is the outward adornment of an inner soul. If this sounds pretentious, it can certainly be said of two social entrepreneurs, Guya Merkle and Sophia Swire.

While Divine Chocolate aims to pay the cocoa-growing farmers of Ghana a fair wage, the Swiss haute jewellery maker Guya Merkle aims to ensure that gold miners in Uganda and Peru also receive a fair wage for their labours.

Merkle is the CEO and owner of Vieri Fine Jewellery, Berlin, founded by her grandfather in Pforzheim, Germany. She belongs to a generation of businesswomen who want to achieve economic success based on ethical principles. She is one of what *Forbes* magazine calls the "impact generation", which is "one of the most significant developments in business today".[10] "According to a study by Deloitte of 5,000 millennials in 18 countries, respondents

9   Farmers' Dialogue newsletter, www.farmersdialogue.org/people-stories
10   *Forbes* Magazine, 26 June 2014

ranked 'to improve society' as the primary purpose of business. This shift in beliefs is compelling businesses to consider not only profitability but also social impact." Such business "will often out-compete its competitors thanks to a new generation of consumers, employees, and investors". Moreover, according to a Nielsen study,[11] "two-thirds of consumers prefer brands that give back to society", *Forbes* reports. "Consumers not only want brands that do good, they also care about the conditions under which the products are made."

Every new jewellery collection produced under Merkle's leadership has used ethically sourced and recycled gold. "Since 2017 we have focussed more and more on the recycling sector", says Merkle, "as gold is an ending resource and we wanted to show alternatives. Nevertheless, I am still using ethically sourced gold and supporting this movement very much."[12] Vieri's website states: "A jewel's true beauty is indicated not by aesthetic standards alone, but also by its ethical quality."[13]

As demand for gold rises dramatically, in line with higher prices, more and more people are also attracted into the labour-intensive, small-scale mining industry. Yet the miners work under conditions that are frequently hazardous or potentially lethal, often in countries that are politically and economically unstable. The miners are exposed to dangerous levels of the highly toxic mercury and cyanide used in gold extraction. Despite major efforts to reduce pollution, very little has been done to protect people and the environment. The damage to health caused by exposure is severe, but few miners are aware of the risks. Merkle aims to address this.[14]

Her father had died in 2007 when she was 21. She was studying communication and management at that time and was working in a social business supporting grassroots projects all over the world. As her parents' only child, she suddenly found herself having to lead the family jewellery business. "Although I had been surrounded by jewellery my whole life, I felt unhappy running the business", she said. At first she tried to continue the business as usual, as her father had run it, but "as no part of me really loved what I was doing, there was no success anymore".

She thought about the possibilities she faced: selling the company or finding out what she really wanted to do with the business and how she could bring her true self into it. Appreciating her family's life work, she chose the second option. Wanting to learn more about jewellery, and to create her own pieces, she went to the GIA (Gemmological Institute of America) in London to gain deeper insights into how jewellery is made and its whole history, including where the materials came from. "I saw pictures of gold mines in

11 Nielsen, 27 March 2012
12 Email to the author, 16 May 2018
13 https://en.vieri.com/
14 As she told Caux TIGE in July 2014

South America and Africa and there was something about them that really touched me."

She found that gold mining is "a very hard and unfair business". Not only is the environment badly affected by it, but also the people working in it. Some 25 million people worldwide work in gold mining, especially in small scale mining. "People working in the field did very disrespected work, under the worst conditions you can imagine. When I first heard of this I was shocked. It was clear to me that I was never going to work in an industry like that. But somehow I couldn't close my eyes to it. I decided to see for myself what the situation really looked like."

She travelled to Peru where she found the working conditions were even harder than she thought. But spending time there, talking to the miners, the communities, the women and children, made clear to her that there was a chance to transform things.

"People there had so many ideas and, suddenly, in Peru, I found the part of myself which I wanted to give to the company. I wanted to create true luxury and a true luxury business because, for me, luxury can't be real luxury if it doesn't bring the best value to everybody who is in touch with it. So, what did I do? I transformed the company into one which produces every single piece out of ethically sourced gold."

This was easier said than done. She faced challenges every day. The market was not ready for it. There was no big demand from the consumer side because customers didn't really know, or care, about the conditions of the gold miners. "It became even clearer to me that just transforming my company into an ethical one is not enough to change the way mining is done today."

Merkle thought more about the possibilities for changing the industry. She decided to create a foundation with the aim of bringing awareness to customers and the jewellery and watch industry, to give miners a voice, a face and the appreciation they deserved, and to picture a positive vision of the gold mining industry, to empower people at its source, and to bring change.

The Earthbeat Foundation was founded in 2012 "and since then we are working hard, every day, to achieve these goals, especially the goals which are not just linked to the gold industry, but the goals which should be achieved for every single activity in the economy. It is about humanity. It is about fairness. It is about empowering people and giving them the chance to express themselves. It is about human beings and that all of us should have the same rights and chances to rise and develop."

The work of the Earthbeat Foundation goes hand in hand with the work of Vieri by working with mining communities at a partnership level rather than exploiting them. Merkle says it is all about finding solutions together—"how we can achieve the right direction and what needs to be done to uplift their standards of living. But it is also about the other side, about why companies in the industry do not work exclusively with ethically sourced gold."

Designing jewellery out of ethically sourced gold is still expensive. "We all know that profit, and maximizing profit, is the biggest driver and decision-maker in businesses, although I do not share this idea", Merkle says. "But it's the reality and this topic is always a matter for jewellery and watch brands. So we try to take this into consideration and, working on business models, aim to avoid extra costs but at the same time making sure that the mining communities are able to sell their gold at fair prices. If one is to bring a change—and I mean a real change—we need a solution that will work for both sides. So, companies need to make small compromises, not big ones, towards humanity and fairness."

Merkle and her colleagues at Earthbeat developed an initiative called Heartbeat Uganda. The aim is to empower communities there towards responsible gold mining, to capacity building and appropriate technology transfer. They have run a pilot project under this initiative called Happy Mine. The aim is to develop a social business including safe mining, agriculture and craftsmanship, by setting up a workshop where women and children in the communities learn how to add value to their gold by designing and creating jewellery.

Yet, surprisingly, their first product has been honey. "Our first success story within the Heartbeat Uganda initiative is heartbeat honey", Merkle reports. "We trained 80 people within the community to become bee-keepers and produce and sell their own honey—so called liquid gold."[15]

The Heartbeat Uganda model, she adds, "should work as an example of how gold mining could work in the future. It should show how mining can become safer, more environmentally friendly and more efficient. In the end, when the mine becomes a social business, and through that a partnership to the jewellery industry directly, the miners will earn much more when they sell their gold, instead of selling it to a lot of middlemen. This should show how they can sustain themselves, how education can be included, and how they can achieve an alternative income to that through debt." Merkle hopes it could become a real social business, where the mining communities will be in partnership at the same level as the "gold demanding" industry.

Explaining the honey initiative further, Merkle adds:

> The focus of the foundation's work has changed slightly as we are still doing a lot of awareness towards ethically sourced gold, but also focussing on alternatives for the mining communities by creating alternative income solutions so they can become more empowered and not so dependent on the gold demanding industry. It is a pilot project and goes hand in hand with business education and education in general. As always, I believe this is the key to a better life.
>
> For me, this is the only way that my company can work in an industry like this. I make no compromises about how I see my company and foundation work, even though it is not an easy way and we have miles to go. Times are changing. We can see that every day in the news and social media, and in stories we hear. I believe in what I am doing and in how I

15 Email to the author, 16 May 2018

am doing it. This is my drive every day. It's about creating beauty. It's about creating true luxury that brings wellbeing to everybody that is in touch with it.[16]

While a fair price for gold miners can change their lives, Sophia Swire believes that jewellery could help to transform the economy of Afghanistan. If this sounds far-fetched, her conviction is based on an assessment of Afghanistan's artisan skills, drawing on vast deposits of gemstones including world-class emeralds, lapis lazuli, rubies, spinels, tourmalines and aquamarines among other stones. Swire, a former investment banker in the City of London, set up Afghanistan's first jewellery school—for Prince Charles' foundation, Turquoise Mountain—before becoming the senior gemstones adviser to the Afghan Ministry of Mines, funded by the World Bank.

Afghanistan is home to the world's oldest lapis lazuli mines, dating back 7,000 years. According to a US Geological Survey report in 2010, Afghanistan's untapped mineral deposits, including gold, copper and lithium, could be worth a trillion dollars or more. "Afghanistan is sitting on treasure", Swire told *The Sunday Times* of London.[17] "I want the world to know that it's not just a land of mortar shells, suicide bombers and Taliban." She believes that the gemstone industry "could become a viable alternative to poppy farming, transforming the economy". Given sufficient development assistance—she suggests $10 million over five years—the industry could be worth $300 million annually.

The need for such investment couldn't be more pressing. The United States has spent $7.6 billion on counter-narcotics programmes in Afghanistan since 2001, says the office of the Special Inspector General for Afghanistan Reconstruction. Britain has invested in similar eradication programmes. Yet by October 2014, opium poppy cultivation had hit an all-time high of 209,000 hectares, worth an estimated $3 billion.[18]

Swire is the founder and CEO of the not-for-profit charity Future Brilliance and the social enterprise it owns, Aayenda Jewellery, *aayenda* meaning "future" in Dari. Aayenda's designs are co-created by Afghan women designers and award-winning Western jewellery designers. They showcase Afghan-sourced gemstones. A royalty from sales of Aayenda through Future Brilliance continues to provide skills training and equipment to the artisans.

Swire believes that it is essential to train Afghan artisans in technical and entrepreneurial skills that give them a sustainable way to earn incomes. Women jewellery-makers are able to work from home, a great advantage should the Taliban ever return to power.

Yet "mining techniques in Afghanistan haven't changed in thousands of years and the men work in appalling conditions", Swire told *The Sunday*

16 www.vieri.com; www.earthbeatfoundation.org
17 *The Sunday Times*, 11 July 2010
18 *The Guardian*, 21 October 2014

Times. "They burrow into the rock and support shafts with branches and twigs." They mine with rudimentary crowbars, as she has seen for herself. Substantial investment in the gemstone mining industry is vital as well as in the development of artisan design and technical skills, if the sector is to grow.

In 2013, Future Brilliance took 36 men and women from Kabul and other places in Afghanistan to Jaipur in India for skills enhancement and business training. Jaipur has been a world centre of the gem and jewellery industry for hundreds of years. Swire also chose Jaipur for the training as it is a safe place to operate and she was able to attract world-class talent for training the students. Leading jewellers Annie Fensterstock and Anna Ruth Henriques from the US and the British designer Paul Spurgeon mentored the students, giving them one-on-one tailored training to improve their technical and design skills. They co-created jewellery designs with the artisans that appeal to the taste of fashion-conscious Millennials. The first collection was snapped up by top boutiques and style leaders such as Fred Segal LA and Donna Karan's Urban Zen, among 25 fashion retail outlets. The Future Brilliance students were trained and certified as master trainers and, back in Afghanistan, are passing on the technical and business skills they learnt in India.

People often tell Swire that they are struck by her courage working in Afghanistan, often in the heart of the gemstone-mining areas, which are many days' drive from safety. She is all too well aware of the dangers of life in Afghanistan. She was "profoundly shocked and saddened" by the murder of her friend Dr Karen Woo, a British doctor whom she had encouraged to serve in Afghanistan, and her American colleagues who, returning from a medical mission close to the lapis mines in 2010, were killed by Taliban gunmen.

"I am so inspired by the [Afghan] women in the project because they've taken a much bigger risk than I will ever take in coming to Jaipur", Swire told *The Mail on Sunday.*[19] For them it is a huge step and I am so proud of them." Swire "wants to close the gap between those who have benefitted from [Afghanistan's] wealth (mainly foreign dealers from neighbouring countries) and those who haven't (the Afghan people)."

She hopes that this investment in people—in "human capital" in the jargon of business—will have an impact on the Afghan economy. So far, she estimates that some 1,200 artisans have benefitted from employment through Aayenda Jewelry, including 300 war widows who work from their homes hand-carving the fine beads in the collection. Some of the Jaipur graduates go on to earn up to $300 (£199) a month as gemstone cutters and goldsmiths— more than six times the average Afghanistan wage. Some earn more than double that, as trainers.

Khala Zainab, who lost her husband to the Taleban some years ago, is the inspiration behind the Aayenda Jewelry brand and a co-founder of the Aayenda Jewelry Cooperative.

19 *You* magazine, supplement of *The Mail on Sunday,* 15 September 2013

"She is a human dynamo, responsible for the economies of two villages in northern Afghanistan with her bead-making business", says Swire. "But when we first met her she was illiterate and lacking in design, business and production skills. We knew that if we could train her in these skills—and the skills to impart them to others—she would be able to access and train hundreds of other women in remote villages, who were beyond the reach of foreign aid because of security challenges."

It took six months to persuade Khala's family to allow her to go to Jaipur for the Future Brilliance training. "When she finally arrived", said Swire, "it was clear who was in charge. She was the elder to whom all the students turned—girls and boys—when they had a problem."

Future Brilliance gave Khala bead-making training, one-on-one design training, trainer-of-trainer skills and training in digital literacy. "She took to her solar-powered, sim-card-enabled tablet computer like a duck to water, and I communicate with her in her village, these days, on Skype", said Swire.

Khaza designed the Zada collection for Aayenda Jewelry. "She told us she was inspired by the ancient Bactrian gold jewellery collection, uncovered by Soviet archaeologists close to her village in 1978. The sun, the star and the moon motifs, which are central to her gold-plated collection, are motifs she found and adapted from this Afghan treasure."

Khala Zainab told Future Brilliance that her dream was to train other women, especially widows like her, so that they could earn a living. With a royalty payment from Aayenda Jewelry, Khala was able to complete the construction of a training workshop in her village and outfit a shop in Mazar-e-Sharif, the nearest town. She receives ongoing support from Future Brilliance and Aayenda to participate in jewellery sales in Kabul and in India. "Most excitingly for me", said Swire, "she has gone on to train over 100 women in remote villages and she continues to market their product locally and internationally."

Future Brilliance also trained her in quality control, which remains a challenge for many of the artisans. "Khala has finally 'got it' and the quality of her beads is now so good that she is supplying major jewellery companies in India and to the legendary Bali-based jewellery designer John Hardy, who is particularly exacting when it comes to quality", Swire said. "He told me he is mesmerised by her deep blue, lapis beads. Donna Karan loved them too. They're so fine, they look like silk thread."

Another of Swire's protégés is Roya Hayat, a half-Afghan, half-Chitral woman born in Kabul and educated in the first school sponsored by Swire and her mother through the educational charity Learning for Life. Roya went on to earn her Masters in Gender and Development at the London School of Economics.

I first met Sophia Swire at an event at the Royal Geographical Society in London in 1998. It was an appropriate place to meet a natural-born traveller and adventurer. The event was the launch of her documentary film about the life of Muhammad Ali Jinnah, the founding father of Pakistan, commissioned

by Channel 4 TV. It was in aid of the UK educational charity Learning for
Life which Swire and her friend Charlotte Bannister-Parker had founded to
support village schools for girls in rural Pakistan, in traditionally patriarchal
communities that actively disapproved of girls' education.[20]

Swire had been a high-flying merchant banker with Kleinwort Benson in
the City of London. But the cut-throat atmosphere on the trading floor after
Black Monday, the financial crash of 1987, appalled her. "Also, I couldn't
justify a career that involved taking commission whether equities went up or
down and didn't really contribute to the world. I wanted to use my life for
something I believed in", she told me.

Even from an early age, she had been motivated "to combat conflict and
fight for fair play since childhood", as she told *Brava* magazine. "I can't tol-
erate abuse. When I was 13, I stormed into my headmaster's study to stop
him from violently beating a foreign student. He was drunk. We were all ter-
rified of him. I remember the girl shaking as I led her by the hand out of his
study to safety. He never looked me in the face again. I think that moment
might have set the tone for my life."[21]

After Black Monday she took herself on a three-week holiday to Pakistan's
North-West Frontier Province (now renamed Khyber Pakhtunkhwa or KPK).
Arriving in Chitral, a magical snow-bound valley in the foothills of the Hindu
Kush Mountains bordering on Afghanistan, she felt she had found her spiri-
tual home.

A local Pakistani district commissioner, Javed Majid, approached her, out
of the blue, on her 25th birthday. He asked her to return to Chitral with
school books and British friends to help him found an English medium
school. This, she told me, was her *kismet*, her destiny.

Swire responded by recruiting friends and family, resigning from her City
job, and returning a few months later with 250 kilos of school supplies,
funded by her final City bonus. The experience of witnessing how a single
school could uplift the economic outlook for an entire community led her to
understand the transforming power of education. And so Learning for Life
was born. The charity helped to establish over 250 schools in Pakistan, India
and Afghanistan. Swire was later honoured with the Pakistan Achievement
Award for empowering the women and girls of Pakistan through education.

Returning to London, but still wanting to retain her connection with the
region, Swire started one of the first ever fairtrade fashion brands, Sophia
Swire London, which developed access to markets for the hand-made products of Himalayan artisans.

The British Council wrote of her: "With corporate social responsibility and
sustainability at the heart of all her work, (Swire) launched and managed an
innovative and profitable, ethical luxury fashion brand, working with artisans
in Nepal and India and spearheading the launch of the global fashion for

20 http://www.learningforlifeuk.org/
21 *Brava Style*, 9 March 2018

pashmina shawls in the 1990s."[22] This led to a significant increase in Nepal's GDP. Her cashmere line sold successfully in stores such as Harrods and Neiman Marcus, among hundreds of fashion outlets worldwide, for 15 years. She became known internationally as the "Pashmina Queen".

In 2007, Swire attended the London film premiere of *The Kite Runner*, whose producers she had introduced to Kabul orphanages. There she met Rory Stewart, former diplomat and now Secretary of State for International Development. He insisted she put her fashion business on hold to go to Kabul and establish Afghanistan's first jewellery school at his charity, Turquoise Mountain, which was developing artisan skills and renovating the ancient heart of Kabul. She flew out there shortly after and, with the support of the local and international trainers she recruited, established the school. She invited the London-based fair-trade jeweller Pippa Small to Kabul to design the first Afghan-made collection and, using her experience in fashion marketing, launched it during London Fashion Week the same year.

Swire lived in Kabul from January 2008 to June 2011—her first year in the Fort of the Scorpions, a building where alarmingly scorpions would fall onto her bed in the night; the second year in a USAID compound; and the third year with an Afghan family. She continued to travel to Afghanistan until 2015, when security conditions became too challenging, even for her.

She co-founded Aayenda Jewelry in 2013 to give Afghan artisans their own brand and give bead-makers, jewellers and gem-cutters from all over the country access to markets. The artisans then formed a co-operative to support each other and help to build a more professional, responsible jewellery sector.

The grant funding for the start-up finished in 2014, but the brand is growing from strength to strength. New orders and new collections are being made in Afghanistan. Royalty payments are funding ongoing training. The Brazilian model and actress Alessandra Ambrosio was featured wearing Aayenda jewellery on the front cover of *Cosmopolitan* magazine all over the world. "It was incredible publicity for the Afghans", says Swire.

"Of course there are still challenges, but four years on, it's now self-sufficient and the brand is being passed to the artisans." The cooperative is up and running and has elected a board of lapidary artisans led by an Afghan management team which is strong and experienced enough to take over the trading company and continue to grow it. "The elected chair is an Afghan-British financier, so can straddle East and West and address all the Know Your Customer challenges that come with doing business in a conflict zone. Future Brilliance has done its job and I am finally free to move on!" says Swire.[23]

In 2015 she received the Humanitarian Innovation Award for Social Entrepreneurship at the United Nations in New York. Speaking on a panel

22   https://creativeconomy.britishcouncil.org/media/uploads/files/cli_2010_london_p rogramme_december_10.pdf

23   www.futurebrilliance.net; www.aayendajewelry.com

there during Women's Entrepreneurship Day she said that economic empow-erment for women is necessary if Afghanistan is going to work its way out of extreme poverty, the fermenting ground of Islamic extremism. Those who are in jobs don't need to take up arms: "Nothing stops a bullet faster than a job."

These days, Swire is a sought-after thought leader and speaker at con-ferences, schools and think tanks all over the world. She told her dramatic story, literally over the world, on International Women's Day 2018 during Lufthansa's remarkable Flying Lab—a special flight from Frankfurt to Houston, Texas, for the SxSW tech, media and cultural festival in March 2018.[24]

She speaks on the importance of "future-proofing" education, skills and business; the importance of incorporating purpose into for-profit companies and the value of gender equity in the workplace. As a result, women founders in tech, education and sustainable businesses, from Silicon Valley to Berlin and London, have reached out to her, seeking mentorship, advice and invest-ment. And, as she told the 500 tech entrepreneurs aboard the Dreamliner at 40,000 feet above the Atlantic Ocean, "The time has come for me to support women back home. I believe in answering calls when they are persistent and the time is right. I won't stop supporting the Afghan artisans. But you can be sure that whatever I do next will include investing in skilled, passionate women entrepreneurs who can turn a profit and change the world, when given the chance."

So, for Swire, life has come full circle—back to finance, only this time with passion and with purpose.

While Swire sees the development of the gemstone industry and jewellery design as a way of developing the Afghan economy, community leaders in Jamaica focused on speciality food products.

They come from the village of Walkerswood in the St Ann district of Jamaica, birthplace of reggae legend Bob Marley and not far from the northern coastal resort of Ocho Rios.

In Walkerswood, a remarkable experiment in social cohesion and commu-nity development has taken place over recent decades. It is the home of Walkerswood Caribbean Foods, an international Jamaican food brand that exports some 80 per cent of its products.

Walkerswood's self-help projects aim to be a model for rural development, countering the drift to the big cities in search of jobs which plagues many developing economies. The experiment attracted the attention of a Vice-Premier of China, Keng Piao, who visited in 1979, and Prince Charles in 2000.

At the heart of the Walkerswood experiment is the relationship of trust built between Afro-Caribbean entrepreneurs, including the late Woody Mitchell, Managing Director of the company and winner of the Norman Manley Award for "excellence in service to the community", and a white land-owning family that might have been mistrusted as members of the privileged "plantocracy".

The story goes back to the 1930s. Minnie Pringle, daughter of one of Jamaica's largest land owners, inherited Bromley, the colonial house overlooking Walkerswood. Her father, Sir John Pringle, had owned 50 estates including Laughing Water, where scenes from the first James Bond film *Dr No* were filmed.

One Bromley visitor was the renowned social reformer Thom Girvan, who in 1940 launched Jamaica's first Pioneer Club in Walkerswood. It spearheaded rural development. Girvan headed up the social welfare programme of People's National Party founder Norman Manley. Walkerswood's Pioneer Club was the first development in this programme. Two villagers, Alton Henry and Peter Hinds, took up the baton. They developed the 800-acre Lucky Hill farm cooperative, the first of its kind in the Caribbean. Henry was a strong Baptist and Hinds was a natural leader despite being illiterate.

Minnie Pringle's daughter, Fiona Edwards and grandsons Johnathan and Roddy continued Bromley's tradition of community involvement. Fiona was "enjoying a wild life" when she encountered the 1930s spiritual revival movement the Oxford Group. This made her "want to do something" to get involved in the Walkerswood community.

Her two sons inherited some of this social and spiritual ethos. Johnathan Edwards helped to develop the Walkerswood Community Council, launched in 1973, while his brother Roddy headed its unemployment committee. They were determined to create local jobs. Roddy had come to realise that he had benefitted from "a grand theft from people who had not been paid properly for their part in the nation's development". Like all Jamaicans, he was well aware of the history of slavery in a country where, at the height of the slave trade, African slaves outnumbered whites by 16 to one.

He and other Walkerswood villagers launched Cottage Industries in 1976, at first selling jerk pork to the eight bars in the surrounding area. It soon became the first company to bottle and market Jamaica's celebrated jerk seasoning. Other products followed and, as the market expanded, villagers found employment in the company, renamed Walkerswood Caribbean Foods, and on nearby farms producing the raw materials.

But then crisis hit. It was caused by a national drought in 1996–1997. As crops dried up, the cost of escellion (spring onions), a jerk seasoning ingredient, shot up from J$15 to J$95 per pound.

The company might not have survived but for the intervention of a new start-up banker, Peter Bunting. The son of a dairy farmer, he was a former MP for the People's National Party. He said he was "captured by the Walkerswood story and the challenge of bringing employment to rural communities at a time when the commercial and the social seemed to be in conflict". He took a risk and made a much needed loan to the company.

The support from his investment bank, Dehring Bunting and Golding Ltd, which he described as a "socially conscious bank", was one sixth of the bank's total assets at the time. Moreover it was not all one-way traffic. Walkerswood, he said, "affected my own thinking and social consciousness within my own company, in the way that we treat our employees—including profit sharing and bonuses".

Bunting never regretted his support for Walkerswood Caribbean Foods, not least because of its "high value brand image" at the quality end of the market, and strong foreign exchange earnings.

The company's image, logo and bottle labels, capturing the sunshine and vibrant colours of Jamaica, were developed by artist and author Virginia Burke, whose *Eat Caribbean* was Jamaica's best-selling cook book in 2006.

In 2005, the company took a further major step, investing US$6 million in a 15-acre plant, across the valley from Bromley. This was largely thanks to a major equity stake from Jamaican businessman, Ray Chang. Chang had been particularly impressed hearing Woody Mitchell, the company's Managing Director, on a radio interview. In its detailed planning, the 3,700 square-metre building was structured to channel rain water and waste water, through a reed bed purification area and into a pond before being made available to surrounding farms. And some of the offices, including Mitchell's and Edwards', were cooled by breeze and fan, and not by air-conditioning.

Logistically, it might have made more sense to locate the new factory near the port of Kingston, to facilitate exports, rather than two hours away in Walkerswood. But the company was keen to maintain its commitment to community and rural development.

The ceremonial ground breaking for the new plant was performed by Jamaica's then Governor General, Sir Howard Cooke, a regular visitor to Bromley since the 1960s. As a young Fabian socialist and politician of the People's National Party, Sir Howard used to attack the privileged plantocracy, accusing them of not making themselves available to educate Jamaicans or make land available. "But", he said, "Walkerswood was unique, in which the great house was very dominant in the life of the people, as a teaching point, as a point to create growth." It was unusual, he said, to find people from the plantocracy who understood and practised a social and community ethos. "Walkerswood is an example of what spirituality can do for the people", he commented.[25]

The "spirituality" was reflected in the food company's voluntary morning worship for any of the staff. On the day I visited in 2006, while researching this story, 15 people took part in the canteen, singing "Let the spirit of the Lord come down" and offering up extemporary prayers. "We want this to be a place where love spreads across the nation", declared Lesept Smith afterwards. He had worked in the packaging area for 13 years and paid tribute to the late "aunt" Zoe Ellis, a packing supervisor whose idea it was to bring daily devotions to the company.

25 Interview with the author in Kingston, Jamaica (Smith 2007)

At that time, the factory employed 160 people, making 23 products, including coconut rundown sauce, Solomon Gundy fish paste, chutney, guava jam, rum marmalade as well as it celebrated jerk seasoning. Equally importantly, it provided a market for some 3,000 farmers and seasonal pickers across Jamaica, who supplied the ingredients, including scotch bonnet peppers, escallion, ackee fruit, callaloo (spinach) leaves, Jamaican ginger (reputed to be the best in the world) and thyme.

A 2005 World Bank report on the Caribbean reported that Walkerswood's success in the market place "has had an economic multiplier effect throughout its community", generating a steady income for local farmers. The company exported 80 per cent of its output, to grocery chains and shops in the Caribbean, North America and Europe.[26]

The company also kept an eye on salary levels, including employees in North America and Europe. Top to bottom salary ratio was 11:1 and top to average was 4:1.

"Walkerswood is an oasis in rural Jamaica", said Hopeton Dunn, an academic at the University of the West Indies and Chairman of the Broadcasting Commission of Jamaica. "It has helped to create a model community in which those who had privilege and prosperity are working alongside those who are dispossessed, in a sharing way, creating a symbol to the whole of Jamaica of what might be when there is a social conscience and collaboration."

Communities such as Walkerswood also counter the destructive side of globalization, commented Doreen Frankson, one of Jamaica's leading business women who was President of the Jamaican Manufacturers' Association, 2003 to 2007. Globalization, she said, "has been very damaging because of opening up markets here to the world. We are struggling to be competitive. Companies like Walkerswood, that are indigenous and have a niche market, are the direction we should be going."[27]

Woody Mitchell, wheel-chair bound since a car accident in 1972, said that Walkerswood's young farmers were finding dignity in working on the land. They were realizing that farming was not just for the elderly. And while unemployment was officially at 12 per cent nationally, there was no "compulsory unemployment" in Walkerswood.

Mitchell, who died unexpectedly in 2017 aged 68, said that he had found dignity and a divine purpose in his role at Walkerswood. He had been a 25-year-old laboratory scientist at Jamaica Reynolds Mines when the car accident broke his back. The driver had gone straight over a traffic island, tipping the Land Rover into its side and throwing Mitchell out onto the stump of a tree.

26 World Bank Time to Choose report, 2005: http://siteresources.worldbank.org/LACEXT/Resources/317250LAC.pdf See also "Tasting local flavour", *The Guardian*, 27 April 2007: https://www.theguardian.com/world/2007/apr/27/outlook.development
27 Interview with the author (Smith 2007, p 83)

Reynolds Mines helped him to take a correspondence course in accountancy, which gave him employment helping small business people, while he lived at his parents' home in Walkerswood.

He got a job with Cottage Industries in the late 1970s, delivering fudge and other products to gift shops in a station wagon with automatic gears and hand controls. But he was "petrified" that he would end up with body sores. Driving was not the best way to avoid this. So it was a godsend to him when he became Managing Director of the fledgling Walkerswood Caribbean Foods in 1983.

Mitchell characterized his relationship with Edwards, the company's Chairman till 2008, as "great partners together. He has his views and at times they might not converge with mine. But at the end of the day we are aiming for the same goals. Roddy and I have got on great over the years."[28]

Mitchell first met his wife, Pat, at the Walkerswood community council meetings. Throughout the food company, stability of employment had an unexpected side effect: encouraging marriage amongst the employees, with some ten marriages taking place. This was significant in a country where many were born outside wedlock, despite the nation's strong Christian traditions.

The company also had a vision that generating enough rural jobs would also prevent vulnerable young women, desperate for an income, from drifting to the cities and being caught up as drug mules in the notorious drug trafficking trade.

Despite the joy at moving into the new purpose-built factory, the next years became as difficult as any of the previous 30, Edwards says. "There were real problems with hurricanes, fluctuations of exchange-rates and management of debt."[29] But three other problems were very much in the company's hands.

Firstly, the rapid growth needed new managers. "Divisions emerged which we could not adequately bridge. All the factors of race, gender, class, personal ambition and jealousy played their parts. This cost us dearly, but the lessons learnt became part of all our experience data banks, and I am glad we didn't choose to remain in a previous comfort zone." The lesson learnt, he says, was to "spare no effort in building teamwork on the basis of conscience-led decision-making, but accept that divisions that have built up over centuries will often elude one's best efforts. This doesn't mean giving up but accepting that the timetable for reconciliation is not in our hands. Some enduring friendships across the divides will be built and remain a yeast in society, and a challenge for future generations."

Secondly there was a case of moral compromise. A dilemma appeared when an export pass was mistakenly granted for a bigger tin of ackee fruit than the size they had sent in for testing. They were told that the mistake could not be officially corrected, despite the urgent need to send off the order. "We wrote out export documentation stating it was the bigger cans leaving the country", recalls Edwards.

28 Interview with the author (Smith 2007, p 85)
29 Interview with the author (Smith 2015, pp 139–140)

This was not absolutely honest, even though the cans leaving had passed the test. I was part of this decision and it wasn't honest. I came to realize that this practice continued to be used if we had urgent orders, and I always felt that my compromise in condoning this played a part in contributing to lower standards in the company. The practice was later stopped, but damage had been done. The lesson learned was that moral standards are key helps when we are faced with moral dilemmas, as well as friends and colleagues with whom one can share the challenges and help one to make a mature decision.

Thirdly there were cases of drugs and corruption. "We discovered drugs were to be shipped in one of our containers. We were never able to conclusively track down all who were involved, but it undermined morale and there were further thefts even though they were not drug-related. Corruption operates at every level—there is dishonesty at the managerial as well as the shop floor level. Change is needed in our national and company cultures. The changes have to do with choices over fairness as well as stopping theft."

The divisions and corruption, says Edwards, added to high debt on the factory, exchange-rate fluctuations and hurricanes affecting crops, drastically hitting the company's bottom line. They took the decision to sell the company in 2008. Thanks to the strong brand name, two well-resourced groups bid to buy it. The new owners cut back on the product range and the number of employees. They created strong profits and 80 people continued to be employed there, ensuring Walkerswood's strong village community spirit.

Edwards concludes: "My belief remains as strong as ever that ordinary people can change, for the better, the way wealth is created, saved and distributed. More of us need to take the plunge and get involved wherever we are."

Some of those who have taken the plunge are recorded here. They include Merel Rumping, Tony Bradley, Bob Doherty, Lisa and Charly Kleissner, Duncan Nduhiu, Guya Merkle, Sophia Swire, Bill Drayton and Jeff Skoll. There are countless others who are creating a whole new paradigm for doing business in the world based on their social awareness and inner conscience. They are committed to social justice and an economy for the common good. From Afghanistan to Colombia, Ghana to Jamaica, and in many other places, they are leading with integrity in the light of global needs.

References

"Hope for landmine casualties", *Changemakers* magazine, December2016; http://cha ngemakersmagazine.org/hope-landmine-casualties/

Smith, Michael, *Great Company*, Initiatives of Change, 2015

Smith, Michael, *Trust and Integrity in the Global Economy: stories of people making a difference*, Caux Books, 2007

12 Thinking heads

The wise owls of academia

Academia, including business schools, plays a critical role in encouraging and nurturing a leadership of integrity, particularly among the next generation of business leaders, in the context of the global economy.

Inside the splendid Beau-Rivage Palace Hotel on the lakeside in Lausanne, Switzerland, Paul Polman, then chief executive of Unilever, is addressing the nearly 150 graduate students of Business School Lausanne at their graduation ceremony on 20 September 2014.[1] They come from all over the world, representing 43 countries. Polman is awarded an honorary doctorate by the university "in recognition of his exceptional contribution to putting sustainability at the core of the corporate world". He in turn commends the boutique university for being "ahead of the pack" in its commitment to global sustainability issues under the leadership of the Dean, Dr Katrin Muff.

Polman was renowned for rejecting demands from institutional investors for quarterly reports of Unilever's results. Quarterly reporting is simply not a sufficient measure of a company's underlying strength and too easily encourages short-term thinking. His company generated annual revenues of more than $50 billion, through products ranging from Lifebuoy and Dove soaps and Surf detergent to Marmite and Magnum ice cream.

He reminds the graduates of their privileged responsibilities. In China, he says, only five per cent of the population graduates. "Put yourself at the service of others", he urges them. "You have enormous liberty and enormous responsibility. How do you get traction on sustainable living from consumers?" asks the CEO whose products are sold to consumers in 90 countries. This is his challenge. Businesses are changing, he asserts. "They are coming together to tackle the global issues. We are still living in a world we should not accept. Eight hundred million people go to bed hungry, not knowing if they will wake up in the morning. We need to lift billions of people out of poverty." He quotes the Oxfam statistic for that year that the world's 85 richest people have the same wealth as the world's poorest 3.5 billion people. (The figure for the richest individuals is now even lower.)

---

1   The author was present at the event, as a guest of Dr Katrin Muff, then the Dean of the University.

Polman makes reference to Unilever's Sustainable Living Plan. With an increasing world population "we can double our business in 90 countries", he says, with an eye to sustaining profitability. But he is also aware that corporations such as his have a responsibility towards the planet's sustainability; towards climate change and the environment. "Half the world's deforestation is caused by the need for food", he says.

The leader of one of the world's mightiest corporations has a simple definition of what constitutes a leader: "A leader is anyone who has the ability to influence others." The urgent need is for people working together "in a high level of engagement, humanity and humility" in order to create "a fairer, more equitable, more sustainable world". It is all a far cry from the profit motive and shareholder value typical of many corporations, though the implication is that these are also well served by doing the right thing, by putting people first.

Polman is not the only Dutchman to have led a multinational corporation with such ideals. The late Frits Philips, the former Chairman and CEO of the Philips Electronic multinational, based in Eindhoven, always maintained that "Profit is important; people are more important."

The theme of the graduation ceremony is "Switzerland as a global sustainability hub", a notion that is predictably supported overwhelmingly from the floor by a mass showing of green cards in favour, rather than red cards against. For her part, Katrin Muff, the Dean, urges the graduates:

> Be a positive force: focus on how to make a significant difference—be part of the solution rather than focusing on the problem;
>
> have the courage to lead: inspire others to do their best as well— don't hide in the shade;
>
> be an entrepreneur—remember what we say at BSL: entrepreneurship is above all an attitude—everybody can be an entrepreneur at any level of any organization;
>
> make responsible choices: respect the planet, your partners and yourself and rather than pointing fingers at others' mistakes, ask yourself, "What can I do now?";
>
> be a professional: keep your agreements, be on time and be prepared;
>
> and keep on learning: you don't need to have all the answers; keep on welcoming change, be open to new things, remain curious and encourage others and yourself to keep asking the real questions.

Muff continues: "Dare to make a tough choice, and be prepared to stop, reflect and correct if you find out that a decision has not led you in the right direction. You don't need to get it right every single time. But choose, take a stand, voice your opinion and trust your gut feeling. We need leaders who dare to be different, who dare to question the status quo and who get the big picture of how to make this world a better place. Be part of the change that we need now, in these shaky and uncertain times. We know that YOU CAN!"

Katrin Muff describes the Caux conference centre in Switzerland (see Chapter 6) as "an exquisite space of transformational beauty, power and depth at all levels brought together at a human scale—simply breath-taking!" She is part of a growing movement of business schools worldwide that are mandated to teach business ethics. This is a fallout of the financial crash of 2008. MBA courses are waking up to their responsibility to teach ethical business leadership. Some universities, says Muff, are scrambling to catch up.

Yet, perhaps surprisingly, this is not new. "Business schools have a rich treasure of wisdom, idealism and vision that they can draw on to move away from the *homo economicus* model", writes the American economist Herbert Gintis, External Professor at the Santa Fe Institute, New Mexico. "It is an inheritance that can be traced to the mission of the university as social institution charged with advancing the public good."[2]

"Nowadays", Gintis continues, "the notion that those who lead and manage our society's major private economic institutions might provide, or be responsible for providing, a public good is quite foreign to our way of thinking about management. Yet this idea was often voiced by those who led American business schools in the early days of their existence." Gintis quotes a speech given in 1925 by Wallace B Donham, the second Dean of Harvard Business School, entitled "The social significance of business". In it, Donham declared that the "development, strengthening and multiplication of socially minded business men is the central problem of business." Even then, over 90 years ago, Donham called for "the multiplication of men who will handle their current business problems in socially constructive ways."

Gintis comments: "The founders of business schools never dreamt that the sole purpose of the corporation was to serve only one master, the shareholder. Nor could they have ever imagined that students would be trained in a world view that conceived of managers as self-interested with no consideration of any other values or imperatives but their own wallets." He concludes: "Business schools need to recover professional ethics. To this end, business schools have an institutional responsibility to present students with a model of behaviour that inspires them to respect other institutions in society, especially basic units such as the family and community, and to inspire students to accept the responsibilities and obligations that come with occupying society's most powerful positions."

Nowadays the worldview of business responsibility also has to adapt to the challenges of climate change, environmental preservation, warring states and the well-being of the planet in which businesses and big corporations operate. Boardrooms have to address the common good of all stakeholders in society.

Such issues are on the agenda of the 50+20 initiative of leading business schools, of which Muff is a moving spirit. It was launched 50 years after the agenda for management education had been reset in the 1950s and in time for the Rio+20 Earth Summit in 2012. 50+20 is described, on its website, as "a

2   *Financial World* magazine, London, August/September 2014

collaborative initiative that seeks to learn of new ways and opportunities for management education to transform and reinvent itself. We are asking critical questions about the state of the world, the emerging societal issues, the dominant economic logic, the purpose of business, the crucial role of leadership, and the challenges facing management education."[3]

Muff spells out more about the 50+20 initiative:[4]

> We presented it in Rio for the Rio+20 conference. We said isn't it high time that we as business educators looked at how we would go about developing different kinds of leaders the world needs for the future. We worked for two years in a collaborative process involving about 300 people from around the world to come up with a radically new vision for management education.
>
> When we presented our vision in Rio...we had some hopes of what this change would create and initiate. But the reality has far exceeded our wildest aspirations. In the meantime the two biggest governing bodies in academia, EFMD (European Foundation for Management Development) and AACSB (Association to Advance Collegiate Schools of Business), have adopted, if you want, a new "law" forcing the top 1,500 business schools in the US and in Europe—and that touches everybody—to include responsibility and sustainability, not only in their teaching and learning, but also in their research and the way they operate as institutions, effective immediately. We never thought this could happen.
>
> So change is happening. What have we actually proposed? When we said we need to change the way business educators worked, we started off by saying, well, what kind of a world do we need? What is our challenge? For that we looked at what is actually happening from a social, environmental and economic perspective. What kind of a world do we live in and what would we like to have? We realized that we wanted to contribute to a society where all nine billion people can live well and within the limits of the planet by 2050.
>
> Then we asked ourselves, what does that mean for business? Very quickly we realized that business needs to shift dramatically from serving a limited amount of shareholders with short term profit maximization to fundamentally rethinking what they are doing to contribute to society and to serve the common good. That's a huge paradigm shift. As a result we said, well, what do we need? There is change at the individual level, there is a change at the institutional level and there is change for all of us at the global level. We need different kinds of leaders to enable business to embrace this paradigm shift, this transformation.
>
> The challenge for business leaders is twofold. If you are a current business leader, not only do you have to transform your business from an

---

3   https://grli.org/resources/5020-agenda/
4   Dr Muff was addressing the 2013 Caux TIGE conference.

existing paradigm that is very strong, and very difficult to challenge, towards contributing to society, but you also need to work on your personal transformation. You yourself are challenged to change. This is different from the new leaders we are educating in school. Of course we've got the personal development challenge there as well. But they don't have these two parallel challenges. So for a business leader in an existing business organization we're really asking a lot. I think we need to accompany such leaders quite differently to how we have in the past.

50+20 is a shared, open platform that belongs to anybody; it's not branded. We said that rather than competing to be the best in the world, which is what business schools have done so far, we need to work together in order to be the best for the world. So we've shifted from competition to collaboration.

All this adds to and reflects the Aspen Institute's Business and Society Programme, founded in 1998 by Judith Samuelson. This began to rank business schools and MBA programmes in how well they integrated social, environmental and governance issues and values into their curricula. The aim is to "support established and emerging business leaders in putting values at the heart of business."[5]

Equally, the UN's Global Compact launched the UN Principles for Responsible Management Education in 2007, drawn up by the deans of some 60 business schools. It now involves over 700 participating institutions. With an emphasis on the UN's Sustainable Development Goals and on incorporating ethics and values-based business education, this over time has the potential to affect the mind-sets of future business leaders.[6]

Another academic who addresses the challenge of "personal transformation" is Professor Roger Steare, Visiting Professor in the Practice of Organizational Ethics and Corporate Philosopher in Residence at Cass Business School in the City of London. Cass is the leading institution for training the City's future bankers and financiers. Steare is the author of *Ethicability*, which is also the name of the training programme he and his colleagues deliver to staff in the big banks and other institutions.[7] Over 120,000 people from more than 200 countries have carried out his online psychometric profiling MoralDNA[TM] test, developed in collaboration with Athens-based chartered psychologist Pavlos Stamboulides.[8] It is described as "a personality test which

5   www.aspeninstitute.org/policy-work/business-society
6   www.unprme.org; the United Nations Global Compact, launched by the late UN Secretary General Kofi Annan, is a voluntary initiative based on CEO commitments to implement universal sustainability principles including employment and human rights, environmental protection and the stance against corruption. Businesses sign up to this commitment and are monitored for their performance each year: www.unglobalcompact.org
7   https://thecorporatephilosopher.org/
8   https://moraldna.org/

throws light on our ethics and moral values; how we make decisions about what's right and wrong." The website says that "the profile it creates is designed to help you understand your moral values, how you prefer to make good decisions and 'do the right thing'. We emphasize the word prefer, because how we make decisions and do the right thing develops throughout our lives and this can also vary according to the circumstances we find ourselves in."

This is a step in the right direction and the test, through the questions it asks, is designed to prevent people from giving the "right" answer rather than their honest answer. It is a moot point whether it really has the power to affect changes in behaviours, especially when people come under workplace pressures to compromise. But such tests do help to raise awareness of the need for personal choices.

Steare spoke at a forum on "Capitalism towards the common good: regulation or culture and character?" in November 2010:[9]

> After becoming a local CEO in a global services business, I dropped out of the dysfunction we call corporate life and became a professional ethicist. My first business partner was Abbot Christopher Jamison at Worth Abbey and we began a journey…to bring humanity back into business; to redefine capitalism not as the all-consuming ethos of the "vampire, blood-sucking squid",[10] but in terms of the morality and sustainability of family, friendship and community.
>
> At some point in recent history, the meaning of the word economy has been corrupted. Economy used to mean "less", "thrift" or, at most, "enough". If I press the economy button on our washing machine, even I know it means "less" not "more" water, detergent and power. Yet if you listen to politicians, the media, business leaders—and of course economists—the word economy now means "more". And whilst three per cent per annum GDP growth doesn't sound like very much, this means doubling the size of the economy every 20 years.
>
> The problem with this all-consuming ethos is that our planetary resources are not only scarce, they're finite. If all seven billion of us were to live the American dream, we'd need about four more planet Earths to sustain us.
>
> Our economic wealth is 16 times what it was in 1950. But when two billion fellow beings live on less than $2 a day, I find it obscene for British citizens to talk about economic misery and material poverty.
>
> It is also clear to me that our addiction to economic growth has created a poverty of the soul that is corrupting our family lives, our friendships and our communities. When a relationship becomes difficult, we

9   Held in the London centre of Initiatives of Change.
10   The derogatory phrase used to describe Goldman Sachs at the time of the financial crash of 2008

trade it in for a new one. And we treat our homes like a commodity to buy and sell instead of the safe place of belonging that our families need. This philosophy of growth for its own sake is as addictive as tobacco, alcohol and crack cocaine. It is also just as deadly. We must again define economy as thrift and fairness—the moral virtues of temperance and justice. Our mantra might be: "For those with nothing, enough means more. But for those with enough, more means nothing for those with nothing."

Next, let's reset our understanding of money. Let's read what it says on the front of a £20 note. "I promise to pay the bearer on demand the sum of twenty pounds." And on the back of a US$20 bill, it says "In God We Trust". We have forgotten that money has no intrinsic value. Money is simply a promise we trust. Corporations don't make money; they simply keep or break their promises. That's how they create or destroy trust. That's how they create or destroy value. The bottom line is deeply rooted in the moral values of honesty and faith.

Steare emphasized that capitalism is a relatively new term:

For most of our history, money has been a means of exchange rather than a factor of production. Human beings have traded and exchanged goods and services for millennia and money has simply facilitated this process. Therefore, we can reasonably argue that financial capital is not, I repeat not, a prerequisite for well-being. Indeed, the contemporary renaissance of mutuals, not-for-profits and social enterprises is further evidence that, at best, capitalism is incidental to human endeavour and prosperity.

Here in the UK we are privileged to live in a more-or-less free market, liberal, social democracy. Yet the joint-stock company represents the antithesis of this ideal. The corporation is a feudal, rapacious plutocracy run too often by an unelected mercenary elite with morals not far different from gun-toting bandits in 4x4s. They might not be firing bullets, but take a look around the abandoned suburbs of Detroit and you will see the desolation of a war-zone. A capitalism that usurps family life, and that destroys homes and neighbourhoods is one that I believe we now need to consign to the history books.

And yet there is hope. If we have the courage to confront the brutal realities of our existence together, then we can overcome not only our economic difficulties, but also our social and environmental challenges. In our research into what we call Moral DNA, three moral values not only define our moral character as human beings. People say that these are the virtues to save us from ourselves. Let us replace what Stephen Young[11]

---

11   Stephen Young, the American author of *Moral Capitalism* (2003)

calls "brute capitalism" with an ethos based on the universal moral values of wisdom, fairness and love.

In October 2014, the UK's Chartered Management Institute published a study entitled The Moral DNA^{TM} of Performance, following interviews with more than 2,500 managers in both the private, public and co-operative sectors conducted by Steare and his colleagues. This found that, according to a report in *The Daily Telegraph*, "top performing businesses have a strong ethical stance". "Bosses doing the right thing ethically build better performing business and organizations", wrote the paper's City News Editor, Alan Tovey. "A report by the Chartered Management Institute (CMI) claims to have found links between management focused on morals and values and successful companies and organizations."[12]

The study, Tovey reported, had found that

> strong ethics and high levels of organizational performance went "hand in hand".... But the biggest surprise was how the managers questioned saw their employers. Just 20 per cent of those working in the public sector rated their employer as excellent when it came to ethical behaviour by giving the top score of five out of five. This is half the amount of managers working for listed companies, and just a third of those employed by top-performing cooperatives. When it came to rating organizations as poor for ethics, 13 per cent of public sector bosses said their employer was poor, more than four times the amount in the best performing partnerships. Just ten per cent of listed company managers and seven per cent of those working in private companies rated their employer as poor.

While such a study is a pat on the back for private and cooperative sector organizations, it seems to be a wake-up call for public sector employers, at least in the UK.

Just how much of a rethink is going on in the academic world about the governance, purpose and contribution of business is illustrated by the Frank Bold forum held at Cass Business School in September 2014, quoted in Chapter 3. Its initial report recommends:

> regulatory reform including reforming the (UK) 2006 Act to address corporate purpose and to address "externalities" such as environmental impact;
> board reform to increase worker voice on boards and other issues;
> changes in business practice to expand partnership models, such as the John Lewis Partnership, and other ownership models;
> changes in education to improve how corporate social responsibility is taught in business schools, ensuring it is universally part of the curriculum.

12 Alan Tovey, *The Daily Telegraph*, 29 October 2014

"Business culture and ethics are critical", says the report. "Companies should foster a sense of accountability and transparency in order to reintroduce ethical responsibility and awareness of the firm's relationship with stakeholders."[13]

Alexander Schieffer, who gained his doctorate in leadership at St Gallen University, where he is now a visiting professor, and Ronnie Lessem, founder of Trans4m and Professor of Management at da Vinci Institute of Technology Management in Cape Town, South Africa, advocate Integral Economics, in their book of that title (2010). It aims to draw together the best economic models from the four worlds of East and West, North and South, as well as the "middle Earth" of the Middle East. The aim, they write, is to "pave the way for a sustainable approach to economics, building on the richness of diverse economic approaches from all over the globe". They have successfully applied this approach to economic development working with local people in countries ranging from Slovenia and Egypt to Zimbabwe.

The Integral Economics approach has had a considerable impact in Slovenia, the small central European country bordering on Italy and Austria to the west, with Hungary and Croatia to its east. Slovenia joined the European Union in 2004 and was able to gain funding from the EU for its Integral Green Slovenia initiative. This aims to help the country to go carbon neutral, building on the country's strong history of cooperatives and social entrepreneurship since before the Second World War. The woman behind Slovenia's integral green programme is Dr Darja Piciga, a policy-maker and analyst for the Slovenian government, who is also an independent expert in integral planning for sustainable development.[14]

Working as a civil servant on low-carbon policies for the Slovenian government, Piciga visited Geneva in 2010. There she picked up Lessem's and Schieffer's book and was so intrigued by it that she met them in Caux that summer. She subsequently invited them to Slovenia. Piciga, a cognitive development scientist by background, felt that, after about three decades of so-called real socialism followed by two decades of a rather coarse form of capitalism, "the cognitive map" of the capitalist economic paradigm "wasn't working anymore". She was searching for solutions to global issues, including climate change, migration and food security, and realised just how much these were interconnected. The need was for an integrated, holistic approach. Lessem's and Schieffer's "integral worlds" emphasis resonated with her. Their research had shown how vital it is that a society's outer economic system is aligned with its inner moral compass. With a moral core at the centre, the four cultural points of the global compass, in their model, represent relationships of nature and community (South), inspiration of culture and spirituality (East), knowledge of science and skills (North), and action of finance and enterprise (West).

---

13 http://www.purposeofcorporation.org/corporate-governance-for-a-changing-world_report.pdf
14 Various EU policies are reflected in the good practices presented in the book *Integral Green Slovenia* which shows that smart integration already works.

Lessem and Schieffer began to work in Slovenia with Piciga and several policy makers and practitioners to develop a new conceptual framework for an Integral Green Economy for Sustainable Development, in the context of EU policies. In building this Slovenian model they have complemented traditional concepts of sustainable development, says Piciga, according to the Integral Worlds approach. They describe sustainable development as having four dimensions: environment, economy, society and culture, and emphasize values of social responsibility.

"They didn't build a new development model from scratch", says Piciga.

> Quite the opposite: their argument is that a number of existing EU, national and regional policies and guidelines, measures and instruments, across several policy domains, are already supporting sustainable development goals and the integral green model of development: green and circular economy, social economy and socially responsible entrepreneurship, ethical banking, sustainable development towns and rural areas with organic food and energy self-supply, and revitalization of cultural heritage. A new concept of "smart integration of European Union policies for sustainable development" has been proposed. This is emphasizing and promoting synergies and a cross-sector approach, relying on all four dimensions of sustainable development and placing the values of social responsibility and sustainability in the centre of the economic model.[15]

Take, for instance, Domel. It is an electric motor manufacturer for appliances ranging from vacuum cleaners to garden power tools, air conditioning and the automotive industry. The company was established over 70 years ago and its products are used in 250 million appliances worldwide. But by 2008–2009 the company was in financial crisis, caused by catastrophic flooding and the global financial crisis. A social knowledge-based economic approach has helped the company.

"Darja was able to get business executives there to reconnect with the company's own story in an integral way", Lessem explains. "The company grew out of a metal works cooperative, working in a very steep-sided, narrow valley. Local people there needed to work cooperatively to ensure the safety of everyone." This cooperation shapes their working practices and decision-making to this day. Identifying this as a core, shared value helped the company to articulate its inner moral core. This means "such values aren't just plucked from a company handbook but from the soil of a place", Lessem says. "The values are authentic and rooted in a company's history. You can't impose a model—you've got to find out and work with what already exists."

Darja Piciga has told this story at the annual business conferences in Caux, Switzerland. In their book, Schieffer and Lessem evaluate the stories and experiences emerging from the Caux conferences as being like a "university of

---

15   Email to the author, 3 May 2018

life". The TIGE conferences (Trust and Integrity in the Global Economy) were launched "to bring change around the interdependent issues of economy, environment, sustainability, food security and social enterprise—all based on inner transformation and personal commitment to core moral values", they write.

It is possible for business schools to instil vision and integrity amongst the next generation of business leaders, as institutions from London to Lausanne, Harvard to Rio, Germany to St Gallen, Slovenia to South Africa, are showing.

References

Elworthy, Scilla, *Pioneering the Possible: awakening leadership for a world that works*, North Atlantic Books, 2014

Lessem, Ronnie, and Schieffer, Alexander, *Integral Economics: releasing the economic genius of your society*, Routledge, 2010

Muff, Katrina (editor) et al., *The Collaboratory: a co-creative stakeholder process for solving complex problems*, Routledge, 2014

Philips, Frederik, *45 Years with Philips*, Blandford Press, 1978

Piciga, Darja and Schieffer, Alexander, *Integral Green Slovenia*, Routledge, 2016

Steare, Roger, *Ethicability: how to find what is right and find the courage to do it*, Roger Steare Consulting Ltd, 2008

Young, Stephen, *Moral Capitalism: reconciling private interest with public good*, Berret-Koehler Publishers Inc., 2003

13 Health and welfare

The human face of business leadership

Nowhere is a leadership of integrity more needed than in the healthcare that saves lives. We have already seen, in Chapter 9, how the Mumbai business-man Suresh Vazirani is providing life-saving medical technology to over 100 countries.

The British National Health Service—in the public sector and "free at the point of care"—celebrated its 70th anniversary in July 2018. For all its short-comings and funding challenges, it is seen as an envy of the world. Yet too often there is incompetence and waste, as Margaret Hodge points out in her book *Called to Account* (2016). Hodge, the MP who was Chair of the influ-ential all-party Public Accounts Committee in Parliament, writes about the disastrous, if laudable, attempt to introduce a comprehensive IT system for patient records, one of the largest civil IT programmes in the world, launched by Prime Minister Tony Blair in 2002:

> The sums involved in developing this national IT system were mind-bog-gling. For the entire system, costs rose from an initial £2.3 billion in 2002 to an estimated £11.4 billion nine years later, when we looked at the care records in the summer of 2011. At the time of our hearing, the Depart-ment of Health and the NHS had spent some £6.4 billion on the project as a whole. Just imagine what that money could buy in terms of front-line doctors and nurses and much-needed medical equipment.

She continues:

> The department [of health] was trying to do something completely new and untested, doing it hastily and without securing the buy-in from the users. Most important, they had not defined the product; they did not know what they were buying—with our [tax-payers'] money....
>
> In the end the Department of Health abandoned the concept, but could not extricate themselves from all the contracts. So they are using money identified for one purpose to introduce different, localized, trust-specific solutions which mean that if you do have a serious accident in Cornwall, doctors will not be able to access your records from Carlisle.

The government signed contracts with four firms. Accenture walked away from the £2 billion contract in 2006 and declared in their accounts a provision of £450 million for expected losses. In 2008, negotiations to "reset" the contract with Fujitsu ended up with the departure of Fujitsu and long-drawn-out negotiations to terminate the contract that cost the Department of Health many tens of millions.

Hodge writes that under a new Secretary of State for Health, Jeremy Hunt, the NHS promised to be paperless by 2018. (Since then the NHS National Information Board has published a framework entitled "Personalized Health and Care 2020", describing the strategic direction for IT and data collection and use.)

Hodge concludes:

In the 2015 Spending Review and Autumn Statement, the Treasury gave the NHS yet another £1 billion for new technology to support and produce integrated care records by 2020. Richard Bacon [on the Public Accounts Committee] described the NHS IT programme as "one of the worst and most expensive contracting fiascos in the history of the public sector", but the government had set off on the same journey yet again. I have no doubt that they sincerely believe that they will do better this time around. But I simply observe that the ambition has not been moderated and the political and electoral imperatives have dictated the timeframe. It feels like a case of plus ça change.

Yet the NHS saves millions of lives, including my own after I suffered from peritonitis.

In the USA, the Affordable Care Act, known as ObamaCare, was signed into law by President Obama in March 2010. It gave more Americans, particularly the young and those from poor backgrounds, access to quality health insurance. It had four goals: to expand patient protections; to make health insurance more affordable; to improve the quality of health insurance and healthcare; and to curb health care costs.[1] By the end of 2014, the number of newly insured was estimated to be around 17 million people.[2] Yet its introduction was seen as an ideological struggle between those on the Right who saw it as increasing public expenditure and those on the Left who saw it as a matter of social justice.

In February 2018, India announced what is thought to be world's largest public health scheme. In his budget, the finance minister, Arun Jaitley, said the flagship health insurance scheme would cover more than 100 million poor families and provide 500,000 rupees ($7,825; £5,520) in medical coverage for

1   https://obamacarefacts.com/obamacare-facts/
2   https://www.forbes.com/sites/scottgottlieb/2015/05/14/how-many-people-has-obama
    care-really-insured/

each family annually. "This will be the world's largest government-funded healthcare programme", Mr Jaitley told the Indian parliament.[3] The so-called "Modicare" initiative, named after the Prime Minister, aims to save the lives of nearly1.6 million people, particularly from poor backgrounds, who otherwise would die each year because they cannot afford healthcare. Some Indian states, however, refused to administer it, claiming it was not cost effective.

These developments in the USA, the UK and India affect millions of people's lives at the macro level. What about the care for individuals at the micro level? For, as the old saying goes, each individual is a royal soul.

Like Vazirani's story, there are cases of best practice in the healthcare private sector, on a small scale, driven by a motive of service and not just the bottom line.

While too many companies pay too little attention to their staff, others have excellent welfare policies for their employees—nurturing the "human capital". James Miller, who ran the occupational health company Abermed, tells an unusual story of employee welfare. It illustrates the notion of empathy in business advocated by Bill Drayton, already quoted in Chapter 11.

Miller was the Chairman and Managing Director of the occupational healthcare business Abermed. He went on to become Managing Director of Stella Maris Yachting in Southampton. Abermed, based in Aberdeen, serves the welfare of employees on the North Sea oil rigs:[4]

> The company employed doctors and nurses, administration people, IT staff. All of us were passionate about our areas and we wanted to develop our skills and knowledge and embed the core value of caring for and protecting one another. It doesn't always come naturally in some business cultures for people to be caring for and protecting one another. A lot of business environments are competitive and people really see other people they work with as competitors for promotion or reward. So applying that care was really important.
>
> One of our managers, Phil, came one day and said his wife had been diagnosed with a neurological condition that was very rare, couldn't be treated and was terminal. He had been told that she would probably live between 18 months and five years. The family decided that they wanted to look after her at home and that she would die at home. He felt that he wasn't going to be able to do his job, and so the right thing to do was to resign.
>
> We could think he was showing real concern and care for the rest of us in that he wouldn't be able to carry out his role. But then the challenge for us as a business was our agreed core value—are we caring for him? We decided that our response was to amend his job description. His priority would now be to look after his wife.

3   BBC News 1 February 2018. https://www.bbc.co.uk/news/world-asia-india-42899402
4   James Miller told his story to the 2013 Caux TIGE conference in Switzerland.

In the early stages she was still able to go around, so he could work part-time. But as time went on, he was able to do less and less at work as her condition became worse. But he was able, and wanted, to work from home. A few times he came to me and said he really thought he ought to resign because he didn't think he was pulling his weight. So, we had to remind him what his job description top priority was. And then he realized he was pulling his weight.

Now, the response to that was interesting. At that time we had a venture capitalist investor who had a seat on the board, and was aware of our purpose and core values. They were very interested in our business and saw great potential for profit.

They believed that, yes, we said all those nice things but, at the end of the day, money would talk and we'll be focused on making as much money as possible. In the end they did actually get a very good return, but their response to what we were saying at that time was interesting. As human beings they couldn't disagree with our application of the "care value". So they rationalized it and concluded that it was a good tactic because we would get commitment from Phil after his wife died and so it will work out in the end. That wasn't how we saw it. It was because we said one of our core values was that we will care for one another, not to get "a return on investment".

Phil's wife lived on for over five years; it was a long and hard time. Then she died and in time he did come back to full-time work. He wanted to get stuck in but after a few months he found that he'd been out of work for so long that he wasn't enjoying it. He didn't really want to carry on working and so he took early retirement. That's what he wanted and it suited where he was in his life.

That was one of the challenges we felt with living our core values. It actually cost us money to keep him looking after his wife, but it was the right thing to do because we had set it as a core value. The value to the business was in the maintenance of a caring, loving and human culture that is beyond measurement!

Such a case story may be comparatively straightforward for a small business to implement, including the buy-in of the management board. But what about transforming the healthcare culture of much larger organizations?

A Bengali Indian orthopaedic surgeon, Dr Amit Mukherjee, tells a remarkable story of how "a spark"—an arresting thought—he received in the middle of a routine operation saved the life of a three-year-old girl called Jaya. She had two deformed feet and in the middle of the operation to correct them her heart stopped beating. Mukherjee and his anaesthetist thought they had lost her. The anaesthetist twice injected her heart with atropine, to no effect. The arresting, compelling thought that Mukherjee had was to "use a larger needle". Taking the atropine from the technician, he injected it deep into her heart. After a few terrifying seconds, Jaya's heart started beating again. With the aid of a resuscitator, they pumped oxygen into her lungs and suddenly with a jerk she started breathing again. The operation was successful. The "arresting thought" had saved her life.[5]

Mukherjee not only saved the little girl's life; he also saved a Tata company hospital from closure. How this came about, Mukherjee also attributes to his obedience to the "inner voice" of conscience and inspiration which Mahatma Gandhi used to talk about.

In India, employees often depend on private healthcare in a society where there are not sufficient numbers of public hospitals and where there is a longstanding culture of corporate responsibility for employee and social welfare. Company hospitals for workers and their families are not an alien concept. A number of companies in the Tata group, for instance, run their own hospitals. Tata, one of India's biggest industrial groups, began with industrial plants in places where there was no infrastructure. Tata Steel arose in the middle of the jungle, in what is now Jamshedpur, Mukherjee's home city, over 100 years ago. There its first steel ingots rolled out in 1912.

The company had to pioneer a comprehensive way of caring for all its employees and their families, including providing housing and healthcare facilities. Today the Tata Main Hospital has 1,200 beds, while another hospital for Tata Motors has 400 beds. Located between the two is the hospital of the Tinplate Company of India Ltd (TCIL) with 200 beds.

TCIL has been India's market leader in supplying most of the tin sheets for making food cans. Dr Mukherjee was an orthopaedic surgeon at the Tinplate Hospital. He has also been a Course Director of the training faculty of the Heart of Effective Leadership courses at Asia Plateau, the Initiatives of Change centre in Panchgani.

On my last visit to Jamshedpur he told me the whole story, during long taxi journeys, of how he and his fellow doctors saved the company hospital from closure.

Back in 1998, TCIL was going through a tough phase. It could not sell what it was producing. Its production process was antiquated and it was facing stiff competition from imports that were undercutting prices. The company was making cash losses of 5 crores rupees (Rs 50 million, approx. £500,000) per month. The management was under pressure to close or sell the loss-making hospital.

This saddened Mukherjee greatly. The hospital was catering to the many employees and their families who would now have to go to the Tata Main Hospital at the other end of town, and stand in long queues for treatment that they received much faster at the Tinplate Hospital. Mukherjee was really concerned about the 150 staff of the hospital, who would hardly get a satisfactory compensation as the TCIL did not have the resources. Many had taken loans to put their children into university or buy houses.

---

5   The story is told in detail by Graham Turner in his book *That Other Voice: in search of a God who speaks* (2017).

Mukherjee had already been introduced, at the Asia Plateau centre, to the idea of taking times of quiet for prayer and silent reflection every morning.

> So the next morning my strong thought was to ask the managing director, Bushen Raina, to allow us doctors to run the hospital. I didn't even think of how to do it, or what the logistics were. I also shared the thought with the director of medical services, Dr P P Chawla, who was due to retire in a couple of years. I was 46 years old with many years ahead of me. The managing director told us, "Are you crazy? Do you know what it takes to run a hospital? This is a management decision." But he also knew about, and respected, the ideas of Asia Plateau. So he said, "OK, if you think like that we'll give you six months to try it."[6]

Mukherjee's first thought was to open the hospital to other corporate houses in Jamshedpur which had no hospitals of their own. He visited the heads of 22 corporations and invited them to send their workers to the Tinplate Hospital. At first they laughed, saying, "Why should we? We have two bigger hospitals in Jamshedpur. If we go to yours, our employees will say we are just trying to save costs." Mukherjee told them three things: "We are a smaller hospital, so we are more efficient; we give more personalized care; and we are more affordable."

Mukherjee also went to the Uranium Corporation of India, 45 km from Jamshedpur. The Managing Director, R N Gupta, said they had four trade unions and even if one agreed the other unions would not. Mukherjee asked to meet the union leaders. Gupta said there was a need for an orthopaedic specialist in the local hospital. Could Mukherjee come at weekends, see some patients and win the union leaders' confidence? So he started to go there every Sunday. Slowly he became good friends with each of the four union heads. When he asked them about coming to the Tinplate Hospital they agreed straight away.

> That process took about six months. By the end of the first financial year of running the Tinplate Hospital ourselves, 31 March 1999, we had earned Rs 97.74 lakhs (Rs 9,774,000; £101,000). We wanted to give a service to outsiders which our previous mindset had not permitted, because we had had a captive market. Now our mindset changed to be more patient friendly, so that outsiders wanted to come back to our hospital. It was a total paradigm shift.

At first, the Tinplate Hospital doctors felt they were losing out as they were only being paid to treat Tinplate employees. So another idea was to allow them private practice in the hospital, to treat their own patients. The hospital

6   The quotes here are from the author's extensive interview with Dr Amit Mukherjee in Jamshedpur, India, and from his book *Great Company*, pp 158–161

would get the bed, medicine and theatre operation charges and the surgeon would pick up his fees. It would be during working hours and, against a lot of opposition, this was accepted.

They started health check-up schemes and improved the pharmacy and pathology. And so they started to make a good amount of money. Then they thought they should expand the hospital with an Intensive Care Unit (ICU) for heart patients and have an emergency centre.

> At first the Tinplate Managing Director was furious, saying don't even think about it. "You guys are mad. Our company will not be able to spend one rupee on you. If we had that rupee it would be spent on the industry but not on the hospital."

So Mukherjee's next thought was to seek help from outside. They approached the Timken Foundation in the USA for a grant. They couldn't help because the Tinplate Hospital was a commercial establishment. So in 1999, with the support of the Tinplate board, the hospital became a charitable trust—the Dr T C John Memorial Charitable Foundation in memory of the first doctor who had converted a small dispensary into the hospital. Approaching the Timken Foundation again, they gave a grant of Rs 65 lakhs (Rs 6,500,000; £67,000). The Sir Dorabjee Tata Trust gave Rs 35 lakhs (Rs 3,500,000; £36,200) and Lafarge cement company gave Rs 2.5 lakhs (Rs 250,000; £2,500) worth of cement. So they started the project with Rs 1 crore, 2.5 lakhs (Rs 10,250,000; £107,000).

However they were shocked that the cost of equipment for an ICU and trauma centre was much more than anticipated. Their estimates were two years out of date. They needed top quality cardiac monitors. In those days Hewlett Packard, considered amongst the best, quoted a price of Rs 33.76 lakhs (Rs 3,376,000; £35,000).

> The purchasing manager and I went to Kolkata to ask the HP officer for a special price. His Delhi boss offered a 10 per cent reduction and his boss in Germany agreed to another 10 per cent. But this was still too costly. So he gave us the phone number of his boss in the USA. He said, "Give me a little time. I'll need to speak to my directors." We called him back 45 minutes later and he said, "OK, we'll give you the whole package for Rs 18 lakhs (Rs 1,800,000; £18,600)."
>
> We negotiated like this for most of our equipment. We finished the ICU and trauma project within cost and within our time frame. This was a record for Tinplate as the company had a reputation for not completing projects within time or cost.

Unfortunately, even with the extra patients, ICU and Trauma Centre, the income was static. This led to a lot of discussion on whether the whole project was worth it. The next thought was to seek further sources of income by enhancing the activities of the new trust. So they offered to take over the medical installations of other nearby industries.

> It was a thought out of the blue. This is why I think that innovation is very thought orientated. I went to the Lafarge cement company and proposed taking over their in-house medical facility. They were delighted as they had been looking for this kind of intervention. We took on Tata Power's and Tata Cummins' medical units as well as another dispensary inside Tata Steel. As these began to bear fruit we started doing pretty well as a trust.

With some of the money saved, the trust started a fund to help the poor who could not afford to be treated in the ICU. They sent two people to Kolkata for operations. And they started a 24-hour medical store and planned to start a dialysis centre.

The result of all this was that instead of losing about 150 hospital jobs they added 67 new jobs: doctors, nurses, paramedics, sweepers, ambulance drivers. "So we beat the wrong effects of competitive globalization", Mukherjee commented.

One day he was at a Rotary dinner when the President and Vice-President of the Tinplate Company, and the General Manager for Human Resources, caught hold of him. They said that the Managing Director, Bushen Raina, wanted him to head the administration of the whole company. Would he agree?

> This was a shock because I had no concept of what it meant. A few mornings later I was playing golf when he called me to his home. He was lying in bed because of a spinal fracture he had sustained in an aircraft accident. He confirmed that he would like me to take this on. So, I found myself as the Head of Administration of the whole company for which I had no training at all. It was the evening of 30 June 2007 and I was to take over the department the next morning, 1 July, at 9.00 o'clock.

Mukherjee was to look after a whole range of things: public relations, the media, government licensing and legal matters; transport, travel, holiday plans; health and sanitation; housing—over 1,700 houses for employees—and the lawns, gardens and land. He also had the power of attorney, signing on behalf of the company.

Reducing costs remained a continuing challenge. For instance, they had an outdated, sluggish internal telephone communications system. They approached Tata Indicom who gave a good price. But they got a much better offer from the state-run telecoms company, BSNL. They installed a new exchange, worth about Rs 7 lakhs (Rs 700,000; £7,700), free of charge. The hospital's efficiency increased 100-fold, Mukherjee said, "and we pay less on the phone".

He continued to practise as an orthopaedic surgeon, though he had to reduce the amount of his time at the hospital. "It was all a great and ongoing challenge. But it was great fun", he comments.

Mukherjee left the Tinplate Company of India in 2012 to become the General Manager of Jamna Auto's plant in Jamshedpur, with 400 employees. But what is perhaps most remarkable about Mukherjee's story is the fact that he is living with a malignant brain tumour, diagnosed in early 2016. His doctor gave him only six months to live. If that was the case, Mukherjee said to himself, "I'm going to enjoy the rest of my life to the full." Two and half years later he was still as cheerful as ever, attending international forums around the world, and showing little sign of slowing down. His doctor apologized to him for getting his prognosis so wrong.

Mukherjee's and Miller's stories reveal the human face of business, as do many of the stories in this book. They go well beyond the bottom line in their human motivations. The need for the human face of business is all the more imperative at a time when big corporations wield more power than many nation states.

Global Justice Now (formerly the World Development Movement) compared the economic might of the largest corporations against that of countries. GJN found that the number of businesses in the world's top 100 economies jumped to 69 in 2015, up from 63 in 2014. GJN's figure was quoted by the World Bank.[7] An earlier Oxfam report in 2011 suggested that, of the world's top 100 economies, 53 were countries, 34 were cities and 13 corporations.[8] There is clearly discrepancy in the way the figures are calculated. But they do indicate the enormous power that multinational corporations wield.

In his book *Beyond the Corporation: humanity working* (2011, p 21), David Erdal, one of the world's leading advocates of employee share ownership companies, addresses the issue of the power and control that corporations exhibit:

> Many companies set out to create among their employees a feeling of ownership, without any real ownership. This can be done through team-building techniques, systems for making continuous improvement and through participative management styles. Managers themselves can be honest believers in these approaches. But the end result is deceitful: the employees feel like owners but have none of the rights and benefits of ownership. The psychological ownership that is induced is good for performance and good for the people involved, but it is false. It can be reversed overnight and the employees can do nothing about it.

7   https://blogs.worldbank.org/publicsphere/world-s-top-100-economies-31-coun
tries-69-corporations

8   https://oxfamblogs.org/fp2p/the-worlds-top-100-economies-53-countries-34-cities-a
nd-13-corporations/

If this is true for employees it is equally true for the communities in which large corporations operate, as they can all too easily up-sticks and switch from location to location, country to country. They have the power to down-size—a euphemism for redundancies—which puts employees in a position of victimhood. The alternative, Erdal says, is to put ownership in the hands of the entire workforce, such as the John Lewis Partnership retail group and Ove Arup engineers, famed for the structural design of the Sydney Opera House. This encourages partnership and a joint sense of responsibility towards one another. Erdal continues (p 246):

> If financial ownership were used for the benefit of wide employee owner-ship rather than the self-enrichment of a few, what a difference that would make. The temptation will be to skew the ownership and power radically towards the senior people, the chief executive and directors who already do so well out of the current system. That has to be resisted. The powerful need a change of heart, to recognize this is worth doing.... But the satisfactions to be gained from doing it are real and deep.

In the post-Second World War era, after the Caux centre in Switzerland first opened in 1946, the West German trade union leader, Hans Boeckler (1875–1951), said in Caux: "When people change, the structure of society changes, and when the structure of society changes, people change. Both go together and both are necessary."[9] Today, changing the structure of companies towards employee ownership often pays dividends for everyone.

Jon Miller and Lucy Parker argue the case for "how big business can fix the world". Contrary to popular perception, and negative practices, big busi-nesses have a huge positive impact on society as a whole, they say.[10] They tell, for instance, of how companies such as Apple are re-examining the well-being of their suppliers in China and other global corporations are investing in developing their suppliers in African countries, creating new jobs. Miller and Parker conclude that businesses act like a prism. The prism refracts their light into five components: purpose, products, practices (which could also be interpreted as behaviours), philanthropy and point of view. They write:

> The Prism is a way of seeing more clearly the intentions and behaviours of business in society. The companies we met on this journey [researching their book] tend to be driven by a strong sense of purpose—a clear idea of what they are for and an ambition that what they do overall will have a positive impact on the world around them. How a company interprets its purpose is the prime mover and it informs the three ways in which any business touches society: through the goods and services that it sells; through how it operates; and beyond the core activities of the business,

9   https://www.iofc.org/frank-buchman-legacy-15
10 In their book *Everybody's Business* (2013)

through the social causes it chooses to support. Products, practices and philanthropy: these are the practical ways that businesses connect with the wider world. Indeed, there aren't any other ways: it's in these areas that businesses act and how intentions become manifest. Finally, the companies we've seen in these stories have a sophisticated awareness of the influence they have in the world and a point of view about how to use their influence to further the contribution they can make on the issues which are relevant to them. The role of business in society is played out in each of these distinct strands. We see it as a prism: one white light refracted into separate streams of colour. Taken as a whole, they describe how businesses can create social value.[11]

The same could be said for all the stories in this book. At their core their priority is the welfare of people and society rather than just the bottom line. Yet there is a deeper dynamic still—a profound sense of inner inspiration, a spiritual dynamic, which the people whose stories are told in this book draw upon. We shall look at this in the next chapters. Such people have a strong sense of purpose for themselves, their businesses and organizations, for what they can contribute to society and to human well-being. They and their companies add value to their investors, to society and to people's lives. In so doing, their employees are proud to work for them, graduates want to join them, and their customers appreciate them. Their supply chains are well served and adequately rewarded. Society as a whole benefits. Moreover, they are a pleasure to work for and to work with. They lead with integrity and are great company.

References

Erdal, David, *Beyond the Corporation: humanity working*, Bodley Head, 2011

Hodge, Margaret, *Called to Account: how corporate bad behaviour and government waste combines to cost us millions*, Little, Brown, 2016

Miller, James and Parker, Lucy, *Everybody's Business: the unlikely story of how big business can fix the world*, Biteback Publishing, 2013

Smith, Michael, *Great Company*, Initiatives of Change, 2015

Turner, Graham, *That Other Voice: in search of a God who speaks*, Darton, Longman & Todd, 2017

11 Miller and Parker, ibid., pp 400–401

14 Culture of trust

So what is the common ingredient, the golden thread, of the stories in this book? They are all about people who are motivated by personal integrity and a commitment to doing the right thing, not just for profit, important as that is. They are trust-builders. Often they reflect what Frederic Laloux calls "teal" organizations: the blue-green companies that are ushering in a new age of human consciousness about the needs of the planet in an era of diminishing, finite resources; a world that emphasises human relationships rather than human resources.[1]

By highlighting stories of positive outcomes in this book, and the human motivations behind them, it is hoped that they might encourage patterns of behaviour that could become the acceptable norm in society, if they are not already so, just as Nudge theory encourages positive behaviours and out-comes—the "done thing". Not, however, just the done thing but the right thing.

What, then, can we deduce about the ingredients of a leadership of integrity from the stories gathered here? As well as the five pillars of trust outlined in Chapter 7, this book proposes eight Cs of trust which affect the culture of organizations: Contracts, Competence, Covenants, Character, Conscience, Commitment, Courage and Change.

Contracts

Contracts are the written, signed agreements between parties in the sale and purchase of goods, services and property, which everyone honours. They are underwritten by the rule of law, encompassed in the whole gamut of jurisprudence, and are the essential way in which we order society.

Contracts were seriously undermined by the sub-prime mortgage crisis leading to the financial crisis of 2008: as interest rates increased, home owners defaulted on their mortgage repayments, unable to pay for them. They had no option but to break their contracts with mortgage lenders. A fundamental dishonesty was built into the system of selling mortgages to people who could

---

1   *Reinventing Organizations*, Frederic Laloux (2014)

not afford them. Mortgage lenders also encouraged customers to dishonestly inflate their incomes in order to qualify for a mortgage. They became known as "liar loans". The bubble was bound to burst.

Competences

We have a fundamental trust in the competence of the person whose skills we pay for—the plumber, electrician, airline pilot, surgeon or anaesthetist—such that they will deliver their skills to their maximum ability, on time and within budget. We trust them to do a great job. Our lives are often in the hands of such professionals. The emphasis is on the pursuit of excellence across all disciplines—musicians, sports stars, and all of us with our various skills and talents. The market dictates that we walk away from those who prove to be incompetent or slovenly.

Covenants

This is an old-fashioned Biblical word which refers to the promises we make to one other over the long term, often agreed by a handshake. It was a traditional concept reflected in the notion of "My word is my bond" in the City of London. It was undermined by the crash of 2008, and destroyed further by rogue traders who manipulated key interest rates for their own or others' greed. Putting such self-interest before mutual interest was unconscionable.

Character

Character is an enigmatic word. We refer to someone fondly as "being a character" when we sometimes mean an odd-ball or even a "shady" character. Alternatively, a person's character includes courage, fortitude, honesty and all the moral qualities which add up to that person's reputation—a moral force in society. In this sense, character means being put to the test and found fit for purpose—morally, mentally, intellectually, emotionally, physically and spiritually. The same could be said for the reputation and character of organizations.

Character is built into our lives by our daily decision-making, right versus wrong, over a life-time. It has been defined as "doing the right thing when no one else is looking". It implies doing the right thing when under extreme pressure to do the wrong thing.

Do I trust the character of a person with whom I have to negotiate? Is he or she really trustworthy? Am I trustworthy for that matter?[2]

---

2   *New York Times* columnist David Brooks tells stories of people in public life who have grown into their roles through their growth of character in his book *The Road to Character* (2015).

Fred Kiel has researched the issue of character in his book *Return on Character: the real reason leaders and their companies win* (2015). It shows that companies led by CEOs of character, as perceived by their employees, outperform companies led by "self-focussed" CEOs, by a factor of 5:1. He describes character as including four ingredients: integrity, responsibility, forgiveness and compassion.

Character, says the *New York Times* columnist David Brooks in his book *The Road to Character* (2015), is formed by the choice between "Adam I and Adam II" in each of us. "While Adam I wants to conquer the world, Adam II wants to obey a calling to serve the world", he writes. "While Adam I is creative and savours his accomplishments, Adam II sometimes renounces worldly success and status for the sake of some sacred purpose. While Adam I asks how things work, Adam II asks why things exist, and what ultimately we are here for." Life, he says, is "essentially a moral drama, not a hedonistic one"(p 241). In this moral drama, "Character is built in the course of your inner confrontation. Character is a set of dispositions, desires, and habits that are slowly engraved during the struggle against your own weakness. You become more disciplined, considerate, and loving through a thousand small acts of self-control, sharing, service, friendship, and refined enjoyment" (p 243).

So, character is built through thousands of accumulated daily choices and habits of a life-time. Character helps to shape our destinies. In the business context, character could be said to be the culture of an organization: what is accepted and acceptable and what is not tolerated. It is the tone that permeates through the whole organization. It builds trust.

Conscience

This can be described as the choice between what is right and what is wrong. Social and ethical entrepreneurs have a strong sense of social conscience about what needs to change in the world. But what about personal conscience—what needs to change in us?

Rogue traders, corrupt officials or politicians who steal resources and salt them away into offshore accounts and tax havens have little sense of personal conscience. The world of business and the economy needs conscience-based decision-making at its heart. Tax avoidance, such as through offshore tax havens, may be legal but is it conscionable?

From where do we gain our sense of conscience? Adam Smith made a single passing reference to the "invisible hand of the market" in his book *The Wealth of Nations*. In his earlier book, *The Theory of Moral Sentiments*, he referred to the Impartial Spectator, which acts like a "demigod within the breast", and the "man within" which is "the vice-regent of the deity"—in other words one's conscience. Subsequent generations overlooked his moral philosophy, which now needs to be rediscovered. The need is to be true to our sense of conscience and consciousness about what needs to happen in the world, and to follow our dreams for what we want to achieve.

Commitment

What are we called to achieve in the world? What is our commitment, our contribution? The contribution of our organizations which defines their purpose? This is far greater than the pursuit of profit. Mumbai businessman Vivek Asrani says, "Profit is like the fuel that propels a vehicle forward. It is necessary but is not the purpose of the journey." The commitment, the purpose, needs to be to provide the goods and services that contribute towards an economy that serves the well-being of humankind.

Courage

It takes courage to act with integrity. "Courage" comes from the same word as heart: *coeur* in French. It is at the heart of ethical decision-making. It is different from being foolhardy. But it may take courage to swim against the prevailing tide, to do what is right. In the end people will trust you for doing what is right in a spirit of courage. It can be decisive in times of ethical dilemmas.

Change

Change is the one constant in any organization and in society: change that is driven by external forces whether they are from competitor organizations, or the impact of climate change, or new technologies such as AI; or change from the need to constantly improve to get things right within one's organization— what the Japanese call *kaizen*, gaining the benefits of continuous improvements. This is a leadership issue for CEOs and board members, but can begin anywhere within an organization. It also needs to allow for mistakes and a culture of encouragement rather than condemnation. It may require forgiveness when individuals get things wrong, which may be inevitable as part of the change process. Above all, it is the notion that "change starts with me".

Readers will think of other Cs which affect the culture of organizations, from community to climate change. An interesting group exercise might be to brainstorm on possible Cs—and why they are important.

References

Brooks, David, *The Road to Character*, Allen Lane, 2015

Dyce, James, *The Rescue of Capitalism: getting Adam Smith right*, Stress Publications, 1990

Keil, Fred, *Return on Character: the real reason companies and their leaders win*, Harvard Business Review Press, 2015

Laloux, Frederic, *Reinventing Organizations: a guide to creating organizations inspired by the next stage in human consciousness*, Nelson Parker, 2014

Norman, Jesse, *Adam Smith: what he thought and why it matters*, Allen Lane, 2018

Smith, Adam, *The Wealth of Nations*, Penguin Classics, fourth edition, 1999

Smith, Adam, *The Theory of Moral Sentiments*, Penguin Classics, 2010

15 Time for self-reflection

So how can a leadership of integrity which builds trust be encouraged at the personal and organizational levels, to bring positive change to organizations and the wider world? What is the methodology? How can it be applied? The need to do so, in an age of great disruptions, has never been more pressing.

We have already seen in Chapter 7 how Adam Smith promoted the notion of an "Impartial Spectator" which acts like "a demi-god within the breast", similar to conscience. A theme from the stories told in this book is also the practice of "quiet time", self-reflection and inner inspiration which act as an anchor—and a springboard to action—to help transform the aims and motives of individuals, leading to positive outcomes for organizations.

All the Cs of trust which affect the culture of organizations, outlined in the previous chapter, start with or involve the individual, from the boardroom to the shop floor. Enlightened CEOs will acknowledge that "change starts with me". And, in this process, a helpful tool is to take time out for self-reflection.

Steve Jobs, speaking at Stanford University in 2005, said: "Don't let the noise of others' opinions drown out your own inner voice. And, most important, have the courage to follow your heart and intuition. They somehow already know what you truly want to become. Everything else is secondary."[1]

Wisdom can be found in intuition, says the business author and thinker Frederic Laloux. "Intuition honours the complex, ambiguous, paradoxical, non-linear nature of reality; we unconsciously connect patterns in a way that our rational mind cannot. Intuition is a muscle that can be trained, just like logical thinking: when we learn to pay attention to our intuitions, to honour them, to question them for the truth and guidance they might contain, more intuitive answers will surface." Laloux adds that "wisdom traditions insist on the need for regular silence and reflection to quiet the mind and let truth emerge from a deeper part of ourselves."[2]

So how to find the space to hear that "inner voice", to listen to one's "heart and intuition", to discover intuition and wisdom? Meditation exercises

---

1 Stanford University Commencement Address, 12 June 2005: https://news.stanford. edu/2005/06/14/jobs-061505/
2 *Reinventing organizations*, Frederic Laloux, Indian edition, 2018, pp 47, 154.

certainly help. The public's appetite for them is shown by the phenomenal rise of Calm, the meditation app developed by Michael Acton Smith. Nearly a million people, and increasing, have paid the $60-a-year subscription for a daily guided meditation.[3]

Yet I believe there is a qualitative difference between meditation techniques which calm the mind and spirit and "quiet time" which prompts the mind and spirit, and can be regarded more as active listening, leading to ideas for action.

In their study of the time-management of CEOs of big companies (with an average annual review of $13.1 billion), Michael E Porter and Nitin Nohria emphasize the need to carve out "alone time". They write:

> It's...vital for CEOs to schedule adequate uninterrupted time by themselves so that they can have space to reflect and prepare for meetings. In our study, CEOs spent 28 per cent of their work time alone, on average— but again, that varied a great deal, from a low of 10 per cent to a high of 48 per cent.... CEOs need to cordon off meaningful amounts of alone time and avoid dissipating it by dealing with immediate matters, especially their in-boxes. This proved to be a common problem among the CEOs in our study, who readily acknowledged it.
>
> Given that time in the office is easily eaten up, alone time outside the office is particularly beneficial. Long-distance travel out of contact with the office often provides critical thinking time, and many CEOs swear by it. To capitalize on it, CEOs should avoid travelling with an entourage.[4]

The Chairman and Managing Director of a British company says he likes to be "in flow, like a raft carried downstream". This is strengthened, he says, by taking time for silent reflection first thing in the morning. It helps him to be aware of priorities and sensitive to "quiet hunches".

At one point he was due to chair an important Board of Directors meeting. Instead he had the insistent thought he should meet an employee, who had asked to speak with him. Initially reluctant, the Chairman nonetheless had a sense he should meet the employee, who explained he had just had the news that his twin brother—himself a former employee—was dying. Later that morning, during the Board meeting, came the news that the employee's brother had indeed died. The Chairman had another insistent thought that he should check whether the employee himself had heard the news. The Chairman broke away from the Board meeting, went to find the employee, and had to tell him personally the news of his brother's death. "Which was really the most important priority of the day—what I thought of as that 'terribly important' Board meeting; or the real person?" asks the Chairman.

3　www.calm.com; *The Sunday Times*, 22 July 2018
4　Porter and Nohria (2018)

Today, employees and their bosses around the world benefit from times for silence, prayer, meditation, mindfulness, visioning, and deep listening for guidance in decision-making, whatever their spiritual inclination. These can be hugely beneficial in preparing for difficult situations; reducing stress; building shared values; listening to others; making intentions and actions congruent; doing the right thing; and addressing a world of great complexity. Meditation-type classes are now held in major corporations such as Apple, Google, Yahoo, McKinsay, IBM and Cisco.

"Spirituality could be the ultimate competitive advantage", writes Professor Ian Mitroff in his book *A Spiritual Audit of Corporate America* (2012).[5]

As I write in my booklet *The Sound of Silence*, "In an age of information real inspiration comes in times of silent reflection.... For many around the world, the daily time of silent reflection has become an anchor, and a springboard to action, over the years."[6]

This is also a hallmark of the conferences held in Caux, Switzerland. In the book *The Collaboratory* (2014), edited by Katrin Muff of Business School Lausanne, a chapter written by Louie Gardiner goes into the long-term engagement of the Caux centre in detail:

> Every year, an extraordinary diverse mix of human beings converge—every continent is represented; multiple nationalities, religions, ethnicities; people with little or great material wealth; those with and without formal status; intergenerational; multilingual—and the list goes on. As human beings we are hard-wired to categorize, judge, and seek alliances with those who are similar, with a tendency to separate from those who are not like us. Daniel Kahneman (2011) illuminates the process in our brains—that thinking "fast" is our default reaction to what happens around us. "Slow" thinking faculties require conscious, effortful attention. So to get beyond our hard-wired categorizing minds and unconscious bias we need to slow down enough to challenge ourselves to open up to each other. People in IofC [Initiatives of Change] are no less mortal than the rest of us, yet countless individuals have embraced courage and forgiveness over fear and shame, let go of hatred in favour of healing, relinquished blame in favour of compassion and righteousness in favour of love, and chosen connection over conflict.

Gardiner detects eight characteristics of Caux:

> Serve and receive service joyfully; Turn judgment into curiosity; Engage in quiet time; Share and learn through honest conversation; Care for others, the planet and ourselves; Engage with purpose; Follow through on promises; Turn scarcity into creativity.[7]

5   http://www.visionarylead.org/spirituality-in-business.html
6   Smith (2017)
7   Chapter 20, "Long-term stakeholder engagement", pp 195, 198.

When it comes to "engage in quiet time", Gardiner traces this core practice back to its origins in the Oxford Group, the university student movement founded by the Lutheran minister Revd Frank Buchman in the 1920s. "In these intimate community gatherings, people engaged in quiet time, learning to listen deeply to 'God' or to the 'still voice within', sharing what arose for them", she writes. She continues:

> It took several years of attending Caux for me to realize that three systemic factors were embodied in quiet time. First, it is simple—which makes it potentially replicable. Second, it connects across scales—from individual to group to global. Sharing quiet time enables individuals to extend their reflections beyond themselves. Listening to the similar and different struggles of others connects people to each other and links their personal change to global concerns. Third, it is iterative—enabling rapid-cycle, regular reflections supporting one's (and the system's) capacity to adapt to complex, shifting conditions. Quiet time invites "connection" to what is; making sense of what needs "correction"; and discerning what "direction" or action to take.

Gardiner sees the "Caux laboratory" as "a place to convene, connect, commune and co-create".

The notion of "quiet time", or "internal reflection" as she calls it, is also advocated by Dr Scilla Elworthy, the founder of Peace Direct and the Oxford Research Group, who has been nominated three times for the Nobel Peace Prize. "Leaders have to be authentic," she told a Tomorrow's Global Leaders event organized by Tomorrow's Company think-tank in the City of London in January 2015. "That can only be achieved by inner reflection—a period of reflection every day. Inner work is a prerequisite for outer effectiveness." Elworthy told the forum that "deep feminine qualities" needed to be welcomed in boardrooms: "empathy, grace under fire, nurture, listening intently to the other, a sense of the sacredness of the earth, thinking long-term and the insistence that we are all connected." She added that "If the mantra of the last century was 'what can I get?', the mantra of this century is 'what can I give?' It is all about contribution"[8]

So what is a suitable methodology for self-reflection? It can be a source of inspiration for both correction and direction: personal correction where I need to change, including in personal or workplace relationships; and direction in workplace commitments and responsibilities, and life in general.

There are numerous different ways to practise this in the workplace—and at the personal level.

---

8   The author was present at this event and took notes. Quoted with her permission.

At the workplace level

- As we have already seen, meditation classes are not alien to some major corporations, not least in Silicon Valley. Encourage this with time out for staff for, say an hour, at least once a week. Limit the size of the groups from around 12 people to a maximum of 20. These can be regarded as quality circles. Encourage a spirit of silent reflection and then honest sharing within the group. But don't allow this to invade people's privacy. Create ground rules so that each member of the group knows that they can say things in confidence without fear. Sometimes there may be the necessity for honest apology—and forgiveness—between individuals which needs personal discretion.
- Encourage a process of feedback through line managers or an "ideas box" that feeds through to personnel or human resources managers, or to the main board itself.
- Organize away-days or weekends every year or every six months for groups of staff. We have seen, in Chapter 10, how Joe Garner, CEO of Nationwide, does this. As well as stimulating talks, allow such away-days to take place in a spirit of silence or self-reflection, followed by written feedback. Include sports and/or nature walks.
- End key group discussion meetings with a pause for a minute or two of silent reflection, followed by the sharing of key thoughts from around the group. This encourages democracy at the workplace, as it allows everyone to have their say, whether right or wrong. No one need feel left out. An unexpected key or breakthrough thought might emerge from such a process. We saw in Chapter 11 how this is practiced at Grampari, the rural development scheme in Panchgani, India.
- It can also be helpful to start key meetings with a minute's pause for silent reflection, which encourages participants to be grounded in the "now" moment and let go of previous distractions.
- Don't condone gross negligence, but equally allow staff to make mistakes from which they and the organization can learn.

Don't be surprised if the fruit of such innovations at work increase productivity and profitability. But don't introduce these practices with the profit motive in mind but because it is the right thing to do to make organizations great companies to work for and their people great company to work with.

The Mumbai businessman Vivek Asrani, whose story is told in Chapter 8, tells how his uncle encouraged him to buy a plot of land some 60 km from Mumbai, next to land that his uncle was buying. Asrani had a "gut instinct" he should go with the suggestion, though he had no business plan for its use other than the possibility of relocating his business to a greenfield site. Asrani secured a bank loan for the land and to build a one-storey factory unit on it. Then the architect told him it would be more cost effective to build a two-storey building. So Asrani secured a second credit loan, still with no real plan for the building's use. But he had a deep sense of being "led" into doing this project. When it was completed, a pharmaceutical company approached him, much to his surprise, wanting to rent the plant for five years. This would pay for his investment. It was, for Asrani, another case of acting in faith in obedience to his inner guidance.[9]

Another telling story comes from the Liverpool businessman and graphics designer Jim Sharp who, true to his name, patented a process to sharpen up the reproduction of images in newspaper advertising. He writes:

> I had a thriving art studio and family but the way business was obtained meant going out drinking with clients most nights. This was having a detrimental effect on my family. Principals of absolute purity, honesty, unselfishness and love led me to make the decision to give up alcohol. As a result of this decision things changed in my life.
>
> One evening in 1975 I was reading an electronics catalogue in bed and, because I was clear headed and sober, I had a brilliant idea of how to improve the quality of images in newsprint. I talked it over with my wife till the early hours and the next day I did a test in my studio darkroom and took the results (halftone images of the first flight of Concorde) to the patent office who advised me to patent the process.
>
> The process was named Schafline and was successfully used to improve the definition of advertisements in newspapers at a time when TV advertising was eroding newsprint sales of space. Asda, Rumbelows, Rover Cars, Tandy Electronics and many more were using the Schafline High Definition System and it reversed the decline in newspaper advertising.
>
> Schafline was franchised world-wide with offices in USA, Canada, Spain, France, Australia, New Zealand, Sweden, Venezuela, London, Birmingham, Manchester, Glasgow, Tunbridge Wells and, of course, Liverpool. The Schafline company was eventually liquidated in 1993 because Apple Macs and Photoshop could create the same high quality results without the use of film.[10]

Jim Sharp's decision to heed the voice of conscience not only saved his family life, it also transformed the direction of his business in those days.

The social entrepreneur Roddy Edwards from Walkerswood, Jamaica, (see Chapter 11) tells how, when he was at school, he was shocked when his car-racing brother became involved in a global movement for spiritual and moral rearmament. "He shared with me the basic idea that if you wanted to change the world the best place to start is with yourself." Edwards could not dislodge this idea from his mind and began to reflect on where he needed to change. "To this day I remember repaying money to a teacher for things I had stolen

9   Asrani told this story to the February 2018 Caux Initiatives for Business conference in Panchgani, India.
10 Email to the author, 20 August 2018

to help create a place far from the school buildings where I and my friends could drink and relax with relative impunity."

A second idea also stuck with him: that of taking a daily time of quiet to listen to the "still small voice" within, which could guide people on what is the right thing to do. "It was in such moments of quiet reflection, as well as discussion with fellow villagers, that the dream grew to aim that every single inhabitant of Walkerswood, who wanted work, would be able to find work."[11]

But what happens when companies and their staff face real dilemmas that are not necessarily easy to resolve, as Antonio Hautle, executive director of the UN's Global Compact Network in Switzerland, points out? His hypothetical case studies become a focus for group discussion.

For instance, a company opens a prayer room to cater to the needs of their staff from different faith traditions. An employee, Robert, complains:

> I work at a fast growing, young company in a quickly changing field, and we are known for attracting employees as diverse as our customers. Like most of my colleagues I am open-minded and enjoy the mix of professionals we have here, over more traditional companies. However, when they opened a prayer room for our religious colleagues recently, I feel things have gone too far. This is an office, not a place of worship. I don't know what these people do all day, but it certainly isn't working when I see how many times they leave their desk.[12]

Are they undermining productivity? Or does the fact that their spiritual well-being is being met increase their productivity? Is Robert justified in his attitude? Or does he lack empathy? Why does he feel the way he does? Without resolution, what kind of disruptive behaviour could he display? What can the management do to resolve such a situation?

Or take the case of a law firm which hires a new employee, Tisha, who does not come from an "appropriate" social environment or background. Other lawyers don't recognize themselves in her and fear that clients will lose confidence in the firm and its abilities. One employee, Juliette, complains:

> So we have this new colleague, Tisha. She comes from a depressed district and has seven siblings, not from the same father of course. Quite an accomplishment to escape from such an environment, needless to say. But why have they hired her? It's a mystery to me. We all have the same social background and this is the image that comes with the legal profession. It's what our clients expect, I hope they won't put her in touch with long-

11 Author's interview with Roddy Edwards in Jamaica
12 Quoted by Antonio Hautle in his presentation of case studies to the Ethical Leadership in Business Forum, Caux, Switzerland, 2017

term clients, because they don't like change and will not be amused when they have to put their faith in the hands of some hip-hop type.[13]

Is Juliette simply being realistic in wanting to protect the law firm's reputation with its clients? Or is she a snob, failing to evaluate the ability of Tisha, or the changing social mores and perceptions of the company's clients? Could Tisha's employment actually attract new clients?

And what happens when a recent employee gets promoted over a long-standing loyal employee? Michael says:

> I have been working here for seven years. I have always invested in myself by taking courses and asking for critical feedback on the way I function with my colleagues, in order to improve myself. My goal was to grow to the role as Head of the Financial Department. I was right on track and so excited when this position finally became available. But now this Isabella, who has worked here for only ten months has been chosen over me. Sure, she has some qualities, but don't tell me this has nothing to do with this whole new nonsense about favouring women over men in promoting them to higher positions.[14]

Is Michael justified in his bitterness? Has the company become too politically correct? Or is the situation simply that Isabella is the better candidate for the role? How does the management convey their decision to him so that they placate him? Or will he simply resign?

Such dilemmas need wisdom and insight on the part of management and all who are involved. They may need transparency and discussion, as well as times for self-reflection which might point a way towards resolution

At the state and public sector levels

Teams from Asia Plateau, the Indian centre of Initiatives of Change in Panchgani, give in-house training, entitled Ethics in Public Governance, to senior executives in some of India's biggest public sector corporations. They include Indian Railways (the world's largest civilian employer with some 1.6 million employees), the Steel Authority of India Ltd (SAIL), and Coal India Ltd, the world's largest coal producing company. (See more on Indian trends towards sustainable energy in Chapter 11.)

From 2007 to 2009, 90 senior executives from the public-sector Bangalore Electricity Supply Company (BESCOM)—the main electricity distribution company for the state of Karnataka—and 300 assistant managers went on training courses at Asia Plateau. Then in 2010, BESCOM sent its entire workforce of nearly 12,000—workers, supervisors and senior managers—to

13 Ibid.
14 Ibid.

training courses in Bangalore. The three-day workshops were called *Parivarthana Dhaare* or "A process of transformation". The emphasis was on "personal challenges, behavioural dynamics and wholesome lifestyles" including listening to the "inner voice" and the core values of honesty, purity of motive, unselfishness and love, presented in practical and interactive ways—including anger management.[15]

The result was that hundreds of the staff gave up smoking and alcohol, taking charge of their health. Thousands decided to take up regular exercise and sport. But the most important consequence, from the company's point of view, was the new-found dialogue between senior management and the workforce. Managers began listening to the employees about the problems they identified, such as theft of electricity, mismanagement and lack of respect, equipment breakdown and poor safety procedures. The productivity gains were palpable, as were the levels of trust.

In the Indian state of Madhya Pradesh, the former Chief Minister, Shivraj Singh Chouhan, set up a State Department of Happiness (*Rajya Anand Sanstham*). Inspired by the Asia Plateau centre, he introduced the notion of silent reflection—what he called *alpviram* or short break (literally meaning semicolon)—across all government departments. All government meetings begin with such a period of initial silence. The aim is to bring "a positive disposition in the outlook of people in general and government employees and officers in particular".[16]

Speaking about *alpviram*, Chouhan said:

> Once you sit in silence and take your mind off everything else to look within and think about all you have done, you will realise you might have troubled someone, might have lost your cool on someone or hurt someone else; have taken away someone's opportunity or money and property. How does it feel then? We do not take the time and effort to look within ourselves. But during this time of silence when people have looked at themselves honestly, many have broken down and cried at their realization. We get so caught up in our busy lives that we just forget our connection with our inner selves.[17]

Iqbal Singh Bains, the state's Additional Chief Secretary, who was put in charge of setting up the Ministry of Happiness, says that they have trained some 200 volunteers to spread the message of *alpviram* throughout government offices. He adds: "We have set up 180 *anandam* (joy of giving) centres where people can exchange their surplus goods. We have trained teachers to run life skills modules in 30 schools in Bhopal."

---

15 https://in.iofc.org/node/464
16 https://www.youtube.com/channel/UCJJ4-BAuKCbbHEonNtwQLNw
17 Ibid. Translated from the Hindi into English by Siddharth Singh.

Chouhan was Chief Minister from November 2005 till 2018 and under his leadership the state saw impressive growth rates. In 2014–2015 Madhya Pradesh achieved the highest growth of all states in India, at over 10 per cent. From 2005 to 2015, the state's per capita income quadrupled.[18]

At the personal level

- Give inner reflection or quiet time an honest daily try, initially for four weeks. Get into the habit of it. You may be surprised at how things develop. Start ideally at the same time and location each day. Some people practice this first thing on waking, before the clamour of emails, phone calls and online media demands our attention. It is a way of prioritising: of getting on top of the day before the day gets on top of you. After all, musicians tune their instruments before the concert begins, not after the concert is over.
- Start with 30 minutes and increase to 45 to 60 minutes. Include "food for thought" (e.g. stories of inspiration, spiritual or scriptural texts, and meditating with the flame of a candle/nature/music).
- End with one or two questions you want to reflect on or resolve, followed by 15 minutes of silence.
- You will discover that there are two kinds of quiet times: the time to reflect on a question or questions; and the still times into which to take nothing but our open spirit. Both are valuable and can be equally practised.
- Write your thoughts down which can be shared with a family member or trusted colleague. This also acts as an *aide memoire* during the rest of the day. By writing down thoughts, uncomfortable or challenging ideas that demand a change of behaviour or mind-set cannot be easily ignored: an honesty to confess; an apology to make; forgiveness to be sort or offered. A helpful dictum is: "Not who is right but what is right." Thoughts that come may be in the nature of *correction*—personal or organizational—or of *direction* for oneself or for the organization and wider society.
- The best way to understand all this is to practise it. You may be surprised by the transformative outcomes.

If all this sounds prescriptive or didactic, the aim is to create a habit. Our habits, after all, determine our character, direction in life and destinies.

Anita Hoffmann writes about influences which help to shape our direction in life, including the need for coaches, "circles of support" and "quiet time" (*Purpose and Impact*, 2018, pp 82–83): "We need to have time for reflection, to make our 'out-sight' into 'in-sight', to rest and regenerate our mental and physical batteries. One of the ways I have found most useful for finding balance, regenerating and thinking clearly is to spend time alone in silence."

18 https://www.shivrajsinghchouhan.org/biography.aspx

She adds that meditation "is increasingly proven to lower stress, promote well-being and alleviate anxiety and depression. There is increasing clinical evidence that meditation actually physically changes our brains, from protecting the ageing brain, helping concentration and focus, to coping better with unemployment by reducing physiological inflammation and stress markers."

For busy executives she recommends to "spend a quiet hour—with the phone off—each week with a journal, either in a café or on early morning flights...to reflect in silence. Yet other executives take away days, longer gap periods, or attend leadership development programmes or retreats. You will know what is right for you."

In the end you may be surprised by how much this affects your leadership of integrity—and how much your colleagues, employees, suppliers and customers regard you as great company to work with.[19]

All this is, of course, much more than just a personal or organizational matter. Those, particularly in leadership, who follow this path of integrity and inner inspiration will find themselves contributing to the transformation of the global village. They will have a global impact. They will globalize integrity and, in so doing, will change the world for the better.

References

Hoffmann, Anita, *Purpose and Impact: how executives are creating meaningful second careers*, Routledge, 2018

Kahneman, Daniel, *Thinking, Fast and Slow*, reprint edition, Penguin, 2012

Laloux, Frederic, *Reinventing Organizations: a guide to creating organizations inspired by the next stage of human consciousness*, Indian edition, Knowledge Partners, 2018

Mitroff, Ian I, and Denton, Elizabeth A, *A Spiritual Audit of Corporate America*, Jossey-Bass, 2012

Muff, Katrina (editor) et al, *The Collaboratory: a co-creative stakeholder process for solving complex problems*, Routledge, 2014

Porter, Michael E and Nohria, Nitin, "How CEOs manage time", *Harvard Business Review*, July–August 2018

Smith, Michael, *The Sound of Silence: how to find inspiration in an age of information*, sixth edition, Caux Books, 2017

---

19 These practices at the workplace and personal levels have been the hallmark of the global Initiatives of Change movement for many decades: www.iofc.org

16 Takeaways from this book

- Leading with integrity has a profound impact on the direction of organizations, wider society and the global economy; change in the world starts with change in individuals.
- A fundamental choice for leaders lies in their core motivation: whether it is one of acquisition or contribution to society.
- Leaders who are motivated by acquisition are driven by profit, self-interest, greed and gain—what is in it for them—and are essentially materialistic in outlook.
- Leaders who are motived by contribution have wider concerns than just the bottom line; they are concerned about the role they and their organizations play in creating a fairer, more just society for all stakeholders—employees, customers, shareholders, suppliers, the wider community, the impact on the environment and future generations.
- Leaders motivated by contribution aim to meet human needs for goods, services, jobs and incomes—the human factor.
- The *way* we do things is as important as what we do: the means *determine* the ends.
- It takes courage to lead with integrity—whether under pressure in the boardroom; whistleblowing against wrongdoing; making a stance against corruption; or pursuing a dream against all odds.
- Banking has a profound impact on the global economy; bankers can be motivated by material acquisition or by service to customers and society.
- Saving the environment and tackling climate change depend on the initiatives that are born out of a leadership of integrity; they are also cost effective.
- The stance against corruption is possible through a courageous leadership of integrity.
- Social entrepreneurs, including those amongst the Millennial generation, have a sense of social conscience about the world; they are having a significant impact on societies across national borders and in the global economy.

- Academia plays a significant role in imparting not just knowledge but also vision and values of integrity to future generations of business leaders.
- The health of society and individuals, and the so-called caring professions, depend on integrity in leadership.
- There is a need to rediscover the moral philosophy of Adam Smith, the founding father of modern economic thought; Smith advocated a notion of "the Impartial Spectator"—an imagined outside observer who approved or disapproved of one's actions and was "a vice-regent of the deity", acting similar to one's conscience; Smith also encouraged the notion of "sympathy" which, in his age, was similar to our current notion of empathy.
- There is a need today to take action out of similar moral and spiritual inspirations;
- Such inspirations can be found by taking time out, at the workplace, and in one's daily life, for silent reflection, inspiration and sense of direction in life—what Mahatma Gandhi called the Inner Voice and what others call "the still, small voice within" or personal conscience.
- Such inputs prompt a leadership of integrity, which is proved true by its outcomes.

Index